THE IMPACT OF HUMAN CAPITAL ON ECONOMIC GROWTH

THE IMPACT OF HUMAN CAPITAL ON ECONOMIC GROWTH

A Case Study in Post-Soviet Ukraine, 1989–2009

Ararat L. Osipian

palgrave
macmillan

First published in 2009 by
PALGRAVE MACMILLAN®
in the United States—a division of St. Martin's Press LLC,
175 Fifth Avenue, New York, NY 10010.

Where this book is distributed in the UK, Europe and the rest of the world, this is by Palgrave Macmillan, a division of Macmillan Publishers Limited, registered in England, company number 785998, of Houndmills, Basingstoke, Hampshire RG21 6XS.

Palgrave Macmillan is the global academic imprint of the above companies and has companies and representatives throughout the world.

Palgrave® and Macmillan® are registered trademarks in the United States, the United Kingdom, Europe and other countries.

ISBN: 978–0–230–61824–4

Library of Congress Cataloging-in-Publication Data

Osipian, Ararat L.
The impact of human capital on economic growth : a case study in post-Soviet Ukraine, 1989–2009 / Ararat L. Osipian.
p. cm.
Includes bibliographical references and index.
ISBN 978–0–230–61824–4
1. Human capital—Ukraine. 2. Economic development—Ukraine. 3. Ukraine—Economic policy—1991– I. Title.

HD4904.7.O85 2009
338.9477—dc22 2009002877

A catalogue record of the book is available from the British Library.

Design by Newgen Imaging Systems (P) Ltd., Chennai, India.

First edition: September 2009

10 9 8 7 6 5 4 3 2 1

Printed in the United States of America.

CONTENTS

FIGURES

TABLES

FOREWORD

The ideas of public spending and foreign investment as major engines of economic growth, especially in developing nations, are now replaced with ideas about the importance of reinvestment and development of domestic market. The theories of growth based on the fundamental assumption that a significant influx of the resources is necessary to initiate sustainable growth do not hold. They might work to a certain degree in the developing world, but appear to be insufficient to explain rapid economic growth in Ukraine and other industrialized nations of the former Soviet Bloc. Theories of import substitution now compete with post-structuralism. In education, long dominated concept of manpower forecasting gives way to market reforms. These two trends—structural reforms with domestic market development and market reforms in the education sector—define the future landscape of transition economies.

The goal of this book is to identify the place and the role of human capital in economic growth in the market-type post-transition economies. It fills the gap between the rapid economic growth as an objective economic reality of Ukraine and Russia and the lack of scholarly literature on the issue. This book focuses on the role of human capital as a necessary ground for initiation of economic growth in transition economies. In our view, the choice of both the object of the research and the time frame is very successful and well-justified. In the future, one would like to see further development of the research on sustainable economic growth in those economic systems that are currently not in equilibrium and only move toward their steady state.

Among the many merits of this book, we would like to highlight the following. The literature review unites in itself the chronology of changes in the theory of economic growth and the analysis of major problems of growth. Such a synthesis appears to be especially appealing, since it allows the following of the process of development of different models of growth that leads to qualitative changes and competition between exogenous and endogenous theories of growth. In the literature review, the author concentrates on the discussion of major ideas of economic growth, expressed by the leading economists in this field. This approach advances the spirit of discussion and debate. In the empirical part of the book, the author concludes that in the countries with high levels of human capital, including educational level of population, it is very difficult to purify the positive effect of education on economic growth. We agree with the author that the next advancement in the pace of economic growth in the transition economies will become possible only based on the process of renovation and long-term investment into principal capital. This is necessitated by the high degree of depreciation of machinery and production facilities in Ukraine and other transition economies and by the outdated technologies of production. The process of renovation itself will result in the continuation of strong economic growth. However, such a renovation is only possible based on significant investments. An increase in the quality of products and productivity overall appears to be impossible even with the relatively high quality of labor force simply because of the physically deteriorated and morally outdated equipment and technologies. After the renovation, the economy will continue to grow on the basis of new production capacities, technological advancements, and further accumulation of human capital needed to use new equipment and technologies. From this perspective, the author suggests further institutional and structural changes in Ukraine.

VICTOR SUPYAN
Deputy Director and Professor
Institute for the USA and Canadian Studies
Russian Academy of Sciences

PREFACE

Ukraine has a strategic location between Europe and Asia and remains geopolitically indecisive and squeezed between the West and Russia. This geopolitical position predetermines high interest to the country. Surprisingly, little has been said about this nation since it gained independence after the disintegration of the Soviet Union in 1991. Recent political events that have become known as the Orange Revolution attracted the world's interest to the country, but changed little in the lives of Ukrainians. Strategic developments in the region, including interests of the European Union, NATO, and Russia, warrant more focus on Ukraine in the near future. More attention to the country's development may be expected over the next few decades. Despite the fact that Ukraine is an industrialized nation of 50 million people and the largest country in Europe, little is known about its economy. Economic life in Ukraine remains terra incognita, indeed. Inferences are often drawn on Ukraine from the research done on Russia. Such inferences, however, are not always precise or appropriate. The developments in the nation's economic thought and the description of the processes in the national economy appear to be the reverse of the economic ideas that have been developed in evolutionary Western economics. First, there were formal models of growth in the Western economic thought that were then extended and applied to the issues of economic development, institutional change, structuralism, and other issues concerned with the Third World countries. In Ukraine, along with other former Soviet republics, a lot is being said about institutional changes, market reforms, and socioeconomic transition, but little to nothing is produced in the tradition of hard core economics, including models of growth. Over the last eight years, Ukraine demonstrated a rapid economic growth. This growth was preceded by the sharp decline in the national production, linked to the exhausting and ill-planned transition from the planned economy to the market economy. Some analytical scholarly work on transition economics is available along with reports by the IMF and the World Bank, but no rigorous empirical work on economic growth can be found. Deeper investigation of potential sources of economic growth in Ukraine is needed. The causes of growth remain unclear, while the growth itself appears to be sustainable, not accidental. This contradicts predictions of poverty trap theories and points to the leading role of internal resources.

In this research, preference is given to the endogenous model of economic growth. As a result of the review of a broad spectrum of literature in historical perspective, it has been found that the exogenous models of Solow-Swan and Leontief do not offer complete and adequate reflection of the transition experience. The purpose of this study is to provide a systematic investigation of the human capital-economic growth nexus. The impact of human capital on economic growth is incorporated within the context of economic transition. Such a contextualization places the research of growth in an appropriate framework, keeping it connected to other aspects of economic transition. The endogenous growth model is used as it is most appropriate for evaluation. This model is developed for cross-sectional analysis and shows the influence and importance of human capital for economic growth relative to other key inputs and to differences across countries. A variety of measures of human capital frequently used in applied growth studies is employed. We also estimate a system of linear equations. While intuition and theories of endogenous growth would point toward a positive effect of human capital on economic growth, empirical evidence on this issue is mixed. In our view, the next economic advancement in Ukraine will become possible based on the process of renovation and investment into principal capital. Further institutional and structural changes in the economy are needed. It will increase domestic and foreign investment, further develop domestic market, and sustain already achieved substantial GDP per capita growth.

INTRODUCTION

Economic growth is one of the fundamental issues in economics. The issue of economic growth has been one of the key issues of economic theory and macroeconomics for a long time, tied to the issues of general equilibrium and economic cycles. The process of growth is traditionally considered as a quintessence of an increased scale reproduction, socioeconomic development, and social progress. Sustainable economic growth within the limits of national systems and regional enclaves is a guarantor of sustainable development.

The ideas of public spending and foreign investment as major engines of economic growth, especially in developing nations, are now replaced with ideas about the importance of reinvestment and development of domestic market. The theories of growth based on the fundamental assumption that a significant influx of the resources is necessary to initiate sustainable growth do not hold. They might work to a certain degree in the developing world, but appear to be insufficient to explain rapid economic growth in Ukraine.

The socioeconomic transition in Ukraine may be considered as successful. Political and economic reforms lead to the creation of a predominantly market economy. By 2004 Ukraine achieved pre-transition level of GDP per capita. The positive economic growth took place since 1999. At the same time, the theme of economic growth did not receive much attention in the scholarly literature in the region. Ukrainian and Russian economists have only produced a very insignificant number of works on this issue. As a result, scholarly publications lag behind the economic realities, at best explaining them, but not analyzing them well enough and not presenting well-grounded forecasts. This may be explained, in part, by the low level of familiarity of the Soviet and post-Soviet economists with the Western literature on economic growth, major concepts and theories of growth, macroeconomics, and analytical techniques, including statistical and econometric analysis.

Works on the issues and different aspects of economic growth in transition and post-transition economies are presented by such Ukrainian economists as Aleksandrova (2003a and b), Bazhal and Odotjuk (2003), Bolhovitinova (2003), Borejko (2005), Chuhno (1996), Danilishin and Kucenko (2006), Dem'janenko (2003a and b), Gal'chin'kij (2004), Heyets (1999, 2000, 2001, 2003), Hrytsenko (1997, 2003), Kendjuhov (2005), Krjuchkova (2000), Kvasnjuk (2000, 2003a and b), Gal'chinskij and Levochkin (2004), Novitskij (2005), Olijnik (2003), Petkova (2005), Pokrytan (1997), Prihod'ko (2003a–f), Shchedrina (2003), Shubravskaja (2005), Sidenko (2003a and b), Suhorukov (2006), Tarasevich et al. (2003), Tochilin (2001), Vahnenko (2000, 2003), Vovkanich (2005), Vozhzhov (2004), Yaremenko (2003), and Yatskevich (2006).

Certain contribution to the research of economic growth in transition and post-transition economies was made by Russian economists Balabanova (2004), Bessonov (2005), Chechelev et al. (2001), Cherednichenko (2004), Dubjanskaja (2005), Evstigneeva and Evstigneev (2005), Fridman et al. (1998), Garipova et al. (2005), Golub (2006), Grushevskaja (2004), Hristenko et al. (2002), Ivanter (2004, 2006), Ivlev (2004), Kalinina (2005), Kosenkov (2005), Koshkin and Shabaev (2004), Kuznetsova (2000), Kvashnina (2004), L'vov (2004), Lashov and Spizharskaja (2004), Ovchinnikova (2004), Pavlova (2001), Perepelkin (2001), Perminov et al. (2004), Ponomarev (2004), Romanova (2002), Saktoev (1999), Salijchuk (2004), Savchenko (2005), Seleznev (2001), Simkina (2002), Sokolovskij (2001), Solovejkina (2002), Spirjagin (2005), Tjurina (2005), Tolmachev (2005), Ungaeva (2005), Veretennikova (2005), Vilenskij et al. (2002), Zas'ko (2004), Zemskova (2005), Zhits (2000), and Zverev (2005).

The major problem with the existing research is that it is fragmented, mostly limited to small journal articles, book chapters, and few dissertations. No complex studies of economic growth have been presented by the local scholars. As a result, there is a widening gap in the scholarly literature on economic growth in Ukraine. The goal of this work is to fill the gap between the rapid economic growth as an objective economic reality of Ukraine and the lack of scholarly literature on the issue. This book presents a theoretical and empirical investigation of economic growth and the possible impact of human capital on economic growth in transition economies of Ukraine. For comparison, it analyses similar processes in Russia, Poland, and Hungary as well as in some other countries in the region during the period of 1989–2009. It defines place and role of human capital in the process of transition from the exogenous to the endogenous forms of growth and socioeconomic development.

A substantial part of the book is devoted to the integrative scholarly synthesis of the Western literature on economic growth with special emphasis on theoretical aspects of growth. We consider economic transition within the set of theories of economic growth and at the same time consider the phenomenon of economic growth in the context of post-Soviet transition. Such a contextualization allows for finding and highlighting certain features and processes within economic transition that were earlier neglected by the scholars.

Part I contains an integrative literature synthesis of the major contributions to the theory of economic growth. It presents both exogenous and endogenous theories of economic growth. In this part, we argue that exogenous economic growth models of Solow-Swan and Leontief do not offer an adequate description of the transition experience. Part II presents an analysis of the process of transition and points to the exogenous and endogenous components of current economic growth in Ukraine. This part argues for the need to move from predominantly exogenous to endogenous type of growth. Part III is focused on the data analysis. It presents a substantial bloc of data on Ukraine. Among the models of economic growth, presented in the literature, endogenous model is chosen as most appropriate for our evaluation. Part IV presents description of the model, the data, and empirical results. It also presents the results of estimating a set of equations and impulse response function. Conclusions and policy recommendations are presented in the Conclusion.

PART I

GENESIS OF THE GROWTH THEORIES

We will start from the review of major developments of economic thought over the last few centuries as related to economic growth. This review is a combination of chronological changes and focuses on particular issues in theories of growth. In this manner, we offer an integrative scholarly synthesis of economic growth. This synthesis allows demonstrating incremental development of the models turned into qualitative transitions and rivalry of exogenous and endogenous concepts of growth. The review is built around the ideas that the economists formulate rather than around the economists themselves. It draws some preliminary inferences for Ukraine. This is done in order to show the high degree of applicability of earlier and modern theories of economic growth to contemporary Ukraine. The explanatory power of early and modern concepts of growth is such that it can be of use in understanding the processes of economic transition in Ukraine and first of all, growth. It is not overloaded with the complex mathematical equations and keeps the major ideas and critiques easily understandable for the reader while placing the topic in the broader scholarly literature. Deeper understanding of economic growth requires evaluating the theory of growth in an historical perspective.

1.1 Early Concepts of Growth

Later mercantilists may be considered as founding fathers of the modern theories of growth. At the early stages of development of growth theory economists considered growth as a process of an increase in the national wealth. Theories of economic growth acquired a major direction during the time of mercantilists' domination in the fifteenth–seventeenth centuries and Physiocrats of the eighteenth century (Kregel, 1973). Mercantilists considered accumulation of wealth as the major source of economic growth and the major goal of economic activities of merchants and the state (McDermott, 1999). Representatives of the early mercantilism gave their preference to precious metals and metallic money as materials with perfect liquidity. The late mercantilists considered economic wealth of a nation in terms of total volume of produced commodities and supported positive trade balance. This tendency can partially be explained by the development of manufacturing and domestic markets. According to mercantilists, opportunities of obtaining profit from commodity production and access to credit resources facilitate multiplication of wealth. Presence of sufficient amount of metal money, that is, golden and silver coins, gives necessary access to credit and relatively low affordable borrowing interest rate in the country. For this reason mercantilists insisted on limiting gold outflow from the country.

Presence of golden and silver coins in monetary circulation was given a status of the necessary ground for economic growth. The active trade and commerce was considered as a precondition for economic growth. This approach can be considered as historically justified. All the capital in that era was represented by the trade capital, while there was no manufacturing capital in substantial quantity. Mercantilists favored export since it was a primary source of metal money and at the same time supported restrictions on import of goods in the country. Such a policy was intended to maintain positive trade balance, sufficient amount of money, and hence stable economic growth. Mercantilists voted for the low wages and thought that high wages will lead to a decrease in productivity and the volume of produced goods, and slow down accumulation of wealth. Weakness of systemic approach and absence of sufficient theoretical grounds were characteristics of mercantilism.

Domination of mercantilist doctrines ended in the early eighteenth century, when mercantilists were replaced by Physiocrats. Physiocrats considered economic life as a natural process that has its own natural laws. They proclaimed a principle of "natural law." Physiocrats opposed interference of the state in economic processes. The major principles of Physiocrats were statements about the leading role of agriculture, surplus product, and a unified system of monetary and commodity circulation. According to Physiocrats, the real product was produced only in agriculture. Other branches of the national economy could only change its form. Physiocrats also accepted an idea about the existence of surplus as a part of the produced product that was not used in consumption or in production. This surplus was accumulated in the society and created increase in the national wealth. Francois Quesnay was a leading Physiocrat. He developed the system of economic reproduction and distribution of national product on the national scale.

1.2 Classics of Economic Growth

The first economist to write about the correlates of growth was David Hume (1711–1776). Hume emphasized foreign trade as a primary engine for economic growth saying that both nations involved get an advantage from international trade (Rostow, 1990). Even though Hume is known more as a philosopher, his contribution to the understanding of economic growth at the early stages of development of economic thought is undeniable.

Adam Smith (1723–1790) focused on the accumulation of capital as crucial for the development of early capitalism. His advice was to accumulate capital and to pay for this accumulation by paying workers minimal wages. Accumulation of capital leads to long-term growth. Competition is in the nature of a contest and the economy is regarded as being propelled forward by technical progress, the driving force of which is the division of labor. The consequences of competition are viewed as equilibrating, with the outcome of the process of equilibration being socially desirable (Reid, 1989).

Thomas Malthus (1766–1834) considered the relationship between the growth of population and the growth of agriculture without technological change. He also supported using tax revenue to fund capital accumulation and investment. Malthus emphasized proportions in development in order to avoid over-saving, idle capacity, and unemployment. In his understanding, proportions in development means proportional increases in population, capital, and savings rates, which in turn lead to full capacity utilization and full employment. Malthus suggested that population was affected by economic conditions, and showed a positive connection between income growth and population growth. However, population was considered a noneconomic factor in the production process; he believed that it did not affect economic growth (Rostow, 1990).

David Ricardo (1772–1823) suggested the existence of a natural market wage, and wrote that new technology leads to a decline in the demand for labor assuming a particular form of technological change. He also emphasized proportions, as did Malthus, and diminishing and increasing returns on capital (Rostow, 1990). John Stuart Mill (1808–1873) supported the general idea that output is a function of labor, capital, and land, and suggested that an increase in output depends on an increase in inputs or their productivity. Mill, therefore, distinguished between the quality and quantity of inputs and between extensive and intensive types of growth. Such progressive ideas are logically explained by the fact that he wrote during the industrial revolution in England. A typical production function is given in equation 1:

$$Y_t = F\ (K_t,\ L_t,\ N_t), \tag{1}$$

Y – output;

N – land is fixed and exogenous and slowly goes out of the model over time;

K – capital, with its primary accumulation and then reinvestment, is a factor in extensive economic growth;

L – labor comes from the outside, but is not generated within the system of production, without consideration of its quality.

Diminishing returns to capital and labor were assumed. The capital stock was modeled as shown in equation 2:

$$K_t(i) = (1 - \delta)\, K_{t-1}(-1) + I_{t-1}(i), \tag{2}$$

t – period,

I – investment,

i – every unit.

There was a physical capital accumulation rule. The key issue is how the level of investment is determined. According to Smith, investment is related to the level of profit. From the neoclassical point of view, investment is proportional to GNP, assuming that land grows with GNP (Rostow, 1990).

1.3 Schumpeter's Creative Destruction and Beyond

Joseph Schumpeter (1883–1950) made a significant contribution to the theory of economic development and business cycles and its historical patterns, in particular. Emphasizing the role of innovator, he supported general equilibrium theory, and at the same time stated clearly that in his view such theory could not cope with innovation. He writes: "But static analysis is not only unable to predict consequences of discretionary changes in the traditional ways of doing things; it can neither explain the occurrence of such productive revolutions nor the phenomena which accompany them. It can only investigate the new equilibrium position after the changes have occurred" (1911, pp. 62–63).

Nelson (1996) notes that Schumpeter was curiously uninterested in where the basic ideas for innovations, be they technological or organizational, come from. "The 'entrepreneur' is not viewed by Schumpeter as having anything to do with their generation. It would appear that it is this passage that lies at the root of the argument, often made, that Schumpeter considered invention and innovation very different acts" (p. 90). Schumpeter is most known for his thesis of creative destruction, which he connects directly with competitiveness and organizational changes. He writes:

> The opening up of new markets, foreign or domestic, and the organizational development from the craft shop and factory to such concerns as U.S. Steel illustrate the same process of industrial mutation—if I may use that biological term—that incessantly revolutionizes the economic structure from within, incessantly destroying the old one, incessantly creating a new one. This process of Creative Destruction is the essential fact about capitalism. (1947, p. 83)

Later, however, Schumpeter realized the importance of technological change and that the venue for innovation is the large firm with an attached R&D laboratory that creates new products that the firm introduces. He wrote: "The first thing a modern concern does as soon as it feels it can afford it is to establish a research department every member of which knows that his bread and butter depends on his success in devising improvements" (p. 96).

Philippe Aghion and Peter Howitt (1998a), drawing implications from their tests for endogenous growth, suggested that the long-run rate of growth should be positively correlated with the flow of patents, the flow of entry of new firms, and the flow of new product introduction. They say:

> The central role in creative destruction in Schumpeterian growth theory can be tested by looking at the correlation between growth and two other variables, the flow of exit of firms and the rate of obsolescence of capital. The former is identical to the flow of entry in a steady-state equilibrium, while the latter is the rate of arrival of new innovations, which we have seen is equal to the rate of growth. Hence, the long-run rate of growth should be positively correlated with the flow of exit of firms and with the rate of obsolescence of capital. (p. 429)

1.4 Modern Theories of Growth

Modern growth theory may be traced to the classical article by Frank Ramsey (1928) "A Mathematical Theory of Savings." In this article Ramsey introduced an inter-temporarily separable utility function and derived an optimality condition from it. He points out that if current consumption were reduced in favor of current savings, then future consumption would increase. Therefore, if the marginal product of capital is high, the cost of foregone current consumption is lower than the benefits from increased future consumption.

Writing on the problem of economic growth, Ramsey (1928) suggested the following:

> The first I propose to tackle is this: how much of its income should a nation save? To answer this simple rule is obtained valid under conditions of surprising generality; the rule, which will be further elucidated later, runs as follows. The rate of saving multiplied by the marginal utility of money should always be equal to the amount by which the total net rate of enjoyment of utility falls short of the maximum possible rate of enjoyment. (1928, vol. 2, p. 5)

The main simplifying assumptions made by Ramsey were the following: the community goes on for ever without changing either in size or in its capacity for enjoyment or in its aversion to work; enjoyment and sacrifices at different times can be calculated independently and added together; no new inventions or improvements in organization are introduced without a certain degree of accumulation. Distributional considerations were also ignored. He assumed that the way in which consumption and labor are distributed among the members of the community depends solely on the total amount of consumption and labor. Total satisfaction is a function of total consumption of goods and labor hours.

Ramsey suggested that the rate of interest is governed primarily by the demand price, and may greatly exceed the rate ultimately necessary to induce abstinence. Similarly, in the accounting of a socialist state, the function of the rate of interest would be to ensure the wisest use of existing capital, not to serve in any direct way as a guide to the proportion of income that should be saved. After Ramsey, John M. Keynes (1935) pointed out that the savings ordinarily do not equal the amount of investment. As a result, the market economy is naturally unstable. Sen (1970) mentioned that:

> While the classical economists—Marx in particular—were much concerned with growth, its modern revival started with a remarkable paper of

> Roy Harrod published in 1939. Interest in growth revived at first slowly and then by leaps and bounds. This was to a considerable extent the result of an immense practical concern with growth after the Second World War. The war-damaged economies were trying hard to reconstruct fast, the underdeveloped countries were attempting to initiate economic development, the advanced capitalist countries being relatively free from periodic slumps were trying to concentrate on raising the long-run rate of growth, and the socialist countries were determined to overtake the richer capitalist economies by fast economic expansion. Growth was everybody's concern and it is no wonder that in such a milieu growth theory was pampered by the attention of economists. (p. 9)

Roy Harrod (1939) and Evsey Domar (1946) attempted to integrate Keynesian analysis with elements of economic growth. They used production functions and mathematical analysis to argue that the capitalist system is inherently unstable. The extended model is concerned with the problem of stability-instability in the system. Harrod (1939) noted that:

> The axiomatic basis of the theory which I propose to develop consists of three propositions, namely: (a) that the level of a community's income is the most important determinant of its supply of saving; (b) that the rate of increase of its income is an important determinant of its demand for saving; and (c) that demand is equal to supply. It thus consists in a marriage of the "acceleration principle" and the "multiplier" theory... (p. 14)

Harrod suggested that if investors anticipate more than the warranted rate of growth, the actual growth rate of demand will exceed even the high expected growth rate, and investors may decide that they expected too little from the economy. If investors anticipate a growth rate lower than the warranted growth rate, then the actual growth rate will fall short of the expected growth rate, and investors may decide that they expected too much rather than too little from the economy. "The market thus seems to give a perverse signal to the investor, and this is the source of Harrod's problem" (Sen, 1970, p. 12). Also Sen noted that Harrod's model of instability is undoubtedly incomplete, but it cannot be denied that he was focusing attention on an immensely important part of growth economics that subsequent preoccupation with growth models with perfect foresight has somewhat tended to obscure (p. 14).

Domar (1946) noted that, in the economic literature on the relation between capital accumulation and employment, Marx made a notable contribution. More recently, Keynes (1935) and his followers suggested that labor productivity is not a function of technological progress in the abstract, but technological progress embodied in capital goods, and the amount of capital goods in general. Even without technological progress, capital accumulation increases labor productivity, at least to a certain point, both because more capital is used per worker in each industry and because there is a shift of labor to industries that use more capital and can afford to pay a higher wage. Domar criticized Keynes on the basis that:

> The standard Keynesian system does not provide us with any tools for deriving the equilibrium rate of growth. The problem of growth is entirely absent from it because the explicit assumption can be justified only over short periods of time; it will result in serious errors over a period of a few years. Clearly, a full-employment level of income of five years ago would create considerable unemployment today. We shall assume instead that employment is a function of the ratio of national income to productive capacity. Because investment in the Keynesian system is merely an instrument for generating income, the system does not take into account the extremely essential, elementary and well-known fact that investment also increases productive capacity. This dual character of the investment process makes the approach to the equilibrium rate of growth from the investment (capital) point of view more promising: if investment both increases productive capacity and generates income, it provides us with both sides of the equation the solution of which may yield the required rate of growth. (Domar, 1946, p. 140)

Following the principle that the total increase of capital is equal to the total saving in the period, the fundamental equation $G = S/C$ may be modified as shown in equation 3:

$$G_w = \frac{S - k - (K/x)}{C}, \tag{3}$$

where G is growth, S is savings, and C is capital.

The simple Harrod-Domar model assumes that investment is determined entirely by planned savings and there is no independent investment function based on expectations of the future. The Harrod-Domar growth model provides a very simple framework within which the relationships among the aggregate macro variables can be examined. Even though it is simple, Chowdhury and Kirkpatrick (1994) noted:

> A host of planning problems and a wide range of possibilities can be analyzed within the H-D framework. In fact, the H-D model or some variant of it is the most widely used quantitative planning technique and, even though

> many plan documents do not explicitly present the H-D model, elements of it can be found in the way investment requirements and the role of savings are analyzed in the formulation of the economic growth plan. (p. 12)

The basic Harrod-Domar model (1946) makes the following assumptions. First, savings is proportional to national income. Hence,

$$S = sY, \tag{4}$$

where S is savings, Y is national income, and s is the average propensity to save. Second, the amounts of capital and labor required to produce a given amount of output are given. The aggregate production function can be presented as in equation 5:

$$Y = min\ (K/v,\ L/u), \tag{5}$$

where $u = L/Y$ is the amount of labor required to produce one unit of output, or the reciprocal of labor productivity, and $v = K/Y$ is the amount of capital required to produce one unit of output, or the reciprocal of capital productivity.

According to this production function, output is determined by the lesser of the available quantity of labor and capital. Capital and labor are not substitutes, but perfect complements. From this assumption, Chowdhury and Kirkpatrick (1994) conclude that "since the developing countries are usually labor surplus (relative to capital) economies, it follows that capital is the determining factor for the growth of output" (p. 13).

Assuming investment (I) is equal to savings, and

$$I = K\Delta K/\Delta t = \dot{K}, \tag{6}$$

where t is time, and $\dot{K}$ is capital growth, we get,

$$S = \dot{K} \text{ and, } sY = \dot{K}. \tag{7}$$

In marginal terms, $v = \Delta K/\Delta Y$,

$$v = \frac{\Delta K/\Delta t}{\Delta Y/\Delta t} = \frac{\dot{K}}{\dot{Y}}., \text{ and} \tag{8a}$$

$$\dot{K} = v\dot{Y}. \tag{8b}$$

By substituting (7) into (8b), we obtain

$$sY = v\dot{Y}, \tag{9a}$$

or

$$\dot{Y}/Y = s/v. \tag{9b}$$

The rate of growth of output is determined by the ratio between savings and capital-output ratios. The rate of growth of capital stock is constant and equal to s/v. Replacement of Y in (9b) by K/v in (8b) gives equations 10a and 10b:

$$\dot{K} = (s/v)K, \tag{10a}$$

and thus,

$$\dot{Y}/Y = s/v = \dot{K}/K. \tag{10b}$$

This fundamental equation of the Harrod-Domar model indicates that with historically determined and constant values of s and v, the maximum rate of growth of the capital stock is determined by the ratio s/v. This relation determines the maximum possible rate of growth under the existing economic and other conditions in each country. In many developing countries, the savings rate (s) is low, and a function of national income, which is also low, and unequal (in per capita terms). At the same time v, that is, the capital to output ratio, is high, implying a low level of technology, low productivity, and inefficiency of investment. Therefore, economic growth is a priori low and insufficient to absorb a rapidly growing population, that is, labor force. This results in a high level of permanent unemployment. From this perspective, in order to absorb a growing labor force, the country has to accelerate economic growth beyond the limit set by the traditional values of s and v. Growth acceleration requires an increase in savings to generate a rate of growth sufficient to absorb the new labor force. For example, if the population is growing by 2 percent a year and the country wants to achieve a steady-state rise in per capita income of 4 percent, GDP must grow at the rate of 6 percent annually. If we assume an aggregate capital-output ratio v of 4, then s must be 0.24 as demonstrated in equation 11:

$$s^{\star} = v(\dot{Y}/Y) = 4 \times 0.06 = 0.24. \tag{11}$$

Hence, 24 percent of GDP must be saved in order to achieve a 6 percent growth of GDP. Savings is assumed to be equal to investment. This is the basis of Lewis's comment (1984) that the key to solving the development problem is to raise the proportion of national income saved from 4–5 percent to 12–15 percent.

Uzawa (1967) formulates the Equilibrium Theorem as the following:

> Let the initial capital stock $K^\star$ and labor forces $L^\star$ satisfy $f_k[K^\star / A(0)L^\star] = \lambda + \mu$, where λ is the rate of growth in labor, defined by $\dot{L}(t) / L(t) = \lambda > 0$, and μ is the rate of growth in the efficiency of labor, defined by $\dot{A}(t)/A(t) = \mu > 0$. Then, for the solution $[Y^\star(t), K^\star(t), L^\star(t)]$ to the neoclassical growth process ($\star$), the capital-output ratio $x^\star = K^\star(t)/Y^\star(t)$ remains constant, output per worker $y^\star(t) = Y^\star(t)/L^\star(t)$ increases at the same constant rate as the capital-labor ratio $k^\star = K^\star(t)/L^\star(t)$. The capital-output ratio $x^\star$ is uniquely determined and may be referred to as the equilibrium capital-output ratio of the process ($\star$). (p. 123)

Stability Theorem is presented as the following: "Let the growth equilibrium exist. Then the neoclassical growth process ($\star$) is globally stable; namely, for the solution $[Y(t), K(t), L(t)]$ to the process ($\star$) with arbitrary initial $K(0)$ and $L(0)$, the capital-output ratio $x(t) = K(t)/Y(t)$ converges to the equilibrium capital-output ratio $x^\star$" (p. 123).

Nicholas Kaldor (1961) summed up the broad facts about the growth of advanced industrial economies that a well-told model must be capable of reproducing six "stylized facts." First, real output per person (or per hour) grows at a more or less constant rate over fairly long periods of time. There are short-run fluctuations, of course, and even changes from one quarter-century to another. But at least there is no clear systematic tendency for the rate of increase of productivity in this sense to accelerate or to slow down. If, in addition, labor input grows at a steady rate, aggregate output must also grow, since output is the product of labor input and output per unit of labor, the rate of growth of labor, and labor productivity.

Second, the stock of real capital, crudely measured, grows at a more or less constant rate exceeding the rate of growth of labor. Capital per person can also be said to grow at a more or less steady rate over fairly long periods of time, subject to qualifications about short-run irregularities and occasional breaks in trend. Third, the rates of growth of real output and the stock of capital tend to be about the same, so that the ratio of capital to output shows no systematic trend. Fourth, the rate of profit on capital has no long-run trend, apart from occasional violent changes, associated with sharp variations in effective demand. Fifth, the rate of growth of output per person can vary quite a lot from one country to another. And, finally, economies with a high share of profit out of total income tend to have a high ratio of investment to output (Kaldor, 1961).

1.5 Solow Model of Exogenous Growth

Robert Solow (1988) notes that an economy growing according to the first three (or perhaps four) of the rules listed in the previous section is said to be in a steady state. Its output, employment, and capital stock grow exponentially, and its capital/output ratio is constant. Steady state is normally defined by the requirement that the output and employment be growing at some constant proportional rates and that net saving and investment be a constant fraction of output. Net investment should grow at the same rate as output and the stock of capital, which is the sum of past net investment. The capital/output ratio will therefore be constant. "Most of the modern theory of economic growth is devoted to analyzing the properties of steady states and to finding out whether an economy not initially in a steady state will evolve into one if it proceeds under specified rules of the game" (p. 4). Solow noted that the fourth fact is more controversial than the others for two sets of reasons:

> First, there are problems of definitions and measurement: (a) the ratio of capital to output is very volatile in any fluctuating economy, because the stock of capital is necessarily a sluggish time series, while output is capable of making wide swings in short intervals; (b) we ought really to be interested in the flow of services from the stock of capital, while we actually have measurements of the stock of capital, and the two can diverge not only through changes in the margin of idle capacity (which is really point made under (a)), but also through variations in shift work, "down time," running speed, and the like; (c) although I shall be reasoning in terms of a model with only one commodity, so that relative prices do not enter, our data do not come from such a world. If we think of capital as a factor of production, it is presumably the "real" capital stock that matters, but if we think of it as a store of wealth, it is presumably the value of the capital stock in terms of consumer goods that matters, and both capital/output ratios can be constant only if the price of capital goods relative to consumer goods is constant, as it has not in fact always been. Secondly, the data are far from clear about the constancy of the capital-output ratio, however the measurement problems are resolved. (p. 3)

Harrod (1937) proposed a new definition of neutral inventions primarily intended for applications to the problem of economic growth. According to Harrod, a technical invention is defined as neutral if at a constant rate of interest it does not disturb the value of the capital coefficient. Harrod's classification was discussed by Robinson (1937) who showed graphically that a neutral invention is equivalent to "an all-round increase in the efficiency of labor" (p. 140).

The model presented by Kaldor and Mirrlees (1969) introduces technical progress in the specific form of the rate of improvement of the design and technique of newly produced capital equipment as the main engine of economic growth, determining not only the rate of growth in productivity, but, together with other parameters, rate of obsolescence, the average lifetime of equipment, the share of investment of income, the share of profits, and the relationship between investment and potential output. In fact, it shows future expected capital-output ratio on new capital. Kaldor and Mirrlees suggested that the model is Keynesian in its mode of operation and considers entrepreneurial expenditure decisions as primary and incomes and profits as secondary. Also the model is non-neoclassical in that technological factors, marginal productivities or marginal substitution ratios, play no role in the determination of wages and profits. A "production function" in the sense of a single-valued relationship between some measure of capital, K_t, the labor force N_t, and of output Y_t (all at the time t) that clearly does not exist. Everything depends on past history, on how the collection of equipment goods, which comprises K_t (as measured by historical cost) if a greater part of the existing capital stock is of more recent creation; this would be the case, for example, if the rate of growth population has been accelerating.

> Whilst "machines" earn quasi-rents which are all the smaller the older they are (so that, for the oldest surviving machine, the quasi-rents are zero) it would be wrong to say that the position of the marginal "machine" determines the share of quasi-rent (or gross profits) in total income. For the total profit is determined quite independently of the structure of these "quasi-rents"... by the factors determining the share of investment in output and the proportion of profits saved and therefore the position of the "marginal" machine is itself fully determined by the other equations of the system. It is the macro-economic condition, and not the age-and-productivity structure of machinery, which will determine what the (aggregate) share of quasi-rents will be. (p. 188)

According to this statement, the technical progress function is very consistent with a technological investment function, that is, a shifting in time functional relationship between investment per worker and output per worker. However, it would not be correct to say that the marginal product of investment in the creation of new capital plays a role in determining the amount per man. Since the profitability of operating the machines and equipment is expected to diminish in time, the marginal addition to the stream of profits, which Kaldor and Mirrlees call the "marginal value productivity," will be something quite different from the marginal product in the technological sense, and it will not be a derivative from a technological function only, but will depend on the all system of the relationships.

The authors raise the question of to what extent the technical progress function imposes some restraint on the nature of technological change. Every change in the rate of investment per worker implies a change in the extent to which innovations are actually utilized. Since the capital saving innovations, which increase the output-capital ratio and output-labor ratio, are much more profitable to the entrepreneur than the labor saving ones that give the same rate of increase in labor productivity, and the balance of technological change will appear with higher capital consumption, the greater the rate of increase in investment per worker.

The main suggestion for economic policy is that any scheme that leads to the accelerated retirement of old machinery and equipment, such as taxes on use of morally and/or physically old equipment, technologies and plants, and environmental pollution, and lower or no taxes on investment funds is bound to accelerate for a short period the rate of increase in output per head y/y since it will increase the number of workers available for the new machines n, and hence investment I, and will involve a reduction in p/y. Kaldor and Mirrlees conclude that "A more permanent cure, however, requires stimulating of the technical dynamism of the economy (raising the technical progress function) which is not only (or perhaps mainly) a matter of more scientific education and more expenditure on research, but of higher quality business management which is more alert in searching for technical improvements and less resistant to their introduction" (p. 190).

Behind technological change only, knowledge acquired by learning and training in the process of production should also be emphasized. Kenneth Arrow (1962) starts his investigation on the economic implications of learning by doing saying:

> It is by now incontrovertible that increases in per capita income cannot be explained simply by increases in the capital-labor ratio. Though doubtless no economist would ever have denied the role of technological change in economic growth, its overwhelming importance relative to capital formation has perhaps only been fully realized with the important empirical studies of Abramovitz (1956) and Solow (1957). These results do not directly

> contradict the neo-classical view of the production function as an expression of technological knowledge. All that has to be added is the obvious fact that knowledge is growing in time. Nevertheless a view of economic growth that depends so heavily on an exogenous variable, let alone one as difficult to measure as the quantity of knowledge, is hardly intellectually satisfactory. From a quantitative, empirical point of view, we are left with time as an explanatory variable. Now trend projections, however necessary they may be in practice, are basically a confession of ignorance, and, what is worse from a practical viewpoint, are not policy variables. (p. 155)

Arrow suggests that the concept of knowledge that underlies the production function at any moment needs analysis. Knowledge has to be acquired before and during the process of production. Different students with the same educational experiences may have different amounts of knowledge and so the different countries, at the same moment of time, have different production functions even with the same natural resource endowment (Arrow, 1991). Two generalizations of psychologists on learning are emphasized. First, learning is the product of experience. Learning can only take place through attempts to solve a problem. Second, learning associated with repetition of essentially the same problem is subject to sharply diminishing returns.

Petrus Verdoorn (1956) applied the principle of the learning curve to national output. He used the "Horndall effect" in Sweden to motivate this extension to the analysis of growth. Horndall iron works in Sweden had no new investment, and therefore presumably no significant change in its methods of production, for a period of 15 years, but productivity rose on the average close to 2 percent per annum. This steadily increasing performance can only be imputed to learning from experience. Verdoorn developed a model in which capital and labor are nonlinear functions of output, assuming the rate of output is a measure of cumulative output including learning. He notes that full employment of capital and labor simultaneously is impossible. Arrow (1962) states that another of Vendoorn's conclusions—that the savings ratio must be fixed by some public mechanism at the uniquely determined level that would ensure full employment of both factors—is wrong. Arrow says that one factor or another will be unemployed (p. 160).

Arrow's model ignores the possibility of capital-labor substitution. Profits are assumed to be a result of technical change. The rate of investment will be less than the optimum. Net investment and the stock of capital become subordinate, with gross investment taking a leading role. The main hypothesis is that technical change in general can be ascribed to experience. Some economic implications can be drawn from the model. We introduce learning into our historical review of growth models by first examining how exogenous technological change affects output. In the Cobb-Douglas production function (Sen, 1970), output is presented as:

$$Y = L^{1-\alpha} K^{\alpha},\ 0 < \alpha < 1. \tag{12}$$

The per capita production function can be written as:

$$Y = f(k) = k^{\alpha}, \tag{13a}$$

$$y = Y/L. \tag{13b}$$

The rate at which saving increases, k, is the rate of saving per person, sy, where saving is a function of personal income. The rate of depreciation of k is the amount of depreciation per person, $\delta\, k$. Population growth causes k to fall at the rate nk. The net rate of increase in k therefore, depends on three factors: the rate of depreciation (δ), the rate of population growth (n), and k, and can be presented as shown in equation 14:

$$k = sf(k) - \delta\, k - nk = sf(k) - (\delta + n)k = sk^{\alpha} - (n + \delta)k. \tag{14}$$

Constant returns to scale are assumed, so that the absolute size of the economy or total output is irrelevant to per capita growth.

In the Solow model,

$$Y = TK^{\alpha}L^{\beta}, \tag{15}$$

where $0 < \alpha < 1$.

$$Y = Q + \alpha L + (1 - \alpha)K. \tag{16}$$

$$Q = a + x + e. \tag{17}$$

In the long run, the rate of growth is independent of the rate of investment. Exogenous improvements in technology generate productivity growth. Solow (1957) modeled economic growth using a standard neoclassical production function with decreasing returns to capital. Taking the rates of saving and population growth as exogenous, he showed that these two variables determine the steady-state level of income per capita. If saving and population growth rates vary across countries, different countries reach different steady states. Mankiw et al. (1992) noted: "Solow's model gives simple testable predictions about how these variables influence the steady-state level of income. The higher the rate of saving, the richer the country. The higher the rate of population growth, the poorer the country" (p. 1).

We start by considering some of the theoretical approaches to exogenous economic growth. The Solow model is our starting point for detailed consideration of exogenous models and their implications. Assume the following production function for national output, Y.

$$Y = A + \alpha L + (1 - \alpha) K, \tag{18}$$

where Y is output, L is labor, K is capital, α is labor's share in total product, $(1 - \alpha)$ is capital's share in total product, and A denotes technical progress. All variables are in logs. Economic growth could be achieved in the short run by increasing capacity utilization, and in the long run by changing capacity (k) itself.

$$Y = Q + \alpha L + (1 - \alpha) K \tag{19}$$

and $Q = a + x + e$.

Where x is capacity utilization and e is efficiency in the allocation of resources (allocative efficiency) (Solow, 1970).

1.6 Leontief's Poverty Trap

Wassily Leontief (1958) emphasized the role of savings in economic growth: "Among the many factors which determine the growth or stagnation—as the case may be—of a national economy, its rate of saving out of current income and the subsequent increase in income resulting from the investment of these savings play an important role" (p. 106). The key point here is that preferences of a given national economy between present and future levels of consumption in terms of a conventional set of social indifference curves affect growth. Of course, the problem of maximizing utility—by planning the allocation of income between consumption and investment—over long intervals of time is certainly of considerable interest itself, despite the fact that it was first brought up by Frank Ramsey 70 years ago.

In the study of linear programming, Dorfman et al. (1958) analyze, among other things, efficient programs of capital accumulation on the assumption of Leontief-type (fixed coefficient) technologies. Except for the fact that their model of capital accumulation permits nonzero consumption, its characteristics are basically the same as those defining the situation with savings presented by Leontief. Rudiger Dornbush (1996) expanded the growth equation to include these insights on savings and growth. Domestic saving and current account deficit are determinants of growth through capital investment:

$$Y = Q + \alpha n + r(S + \lambda), \tag{20}$$

where S is the national saving rate, λ is no interest current account deficit expressed as a fraction of GDP, r is the marginal return on capital formation, and n is labor. This equation highlights the role of domestic savings. Higher saving rates (S) finance capital accumulation and growth. However, the equation makes the important point that the immediate impact of saving on growth is minor. Assume that the return to capital is 10 percent. Raising the saving rate by 5 percentage points of GDP will then raise the growth rate of output by only 0.5 percentage points. Of course, the compound growth effects of an extra 0.5 percent growth are considerable, but only in the long run.

Michael Carlberg (1997) examined the effects of savings, labor, and the interest rate on international economic growth and obtained the following results:

> An increase in the saving rate does affect neither capital per head nor output per head. It reduces foreign debt per head. And it improves consumption per head. An increase in the rate of labor growth leaves no impact on capital per head and output per head. It increases foreign debt per head and worsens consumption per head. An increase in foreign interest rate depresses both capital per head and output per head. Besides, it brings down foreign debt per head. As long as the foreign interest rate is low, the shock deteriorates consumption per head. But as soon as the foreign interest rate is sufficiently high, the shock improves consumption per head. (p. 5)

Foreign credits and saving were introduced into growth models by Leontief (1990).

The Leontief model is presented graphically in figure 1.1. TP measures the marginal time-preference (slope of indifference curves). Starting with a very small stock of capital and income below the lowest equilibrium point, A, the system expands toward A. If its initial position in the economy were located some place between A and B, equilibrium also moves toward A. In this case, the process is a regressive one characterized

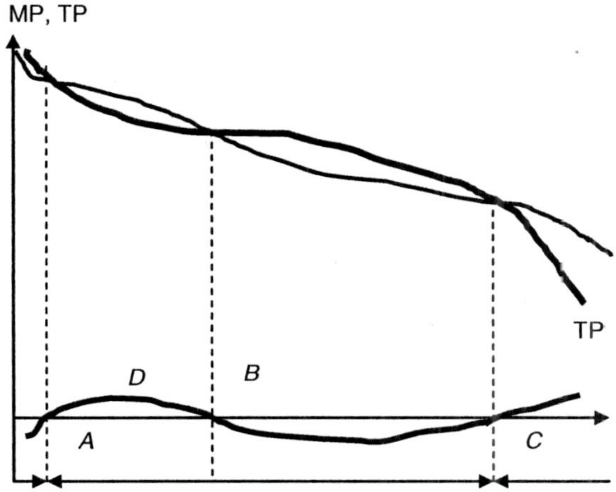

Figure 1.1 Leontief's poverty trap.

by gradual diminishing of the stock of productive capital, reduction in the rate of output (income), and incidentally—as the MP (marginal productivity of capital, slope of the capital-output line) curve shows—an increase in the real rate of interest. Once *A* is reached, the system "stagnates" at that low but stable equilibrium position. When pushed to the left by the action of some outside force, such as an accidental loss of productive capital, it would move back again toward *A* but not beyond.

If, as beneficiary of a foreign loan or gift, this country finds itself in the possession of some additional capital and correspondingly increased income, our country at once proceeds to "live above its means," that is, consume its capital and gradually reduce its output until the stationary state at *A* is again reached. Even a constant flow of foreign aid could, in such a case, do no more than help the system to maintain its income and consumption at some point between *A* and *B*, without, however, releasing any tendency toward further growth. Robert Barro and Xavier Sala-i-Martin (1999) point out: "We can think of a poverty trap as a stable steady state with low levels of per capita output and capital stock. This outcome is a trap because, if agents attempt to break out of it, then the economy has a tendency to return to the low-level steady state" (p. 49).

These observations apply, however, only to gifts or loans not large enough to push the rate of output beyond *B*. Once on the other side of that unstable equilibrium position, *B*, the economy begins to save, accumulate, and increase its revenue; in short, it proceeds to develop under its own power. According to the graph, the new stable equilibrium is approached from the much higher income level, *C*. Had the structural conditions been such as to keep *MP* above *TP*, and thus the *D*—curve below the zero line throughout its entire stretch to the right of *B*, the process of economic growth—once that threshold has been passed, would go on indefinitely until high income level, *C* (Leontief, 1966). The entire scheme assumes that all complementary factors except capital are held constant. Later Leontief notes that changes in the basic structural conditions of the economy shift the equilibrium positions *A*, *B*, and *C*. He even assumes that "some of these positions of stationary state might even disappear or new ones might be created" (Leontief, 1966).

The poverty trap theories were offered even before Leontief's works. John Keynes offered a theory based on the dominance of effective demand and focused on explaining the persistence of high level of unemployment during the Great Depression of 1929–1932 and the following crisis of 1937. The low level development trap was extended by Ragnar Nurske (1953), Richard Nelson (1956), Paul Rosenstein-Rodan (1957), and Albert Hirschman (1958). These authors believed in the need for a big external impact to initiate economic growth. This external impact should be significant enough to move the system to a new equilibrium at a higher level. The external force may be either the government, that is, public sector, or a foreign aid agency.

Some of the most recent studies that consider impact of foreign financial aid on economic growth are by Barro and Sala-i-Martin (1999), Boon (1996), Burnside and Dollar (2000), Hansen and Tarp (2001), Lensink and Morrissey (1999). The authors examine the interaction between foreign financial assistance and growth. During the recent decades unilateral and multilateral donors provide a substantial amount of financial assistance to the developing countries. The stated goals of this aid are often formulated as poverty alleviation and promotion of economic growth. The results of such projects are not satisfactory in many cases. This necessitates further research on the issue.

Peter Boon (1996) investigates possible correlation between foreign aid effectiveness and government macroeconomic policy. He studies mechanisms through which foreign aid helps to alleviate poverty and initiates economic growth. He uses Barro's model of endogenous growth according to which foreign aid has a significant impact on growth because aid inflow contributes to an increase in investments and growth. Boon finds that a positive impact of foreign aid on investment and growth is conditional on government policy. Government policy, in its turn, can be represented with the three different approaches: elitist, egalitarian, or "laissez-faire." Boon states that elitist governments are concerned only with the welfare of a rich group in the population that supports the political elite. Egalitarian governments attempt to maximize the welfare of the poor.

The laissez-faire approach in governmental policy is characterized by minimal government intrusion into the market-based system of distribution of wealth. In this case the government attempts to maximize only the welfare of the most economically and socially vulnerable stratum of the population. Boon concludes that the best condition for foreign aid effectiveness is the elitist regime. Foreign aid in this case does not have significant effect on investments and growth, but substantially increases government size, government consumption, and the welfare of the political elite (Boon, 1996). Boon established that foreign aid "does not promote economic development for two reasons: Poverty is not caused by capital shortage, and it is not optimal for politicians to adjust distortionary policies when they receive aid flows" (p. 322).

Lensink and Morrissey (1999) assume that foreign aid does have an impact on growth, and there are government policies that make aid more effective. They argue that "the principal factor determining the impact of aid on growth appears, in many results, to be investment" (p. 3). The authors point out that macroeconomic performance determines country vulnerability to shocks and aid instability and thus the lack of aid efficiency with regard to its impact on growth. Using cross-country growth regressions Lensink and Morrissey (1999) conclude that aid has a positive impact on investment and a significant effect on growth if to control for aid inflow uncertainty.

Leontief does not offer broad explanation for the meaning of the zero line in his model. However, Barro and Sala-i-Martin (1999), using the neoclassical model of Solow (1957) and Swan (1969) and the golden rule of capital accumulation and dynamic efficiency, derived this line. The fundamental differential equation of the Swan-Solow model is:

$$\dot{k} = sf(k) - (n + \delta)k_0. \tag{21}$$

Where $n + \delta$ is the effective depreciation rate for the capital-labor ratio, $k = K/L$. If the saving rate, s, were 0, then k would decline partly due to depreciation of k at the rate δ and partly due to growth of L at the rate n. In fact, $(n + \delta)$ is Leontief's zero line.

Robert Barro and Xavier Sala-i-Martin (1999) noted the following: "We define a steady-state as a situation in which the various quantities grow at constant rates. In the Solow-Swan model, the steady-state corresponds to $k = 0$, that is, to the intersection of the $sf(k)$ curve with the $(n + \delta)\ k$ line. The corresponding value of k is denoted $k^\star$." Algebraically,

$$s\,f(k^\star) = (n + \delta)\,k^\star. \tag{22}$$

> Since k is the steady state, y and c are also constant at the values $y^\star = f(k)$ and $c^\star = (1 - s)\,f(k)$, respectively. Hence, in the neoclassical model, the per capita quantities k, y, and c do not grow in the steady state. The constancy of the per capita magnitudes means that the levels of variables—K, Y, and C—grow in the steady state at the rate of population growth, n. (p. 19)

Development of the production forces in society, changes in technique within firms, and technical progress lead to changes in the skills of workers, income, and consumption. With the increasing importance of human capital in development, the shifts along the horizontal axis in figure 1.1 should be considered with the new current rate of savings and accumulation of capital. These ideas are more clearly presented in figure 1.2.

A sufficiently large donation would place the economy on a path that leads eventually to a high level of the steady state or possibly to endogenous steady-state growth. Thus, a relatively large quantity of foreign aid might allow an escape from the poverty trap. Note that the policy of high saving can help a country escape the poverty trap even if the high saving is only temporary. It will also work if the economy's temporary high ratio of domestic investment to GDP is financed by international loans, rather than from domestic saving (Barro and Sala-i-Martin, 1999).

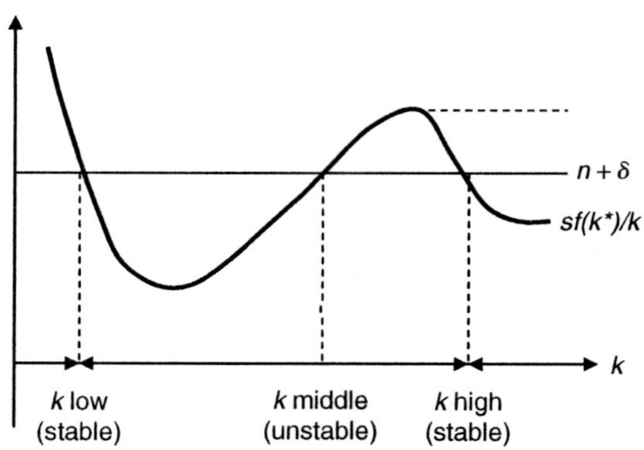

Figure 1.2 Poverty trap according to the modern interpretation by Barro and Sala-i-Martin (1999).

It is important to note, however, that technological change, the utilization of new production technologies, and quality and productivity of labor force would shift the system to the left.

Craig Burnside and David Dollar (2000) analyzed the relationships among foreign aid, economic policies, and economic growth using neoclassical growth theory as a theoretical framework for their study. According to the theory poor countries have a higher marginal rate of return on capital than rich countries and, therefore, a faster growth toward the steady state. The theory also suggests that foreign aid has a positive impact on growth when a recipient country is in transition to its steady state and there is a negative correlation between tax distortion and growth. Burnside and Dollar suggest that unsuccessful government economic policy might decrease the rate of return on capital and slow down the rate of growth. The authors state that the aid impact on growth depends on such macroeconomic factors and processes as budget surplus, inflation, and other measures of monetary policy and trade openness can have a positive or negative impact on growth, depending on the level of inflation and the budget deficit. If inflation is relatively low and manageable and the budget deficit is insignificant, the policy indicator is positive. Burnside and Dollar conclude that there are diminishing returns to foreign aid, a small, on average, impact of aid on growth, but a positive impact of aid on growth in the "good" policy environment that busts macroeconomic performance.

Henrik Hansen and Finn Tarp (2001) disagree with the empirical results obtained by Burnside and Dollar and argue that relationships between foreign aid and growth are not conditional on recipient country economic policy. The authors take into consideration the fact that aid affects growth via capital investments, both physical and human. Inclusion of human capital and investment in the model may be considered as an innovative step toward investigating the relationship between foreign aid and growth.

1.7 Growth Reconsidered: Endogeneity of Human Capital

Paul Romer, in his 1990 paper entitled "Endogenous Technological Change," includes technological changes into the model of growth. He considers technology as the method used in a production process that transforms inputs into output and specifies research and development as sources for technological changes. He emphasized ideas that drive progress are specific types of goods considering them as non-rival in contrast to other goods. According to Romer non-rivalry nature of ideas implies increasing returns to scale.

The implications of Romer's model might be found to be very similar to the neoclassical ideas. His model can be viewed as a "semi-endogenous" model because it predicts sustainable growth only in the case of endogenous technological progress and exogenous population growth. The labor force participates in the production process making capital productive and produces ideas that drive technological progress and, therefore, economic growth. Hence, investments in human capital are necessary in order to increase the productivity of labor and capital. For Romer, education is the main source for knowledge and a guide for the implementation of this knowledge in the production process. Health care development is another way to increase labor force productivity (Pomfret, 2000).

Gregory Mankiw et al. (1992) developed an Augmented-Solow type model. They conclude:

> We have suggested that international differences in income per capita are best understood using an augmented Solow growth model. In this model output is produced from physical capital, human capital, and labor, and is used for investment in physical capital, investment in human capital, and consumption. (p. 432)

The production function that is consistent with the empirical results is:

$$Y = K^{\frac{1}{3}} H^{\frac{1}{3}} L^{\frac{1}{3}}. \tag{23}$$

The model has several implications. First, the elasticity of income with respect to physical capital is not substantially different from capital's share in income. This conclusion indicates that capital receives approximately its social return. There are no substantial externalities to the accumulation of physical capital. Second, the accumulation of physical capital has a larger impact on income per capita than the Solow model implies. A higher saving rate leads to higher income in the steady state, which in turn leads to a higher level of human capital. Third, population growth also has a larger impact on income per capita than the Solow model indicates. In the augmented model, human capital must be spread more thinly over the population of workers as well as capital because the higher population growth lowers measured total factor productivity. Fourth, the model has implications for the dynamics of the economy when the economy is not in the steady state. In contrast to endogenous growth models, this model predicts that countries with similar technologies and rates of accumulation and population growth should converge in income per capita.

> More generally, our results indicate that the Solow model is consistent with the international evidence if one acknowledges the importance of human as well as physical capital. The augmented Solow model says that differences in saving, education, and population growth should explain cross-country differences in income per capita. Our examination of the data indicates that these three variables do explain most of the international variation. (p. 433)

There is research on low-development traps within the endogenous growth theories as well. Aghion and Howitt (1998b) consider the model, based on Acemoglu (1994, 1997) and developed by Redding (1996). The model concludes that complementarity between workers' education decisions and firms' R&D decisions surprisingly will not open the possibility for multiple steady-state growth paths, including a low-development trap. The more workers invest in education, the more will entrepreneurs invest in R&D. This can be formalized as shown in equation 24:

$$\mu^\star = 1, \quad \text{if } \alpha < \rho\,(\lambda - 1)(1 + \gamma v^\theta)(1 - \beta), \quad 0 \text{ otherwise.} \tag{24}$$

Thus, the more workers invest in education, that is, the higher the value of υ, the more will entrepreneurs invest in R&D. Such a trap will involve $\mu = 0$ and therefore $v^\star = v(\beta\rho\theta\gamma)^{\frac{1}{1-\theta}}$. For it to exist we simply need

$$\alpha > \delta(1 - \beta)(\lambda - 1)(1 + \gamma\,(\beta\rho\theta\gamma)^{\frac{1}{1-\theta}}). \tag{25}$$

Conversely, in order to a high growth steady state path to exist, we need

$$\alpha < \delta(1 - \beta)(\lambda - 1)(1 + \gamma\,(\beta\rho\theta\gamma)^{\frac{1}{1-\theta}}). \tag{26}$$

The corresponding growth rates will be $g = g = ln\lambda$ in the high-growth equilibrium and $g = g = 0$ in the low-development trap (Aghion and Howitt, 1998b, p. 342). Aghion and Howitt (1998b) conclude that

> Because of the strategic complementarity between R&D and education, we did not have to introduce threshold externalities in the accumulation of human capital in order to generate multiple equilibria and

low-development traps. Second, targeted education policies and R&D subsidies appear as substitutable instruments for moving the economy away from a low-development trap. In practice, however, education subsidies may be easier to monitor than R&D subsidies to industries (the scope for diversion and manipulation being presumably larger in the latter case). (p. 342)

In summary, we find from our review of the literature that, historically, economic growth was considered indivisibly from industrial capital. However, empirical evidence indicates that the primary accumulation of capital was not confined to the industrial sector. Technological changes before the industrial revolution were exogenous to the production process.

With technological maturity (Rostow, 1990), industry became the engine of production, and the accumulation of capital occurred within manufacturing and was followed by reinvestment. However, technological change was still assumed to be exogenous to production, and the theory of exogenous economic growth dominated until 1970s. Beginning in the 1980s economists began to conceptualize technological changes from within production. Emphasis was placed on R&D, and the problem of the accumulation of capital was transferred into the problem of investment and the balance between saving and consumption. Labor was an input that could be developed by investing in human capital, and growth was stimulated by improvements in labor quality. The quality of labor was considered as accumulated capital, and firms faced new choices among physical capital and human capital investments. The endogenous theory of economic growth currently dominates the literature on economic growth. As Benigno Valdes (1999) points out:

Ever since the new wave of research on growth theory began in the late 1980s, proponents of the two theories have been (on and off) arguing over which of the two approaches is better. One (possibly the first) round of the dispute was fought in the empirical arena. To meet the empirical finding that $\lambda = -0.\ 022$, *(α)* the parameter in the aggregate production function $Y_t = K_t^{\alpha}\left(A_t L_t\right)^{1-\alpha}$ has to be approximately to 0.7 (consequently, $1 - \alpha = 0.3$). In the Solow-Swan (S&S) model factor inputs are paid their marginal products, thus in this model is the share of K (and $1 - \alpha$ is the share of L) in national income. So the model predicted (this was the interpretation at the time) that K must receive about 70 percent of the national income and L about 30 percent of it. However, the national income accounts were indicating the opposite: a 30 percent share for K and a 70 percent for L. The proponents of the new theory took it for certain that it was the S&S model

> which failed. Specifically, it assumed that K and L were paid their marginal products but in reality K is paid less and L more than that. Why? Because each new bit of K generates an externality for which it is not compensated. The important point is that the new theory, by means of this externality effect, could explain the observed discrepancy between each factor's marginal product and their actual redistributions. Then, as it often happens in intellectual disputes, the old theory had its turn on the issue and the human capital augmented S&S model came to its rescue. Another round in the debate between the two theories seems to have been constructed over their (as-of-today-known) implications for economic policy. (pp. 168–169)

1.8 Institutions and Growth

Market-based institutions facilitate the processes of transmitting information efficiently, enforcing property rights and contracts, and securing free competition. All of these functions, performed by the market institutions, strengthen the incentives of agents to participate in a market economy. Economists follow closely development of market institutions and their functioning. Many argue that the functions that market-based institutions perform and the processes they facilitate are of key importance to national economies. Douglass North (1990, 1992, 2006, 2007) and Mancur Olson (1982, 1996, 2000) as well as their followers point out the significance of organizational changes for development and growth. De Haan et al. (2006) summarize that "Since the time of Adam Smith, if not before, economists and economic historians have argued that the freedom to choose and supply resources, competition in business, free trade with others and secure property rights are central ingredients for economic progress" (p. 182).

Timothy Yeager (1999) places major emphasis on institutions and their role in developing and transition societies:

> Over time, a nation increases its wealth via technological advancements. For this to occur, a nation's institutional framework must promote the process of creative destruction, which forces firms to improve their products and technology over time or be driven out of business by a competitor. Many nations do not generate this dynamic growth because their organizations are permitted to remain inefficient, shielded from domestic or international competition. (p. 158)

Economic freedoms embedded in market-based institutions are considered as fundamental for economic growth (De Haan and Siermann, 1998; De Haan and Sturm, 2000). Democratic institutions and democratic political regimes overall are guarantors of economic freedoms and instrumental in forming economic regulatory institutions. Some authors point to the importance of democratic freedoms for economic growth (De Haan and Siermann, 1996; De Haan and Sturm, 2003, 2004; De Vanssay and Spindler, 1994; Perotti, 1996). Political institutions are inherently unstable, because political processes change and political life can become turbulent. Accordingly, they may contribute to the instability of the economic system and high volatility in the growth rate. Haber, Razo, and Maurer (2003) offer a study of instability and economic growth in Mexico in the period 1876–1929. The authors link these issues with the historical changes in property rights.

Alesina et al. (1996), Fosu (1992), Haber et al. (2003), Nehru and Dhareswar (1994), and Perotti (1996) suggest that political instability can undermine growth. Several economists, including Bhagwati (1982), Easterly (1993), Fischer (1993), Krueger (1990), Little (1982), Murphy et al. (1991), Olson (1982, 1996, 2000), and Sachs and Warner (1995), have observed significant losses from bad economic policies, especially in developing countries. Some economic historians, such as Mokyr (1990), North (1990), and Rosenberg and Birdzell (1985), have concluded that differences in governance and institutions are crucial for explaining innovations and implementation of technological achievements. Politically powerful groups use the state redistribution function in order to further enrich themselves. Krueger (1974), Posner (1975), and Tullock (1967) point out that political and bureaucratic processes by which this redistribution occurs are responsible for losses from the distortions caused by the state policies.

Jones and Williams (2000) consider research and development as a key determinant of long-run productivity and welfare. They develop an endogenous growth model that incorporates parametrically important distortions in R&D: the surplus appropriability problem, knowledge spillovers, creative destruction, and duplication externalities. The authors assert: "Calibrating the model, we find that the decentralized economy typically underinvests in R&D relatively to what is socially optimal" (p. 67). Aghion and Howitt (1998a) examined heterogeneity in the structure of innovative activity by making a distinction between research and development. They pointed out:

> One advantage that Schumpeterian's growth models is their greater specificity concerning how knowledge is used, how it is generated, and how it creates losses as well as gains ... There are many kinds of innovative activity, generating many different kinds of knowledge. An aggregate theory that

> fails to distinguish between these different activities is potentially misleading if the distinction matters. (p. 36)

They concluded that the level of research tends to covary positively with the rate of growth, even in the extreme case where the general knowledge that underlies long-run growth is created by secondary innovations arising from the development process. R&D effects on long-run growth were researched by Segerstorm (2000) and Sorensen (1999).

Graeme Snooks (1999) points to the North's argument (1990) about fragmentary character of information that causes significant costs in the process of individual decision making. These costs are referred to as transaction costs. Institutions are designed to reduce transaction costs. North (1990) suggests that

> Institutions provide the structure for exchange that (together with the technology employed) determines the costs of transacting and the cost of transformation. How well institutions solve the problems of coordination and production is determined by the motivation of the players (their utility function), the complexity of the environment, and the ability of players to decipher and order the environment (measurement and enforcement). (p. 34)

Transaction costs can be minimized and eliminated only under the condition of perfect information, equally accessible to all the economic agents.

Yeager (1999) outlines the role of institutions in static and dynamic sense:

> In a static sense, institutions define the costs of transacting and the ability of organizations to capture the gains from specialization and division of labor. In a dynamic sense, institutions define the incentive structure under which organizations operate and determine whether or not organizations undertake activities that advance technology. (p. 8)

He also delineates the meanings of institutions and organizations, pointing to the differences and using the "rules of the game" term The central hypothesis of Yeager's work is that "a nation's institutional framework is the key to unlocking its wealth potential" (p. 8). Integration of institutions into economic theory and suggestion of the leading role of institutions in encouraging and promoting economic growth are central ideas of the author. Yeager reminds us that "transaction costs are the costs of making, measuring, and enforcing agreements" (p. 117).

Many authors traditionally attempt to answer the question about why cross-country evidence shows that a subset of developing countries is growing very rapidly, taking advantage of opportunities while other developing countries are growing slowly. Olson et al. (2000) argue that the difference in the rate of growth among developing nations is due to differences in the quality of governance. They show that productivity growth is higher in better-governed countries. Institutions may be measured differently, and so their operationalization may vary. Knack and Keefer (2008) study possible links between institutions and economic performance. They conduct cross-country tests using alternative institutional measures. Glaeser et al. (2004) challenge conventional operationalization of institutions in quantitative analysis along with the measurements and regression techniques. They offer new approaches in measuring impact of institutions on economic growth and seek for possible causalities in the relationships of institutions, human capital, and economic growth.

Institutions define patterns of behavior in organizations, often dictate them, and regulate their functioning and structure. Institutions are intended to reduce and indeed minimize transaction costs. By reducing transaction costs for the agents, institutions facilitate creation and development of markets. Markets bring competition among producers and encourage specialization and division of labor. Specialization by functions, operations, and products leads to an increase in productivity that indicates improved economic performance. As a result, the society experiences an increase in its total welfare and population's well-being.

The statement about the importance of the positive influence of state institutions for the national economy, including processes of economic development and economic growth, is not beyond the arguable. State institutions cause distortions to the market. Such possible distortions are studied in works of Easterly (1993), Fischer (1993), Krueger (1990), Posner (1975), Tullock (1967), to name but a few. Krueger (1974) points out to the detrimental effects of rent-seeking behavior on economic growth. Along with functions that facilitate economic growth, rent-seeking behavior can also be institutionalized. In that case, institutions will play a negative role in economic development and slow down economic growth.

Glaeser et al. (2004) take a part in the debate over whether political institutions cause economic growth, or if it is growth and human capital accumulation that cause further institutional development. Based on simple regression results and some additional evidence, the authors suggest that "(a) human capital is a more basic source of growth than are the institutions, (b) poor countries get out of poverty through good policies, often pursued by dictators, and (c) subsequently improve their political institutions" (p. 271). Accumulation of human capital within the educational systems is indivisible from the process of institutionalization of educational policies. Storesletten and Zilibotti (2000) investigate education, educational policy, and economic growth.

Referring to Lucas (1988), Storesletten and Zilibotti (2000) suggest that "In the *human capital accumulation approach*, economic agents purposefully devote effort, time and resources to increase their productivity" (p. 43; emphasis in the original). But institutions influence the allocation of talent and the way human capital is distributed among public and private sector and different branches of the economy. Murphy et al. (1991) address the importance of allocation of talent in the national economy. Continuing the line of North (1990), Nickell and Layard (1999) trace links between labor market institutions and economic performance.

1.9 Dependency Theory and Structuralists

In line with the economic pessimism of 1990s, it was popular among some Ukrainian economists, as well as the public in general, to search for a cause of economic problems outside the country. There were suggestions that the West now lives even richer because the former Soviet Bloc is experiencing economic downturn. Such a view had a certain ground in the dependency theory that relates developed and developing countries. Yeager (1999) formulates this in the following way: "In its simplest form dependency theory argues that poor countries are poor because rich countries are rich" (p. 13). According to the dependency theory, all countries are grouped in two camps, the center or the core and the periphery. The center is comprised of developed nations while the periphery consists of developing nations. The center exploits the periphery and prefers to maintain the periphery's status as of a major supplier of raw materials. Thus, the center is not interested in a comprehensive economic development of less developed countries.

The solution for the negative trade balance and vulnerability of developing countries was searched for in industrialization, that is, traditional way of moving to the stage of development. Technological advancements and development of domestic market is expected to make national economies in the less developed countries more independent from the global market volatility. Structuralists, among who are Amendola et al. (1992), Cantwell (1989), Chesnais (1986), Dosi et al. (1990), Ernst and O'Connor (1989), Freeman and Foray (1993), Guerrieri (1992, 1998), Guerrieri and

Tylecote (1994), Justman and Teubal (1991), Lall (1990), Pavitt (1984, 1988), Rosenberg (1976, 1982), and Schmookler (1966), point to the need of structural change and the reduction of external dependency. Yeager (1999) summarizes this idea in the following way: "The foreign exchange earnings from raw-materials exports had to be channeled into capital equipment for new industries, a policy known as import substitution industrialization (ISI). The goal of ISI was to develop a domestic manufacturing sector that would produce the previously imported goods" (p. 14). The goal of import substitution raises the issue of protectionism in foreign trade and prevents from using the country's comparative and absolute advantages in international trade. Accordingly, it can be useful as a policy for few decades, but not a permanent solution.

Paolo Guerrieri (1998) suggests that the successful outcome of the transition to new market-type economies in the former Soviet Bloc countries depends on their ability of ensuring an upturn in their medium-long term economic growth prospects. This requires investment both to restructure and modernize production capacity in such a way so as to generate endogenous sources of investment, innovation, and economic growth: "All that implies and requires structural changes in the economy" (p. 15). He points out that:

> In the traditional orthodox neoclassical framework, restructuring, in terms of structural change, can simply be considered a nearly automatic result of an efficient resource allocation among sectors, which is entirely driven by market incentives (a set of relatives prices) according to individual country's comparative advantage (domestic versus world prices). In the traditional model the openness of the economy can be regarded as a very powerful device for rapidly importing efficient world prices and creating these strong incentives for efficiency in resource allocation (restructuring) and long-term growth. Trade specialization is not a problem, because there is always something each country can profitably produce and trade, as long as markets are open and domestic relative prices free to move. (p. 16)

There are well-known theoretical and empirical arguments to cast serious doubts on this conventional explanation of the sequence between trade openness, structural change, and economic growth-development. Although a proper set of market incentives such as those created by "outward oriented" growth strategy is very important, it can be at most considered a necessary condition for the success of the restructuring process. The structural features of industrial restructuring in a transition economy and the role played in it by technology calls for a more articulated approach. Guerrieri uses an alternative sectoral taxonomy to analyze the relationship between technological capability and international trade performance of the major countries, which is consistent with the earlier mentioned theoretical works on technological change and trade specialization. It identifies five types of industries, primarily through a combination of technology sources, technology user requirements, and means of technology appropriation: natural resource-intensive, supplier dominated, or traditional sectors, science based, scale-intensive, and specialized suppliers.

1.10 Economic Development-Growth-Transition Triangle

Bruce Morris (1961) points out that "The terms 'economic growth' and 'economic development' seem to be used interchangeably and refer to a rise in the per capita national output" (p. 7). The author considers a country as experiencing economic growth if it "undergoes a persistent increase in its national output of goods and services per capita over a period of years" (p. 7). Shearer (1961) points to a distinction in these two terms:

> Economic growth to refer to an increase in the output of goods and services, and economic development to imply a more general development, including personal and social values. Thus, a country might be growing economically but failing to develop (or even may be retrogressing) because other values were being lost. (p. 499)

Economic growth does not necessarily lead to higher levels of human development and well-being for all the socioeconomic strata of population. Empirical evidence shows that in some developing nations, economic growth combined with the growing inequality in income distribution leads to a decline in per capita income in the lower strata of population (Foster and Székely, 2000; Page, 2006). As a result, poverty is not being eradicated or even reduced based solely on economic growth.

According to Snooks (1999), "The pioneering development economists and development agencies equated economic development with a growth in real GDP per capita, while many today see it in terms of 'poverty reduction,' 'equity,' 'basic needs,' and 'human development' (p. 4). Snooks points out that such a change in understanding of development and growth has important policy implications. He refers to Paul Streeten (1995) in an assertion that "the evolution from economic growth, via employment, jobs and justice, redistribution with growth to basic needs and human development, represents a genuine evolution of thinking and is not a comedy of errors, a lurching from one slogan to the next" (pp. 17–18).

Snooks offers a new theory of economic development based on the concept of the global strategic transition.

Morris (1961) points to the difficulty in measuring different aspects of economic development and gives preference to economic growth as it is defined classically. He says that

> it is, of course, possible to define growth in terms of any measure, such as population, accumulated wealth, productive capital, material goods, technological information, or quality of the people. However, many of these are unmeasurable, and the chief concern seems to be goods and services available for use. (p. 7)

In this sense, economic growth and its reliance on GDP per capita as a major indicator appears to be most applicable. Problems start, however, when international comparisons come into play. Even adjusted for purchasing power parity (PPP), indicators of per capita GDP often do not reflect the reality as accurately as one would want. Other indicators, including those that come from the realm of economic development, become of a high value, including in quantitative analysis.

The key point in the discussion on the differences between economic development and economic growth is that economic development is traditionally applied to the Third World countries. Third World countries are developing, not developed, nations. This heuristics anchors the discussion about development to countries of Africa, Latin America, and Asia. Another aspect of this duality is in the attribution of social problems and issues to economic development and not economic growth. For instance, access to clean water, education, higher education, health services, and even security are included in economic development. Human development is considered as one of the key components of economic development. While economic development analysis is applied to the developing nations, the tools of analysis come from economics developed in the developed nations. And macroeconomics is traditionally based on economic growth rather than development. Economic growth is more specific while economic development is more inclusive. It may appear to some that economic development, indeed, includes economic growth. At the same time, economic growth measured in terms of GDP per capita growth can coincide with digressions in human development. This may happen, among other reasons, because of the growing inequality in income distribution. GDP per capita is an aggregated average indicator, while higher level of income inequality may lead to a decrease in the aggregated average level of human development.

Barro (2000) examined data from a broad panel of countries and found little overall relation between income inequality and rates of growth and investment, but he did find a negative relationship in low-income countries. "For growth, there is an indication that inequality retards growth in poor countries but encourages growth in richer places. Growth tends to fall with greater inequality when per capita GDP is below around $2000 and to rise with inequality when per capita GDP is above $2000." However, Sokoloff and Engerman (2000) found, using a broader historical perspective and starting from the nineteenth century worldwide, that countries with greater income inequality had lower growth (Argentina, for instance), but countries with lower initial inequality grew faster over time.

Transition societies and Ukraine in particular inherited planned economy from the disintegrated Soviet Union. The national economies that emerged from the socialist economy were not at the level of developing countries but at a much higher level. Soviet economy had relatively strong indicators even decades prior to the stage of transition. Per capita income of the USSR in 1961 was equal to $986, as compared to $2,790 in the United States. At the same time, the Soviet economy was able to produce per capita income at par with the developed nations such as Switzerland with $1,010, Sweden with $950, and Belgium with $800. Countries in Eastern Europe had average income per capita of $850. Developing countries with large population had drastically smaller per capita income than did the USSR. Per capita income in India in 1961 was equal to only $140 and in China $167. The data is presented in Rosenstein-Rodan (1961) with the per capita income translated into an estimate of the equivalent purchasing power of U.S. dollars in the United States.

Snooks (1999) suggests that the deficiency of the Soviet system was in that it was nonstrategic and thus, what it needs is not an institutional transition per se, but the strategic transition. He points out that transition "involves a dismantlement of the institutional apparatus of centralized government planning, control, and production in favor of freely operating commodity and factor markets and the primacy of individual enterprise. Essentially, transition is conventionally interpreted as a complete change in a society's economic and political institutions" (p. 83). Snooks criticizes theories of poverty trap as being orthodox and based on the standard aggregate production function. He also points out the commonly accepted practice of considering demographics as exogenous to economic development. Instead, Snooks suggests considering population as an integral part of the dynamic process and must be examined in this complex context (p. 253).

Both concepts of economic growth and economic development are readily applied to transition economies. This may be justified by the need to replace the outdated set of tools and instruments of economic analysis, used in the Soviet times, with more modern and appropriate ones. Indicators of human development, such as the human development index, along with other indicators of development, such as social environment and access to water, food, and social services, are all of use in order to monitor and analyze the situation in the transition economies. However, one missing point in such an analysis is that Ukraine, along with some other former Soviet republics, is an industrialized nation. It has been an industrialized nation for over half a century and certainly does not fit the profile of a developing nation. In this sense, the applicability of standards normally applied to the Third World nations is not very appropriate. Economic development is more about the move from preindustrial to industrial mode of production, while Ukraine undergoes transformational changes in the organization, and so less technological changes. It remains on the level of an industrial nation being on the path to postindustrial society.

One may speculate that economic development is more of a process, while economic growth is more of a result, with the clearly defined indicator, that is, GDP per capita. Equally valid is the discussion that would address economic development as a result, accounting for achievements in human development, social environment, and such, while economic growth is nothing but a continuing process of annual changes in per capita GDP. Both of these approaches are credible and have the right to exist. The solution to this imaginative dichotomy lies not in the real of these tow determinants, that is, economic development or economic growth, but in the process of analysis itself. For instance, economic growth, and more specifically, achieved GDP per capita, may be considered as a basis and necessary ground for economic development. Indeed, it is routinely used to explain the ground for advancements in a nation's development, including access to education, health services, and even democratization. This may be considered as a well-grounded orthodox approach, when growing economic well-being supports broader betterment of the society. On the other hand, same social and economic indicators are used to seek for causes of growth. Literacy rate, enrollment in higher education institutions, number of physicians per certain number of population, access to medical services, and such may play a crucial role in initiating and maintaining sustainable economic growth. Some of these factors, and primarily access to education and health care, facilitate the formation of human capital used in production. Similar to unemployment, which may be considered as a social problem and as a number of people who are not currently in the workforce and do not contribute to production, education may be considered as an indicator of human capital accumulation or an indication of human development.

The use of economic development concepts for Ukraine comes in that the country changes the rules of the game. This process implies institutional reforms and even more fundamental institutional changes. Economic development is broader than economic growth because it includes, along with other determinants, institution building and institutional transition. In distinction of developing nations, where many social and economic institutions have yet to emerge, in Ukraine the task is to transform already existing institutions. There are exceptions, however, such as the establishment of the Currency Exchange, Stock Exchange, and Commodity Exchange. Institution building, combined with the high level of human capital in transition economies, led scholars to believe that economic transition will eventually end up being a success story. Few years later, however, many started thinking that negative economic growth will lead to the decline in economic development. This explains pessimistic views of late 1990s. While the positive role of institutions and human capital in economic well-being and growth worldwide is undeniable, the issue was left mostly unattended by scholars in Ukraine, Russia, and other former Soviet republics.

The recognition of access to health care and education, along with other indicators of literacy and involvement in social life as indicators of the level of development, is not new. Measures of welfare progress offered by Morris (1961) include physicians per 100,000 population, number of students per 100,000 population, and newspaper circulation per 100,000 population. Morris asserts that these indicators "reflect, roughly, the health standards, educational effort, and general literacy at a level sufficient to read newspaper (and afford one)" (p. 15). Pasquale Tridico (2007) investigates the issue of whether human development was concurrent with economic growth during the transition toward a market economy in Central Eastern Europe and the former Soviet Union. His main hypothesis is that economic growth is not always concurrent with human development. The author uses simple ordinary least square (OLS) regressions, looking for a possible correlation of human development variables with GDP per capita. Tridico suggest that in transition economies human development is a sufficient but not a necessary condition for economic growth. A Granger causality test confirms this finding. The author concludes that "investing in human development is crucial for obtaining GDP growth. However, since human development is strictly correlated with institutions, appropriate institutional policies are crucial to a development process" (p. 592).

The literature on growth has examined other issues that are important to the understanding of the growth process. It is useful to highlight some of this research. First, within the broad discussion of exogenous versus endogenous growth, we find the following research particularly noteworthy: Grafts (1995), Johansen (1959), Kelly and Hageman (1999), Kendrick (1976), Vanek (1968), Von Neumann (1946), who reconsiders the British industrial revolution in historical perspective staying on both positions of exogenous and endogenous growth theories; effects of inequality on growth (Barro, 2000; Easterly, 2001; Gould et al., 2001; Sokoloff and Engerman, 2000); institutional structure and economic growth (Barro, 1997; Benhabib and Spiegel, 2000; Bleaney and Nishiyama, 2002; Durham, 1999; Ghost, 1999; Lal, 2000; Lensink and Kuper, 2000); human capital and economic growth (Aghion and Howitt, 1998a and b; Berthelemy et al., 2000; Black, 1962; Galor and Tsiddon, 1997; Kalaitzidakis et al., 2001; McDermott, 1999; Mincer, 1996; Romer, 1986, 1989a,b, 1990, 1994; Ruth, 1998; Schultz, 1963, 1970, 1981, 1990, 1993; Scott, 1989; Zagler, 1999); growth in the Commonwealth of Independent States (CIS) (Havrylyshyn, 1999). These issues are briefly discussed in the following paragraphs.

Measurement of human capital and issues of allocation are presented by Barro (1999), Mincer (1996), Mulligan and Sala-i-Martin (2000), and Ruth (1998). Emphasis on measurement of human capital and its implication for economic growth are made by Kalaitzidakis et al. (2001). In cross-country growth regressions and measures of human capital presented in studies by Barro (1997), Barro and Sala-i-Martin (1999), Benhabib and Spiegel (2000), Krueger and Lindahl (2000), Mankiw et al. (1992), and Pritchett (1996), they argue that a semiparametric, partially linear regression model specification of the cross-country growth regression function is a particularly useful way of studying the contribution of human capital to economic growth. The semiparametric partially linear regression model is written as:

$$Y_{it} = x_{it}^T \gamma + q(Z_{it}) + U_{it}, \tag{27}$$

where x_{it} is a variable of dimension q, γ is $q \times 1$ vector of unknown parameters, Z_{it} is a continuous variable of dimension p and $g()$ is an unknown function. Z_{it} refers to various measures of human capital. Human capital is measured by the level of education and gender. They conclude that the effect of human capital accumulation on growth is nonlinear and that there are threshold levels of human capital and growth for each country.

Shioji (2001) incorporates human capital into his conception of public capital, and he estimates dynamic effects of public capital on output per capita. The other components of public capital are: infrastructure, conservation of national land, and agriculture and fishery. Based on an open economy growth model, he derives an income convergence equation augmented with public capital (*PUP*). The relationship between steady-state output per unit (*Y*) of labor and public capital (*PUP*) is presented by the following equation:

$$Y_{it}^{\star} = \sum_{j=1}^{J} \phi_j \times PUP_{jit-\tau} + Y_i, \tag{28}$$

where $\phi_i = C_i / (1-a)$. ϕ_i represents the long-run elasticity of output with respect to public capital per capita, and *C* is a short-run elasticity.

Shioji found that each component of *PUP* had positive effects on *Y*, but infrastructure was more important to growth than education and had a more significant positive effect on productivity than education. These results can be interpreted as support for endogenous growth. To sum up, it appears that the concept of economic development anticipates production for human, while economic growth considers human as a resource to be used in production.

1.11 Growth Theory in the Post-Soviet Ukraine

1.11.1 Inferences for the Post-Soviet Ukraine

There are quite a few inferences for the post-Soviet Ukraine that may be drawn from the presented literature synthesis. Similar settings, trends in economic processes, and economic conditions revive and make relevant economic ideas that come from early stages of developing economic thought. These issues include foreign trade, accumulation of wealth, wages, and many others and are all linked to economic growth.

Mercantilists raised the issue of priorities in economic policy that is so important for modern Ukraine. This issue includes the trade-off between the directions of future economic development, moving toward export oriented economy or import substitution. Mercantilists were the first pointing out the need for economic policy, but their major emphasis was on foreign trade. These issues, that is, balance of payments, foreign debt, and positive trade balance in foreign trade appear to be as important for

Ukraine as they were in the era of mercantilism. The idea that wealth is created in exchange, that is, in trade, made its way from mercantilists to the transforming Ukraine. The national economy with traditionally strong industrial production suddenly turned into trade. While the production in certain industries was declining rapidly, many households found their new sources of income in trade, and, later in the developing service sector.

After independence, Ukraine faced numerous challenges, including organizational and institutional ones. Raising inflation, a need for budget austerity, well-planned monetary policy, and establishing and proper functioning of the National Bank are all issues that were addressed by mercantilists and well applicable to modern Ukraine. There are numerous analogies that may be drawn between economic policy in Ukraine, especially in earlier stages of its economic transition, and ideas and suggestions of mercantilists.

Earlier mercantilism placed emphasis on money, that is, golden coins. For Ukraine, this process found its expression in the rapid dollarization of the national economy. The U.S. dollar was considered as a replacement for the national currency. All large transactions were conducted in U.S. dollars and firms and even households appraised their assets in this foreign currency. The process of dollarization pointed to the transition from material assets as means of exchange to the monetary exchange. The analogy with mercantilism is obvious. The proposed system of bimetallism, including silver and golden coins, reminds the suggestion to reform monetary system in Ukraine not overnight, but through the introduction of parallel currency that would be backed by the gold standard or hard currency. This suggestion was dismissed on the ground that it did not take into consideration the credit nature of the modern money.

Later mercantilism valued commodities and advises to accumulate commodities as material assets within the country. Similarly, Ukraine's galloping inflation in the 1990s pushes the population toward accumulating durable goods, that is, material assets. Households were buying numerous TV sets, tape recorders, refrigerators, gas stoves, vacuum cleaners, and such. At one point, bottles of vodka had the same level of liquidity as did the national currency. The importance of trade manifested itself in the phenomenal growth of small merchants, called "chelnoki" [shuttles], that is, individuals traveling abroad in order to buy clothes, electronics, and other goods and sell them on the local flea markets. This phenomenon reached significant proportions in 1990s and in many cases caused an erosion of the workforce. Many skilled employees left their work in order to make their living out of street trade and shopping tours abroad. The notorious deficit of consumer goods during the Soviet times suddenly gave way to the liquidity crisis, when the combination of large amounts of consumer goods and high prices underlined the lack of money on the side of consumer demand.

Another interesting aspect of mercantilism is its emphasis on low wages, made for the sake of a continuous increase in the total volume of produced goods. Low wages remains Ukraine's largest problem even now, after nine years of sustainable economic growth. Ukraine is distinct with its highly skilled workforce, but the wages are inadequately low. For mercantilists, low wages were justified by the argument of an increase in productivity and rapid accumulation of wealth. Minimal wages of Ukrainian workers along with the long arrears in salaries seem not to have any justification. Wage arrears also contributed to the liquidity crisis.

The process of dollarization of the national economy lead to a remarkable urban landscape with numerous currency exchange offices being located on major streets, farmers markets, in banks, grocery stores, and so on. Working in a currency exchange facility became more beneficial than being an engineer or a physician. One could develop an impression that everyone was moving away from real production into trade, currency exchange, and other commercial activities that had little to do with production of material values. This was especially surprising for the country with a large industrial sector, dominated by machine building, defense industry, extraction industry, and such. While dollarization was commonplace in large cities and industrial centers, in rural areas money circulation was replaced with the natural exchange. Households in countryside often traded goods in exchange for other goods. This situation led to the understanding of the much needed comprehensive agricultural reform, including the land reform.

The idea of reemerging agriculture, along with the need for a comprehensive land reform, moves some aspects of economic transition closer to the ideas voiced by Physiocrats. The major principles of Physiocrats were statements about the leading role of agriculture, surplus product, and a unified system of monetary and commodity circulation. According to Physiocrats, the real product was produced only in agriculture. Other branches of the national economy could only change its form. In Ukraine, with its richest soils in the world, the idea of self-sustainability in terms of food and other agricultural products gains strength. Traditionally strong branches that offer products in high demand, including for export, include sugar beet and sunflower seeds used to produce high quality sugar and sunflower oil, respectively. These products were even reflected in the strategic reports made by the International Monetary Fund (IMF). Further development of traditional branches may be on the way.

Physiocrats considered economic life as a natural process that has its own natural laws. They proclaimed a principle of "natural law." Physiocrats opposed interference of the state in economic processes. This reminds one of the current situation in Ukraine, where turbulent political life only adds instability to the economic process. Many former supporters of the strong state now turn to liberal ideas of free market economy and laissez faire capitalism, and limitation of the state leviathan. The state that has yet to restructure and reorganize many of its regulatory and supervisory institutions in many instances appears to be detrimental to the normal development of the national economy. Physiocrats also accepted an idea about the existence of surplus as a part of the product that was not used in consumption or in production. This surplus was accumulated in the society, increasing the national wealth. The idea of capital accumulation transforms to be a number one priority in Ukraine. The country prepares for a much needed massive renovation of principal capital, including production capacities, buildings, machinery, and equipment. This can only be realized through the continuing accumulation of capital. Finally, the system of economic reproduction and distribution of national product on the national scale, first offered by the Physiocrats, is still being taught to economics majors in Ukraine.

Classics of economic thought consider issues raised by Mercantilists and Physiocrats. The minimum wage issue, so relevant for contemporary Ukraine, continues in the works of Adam Smith. In distinction from Smith, David Ricardo suggested the existence of a natural market wage, and wrote that new technology leads to a decline in the demand for labor assuming a particular form of technological change. More fundamentally, Smith's "invisible hand" served as one of the major justifications for the market transition, launched in an expectation of higher effectiveness of the new system. It is a challenging task to turn the egalitarian society with highest values placed on income equality toward the new system where efforts of particular individuals are rewarded based on the market principles. In such a system, governmental regulation that was immanent for the planned economy of the Soviet Ukraine is being replaced with the invisible hand of the market. It is presumed that striving for better material conditions by each particular individual or economic agent eventually makes everyone better off.

Foreign trade was considered a moving force in economic development starting from works of David Hume, a classic of economic growth. Hume, Smith, and Ricardo pointed to an increase in foreign trade and national export as an engine of growth. Unlike in the period of transition, now Ukraine starts moving more toward the ideas of structuralism, development of the domestic market, and reestablishment of many fundamental branches of the economy. This trend demonstrates a slow move from prioritization of export oriented industries. Other issues, raised by the classics of economic growth remain relevant, including capital accumulation, technological progress, and division of labor.

Thomas Malthus considered the relationship between the growth of population and the growth of agriculture. It is hard to single out a more important problem for Ukraine than the demographic one. A steady decline in population necessitates the concept of economic growth that would combine reduction in the total labor force with steady growth of per capita GDP. Malthus emphasized proportions in development in order to avoid over-saving, idle capacity, and unemployment. Proportional increases in population, capital, and savings rates, which in turn lead to full capacity utilization and full employment would be an optimal scenario for Ukraine. In the 1990s, there was a fear of possible mass unemployment (Osipian, 1997a). Few organizational forms of employment in the stage of unemployment rate increase were implemented (Osipian, 1998c), including public works, but they were not particularly effective, nor were they efficient. In any case, using a traditionally high level human capital of Ukrianian workers in low skill public works does not seem to be the best possible strategy. The national economy now faces the need to load production capacities, renovate principal capital, and reverse the negative demographic trend. Malthus's suggestion to use tax revenue to fund capital accumulation and investment is fully applicable to modern Ukraine.

John Stuart Mill suggested that an increase in output depends on an increase in inputs or their productivity, distinguishing between the quality and quantity of inputs and between extensive and intensive types of growth. In this sense, Ukraine continues to suffer from the legacies of the Soviet economic system, demonstrating so far unsuccessful attempts to move from extensive to intensive growth. Little presence of technology transfer is compensated with conversations about innovations and growth. Mill's progressive ideas are logically explained by the fact that he wrote during the industrial revolution in England. Similarly, the industrialized society in Ukraine requires major renovation of production capacities that would allow for implementation of technological advancements and sustainable growth.

Schumpeter's contribution to the theory of business cycles may be used in making projections on the future economic growth in Ukraine, including its move to periodic economic fluctuations. The changing dynamics of the Ukrainian economy will eventually bring the system to the new, higher level equilibrium. The emphasis placed by Schumpeter on entrepreneurship was in high demand during the initial stages of economic transition in Ukraine, when the authorities were appealing to the entrepreneurial spirit of the population. The ever popular idea of the emerging middle class as consisting of small entrepreneurs is being actively promoted now. Innovations and inventions were considered separately by Schumpeter. R&D laboratories that existed in the planned economy as attached to large plants are now transforming into independent research institutes. Some are successful in adaptation to new market realities, while others are just surviving. Institution building is yet another parallel that can be drawn between Schumpeter's works and contemporary Ukraine. Schumpeter (1947) emphasizes the role of the new type of organization:

> But in capitalist reality as distinguished from its textbook picture, it is not [pure competition] which counts but the competition from the new commodity, the new technology, the new source of supply, the new type of organization (the largest-scale unit of control, for instance)—competition which commands a decisive cost of quality advantage and which strikes not at the margins of the profits and the outputs of the existing firms but at their foundations and their very lives. (p. 84)

John Stuart Mill supported the general idea that output is a function of labor, capital, and land, and suggested that an increase in output depends on an increase in inputs or their productivity. Mill, therefore, distinguished between the quality and quantity of inputs and between extensive and intensive types of growth. Such progressive ideas are logically explained by the fact that he wrote during the industrial revolution in England. Ramsey's theory of savings and growth points to the lack of savings, low level consumption, little reinvestment, and a significant capital flight in Ukraine in 1990s. This situation promised bleak perspectives. The steady growth of 2000s places most emphasis on current consumption. The issues of optimization of savings along with the continuing capital flight remain on the agenda. The continuing presence of dollarization of the national economy along with the growing rate of inflation makes interest rate unstable. The two points made by Keynes: that the savings ordinarily do not equal the amount of investment; and that as a result, the market economy is naturally unstable, are well applicable to Ukraine. Savings made by population are not being channeled to production through the process of reinvestment. The undeveloped capital market adds to the potential instability of the national economy.

Harrod and Domar's integration of Keynesian analysis with economic growth raises the issue of instability. This instability, however, takes place under the constant rules of the game. In Ukraine, the period of transition was characterized not only by the instability, but by the changing rules of the game. Solow points out that the modern theory of growth is devoted to analyzing the properties of steady states. It also focuses on finding out whether an economy not initially in a steady state will evolve into one if it proceeds under specified rules of the game. For Ukraine, the rules themselves are changing under the pressures of the changing economy.

Kaldor and Mirrlees introduce technical progress in the specific form of the rate of improvement of the design and technique of newly produced capital equipment as the main engine of economic growth. In Ukraine, massive renovation of principal capital remains one of the fundamental tasks. Technological improvements determine not only the rate of growth in productivity, but, together with other parameters, rate of obsolescence, the average lifetime of equipment, the share of investment of income, the share of profits, and the relationship between investment and potential output. The rate of depreciation of principal capital in Ukraine is such that massive investments in equipment are needed. Since the Soviet times, inventions were routinely not implemented. The decline in the R&D and poor management exacerbate the problem of the lack of innovations. Unfavorable distribution of property and high level of concentration of property rights in the hands of few lead to the lack of competition among producers, and hence, lack of incentives to implement new technologies and innovations.

It is interesting that despite the well-grounded pessimism of 1990s and popularity and heavy reliance on the external help, including that from the IMF, the World Bank, the EBRD, and other international agencies, Leontief's theory of "poverty trap" did not find any reflection in works of Ukrainian economists. It is unlikely that the scholars did not accept its statements and did not believe in its theoretical merits or their applicability to Ukraine. Rather, it was mere unawareness of this fundamental work as a part of greater unawareness of the achievements of Western economic theory. It is exactly because of this unawareness that local economists were unable to either accept or reject postulates of Leontief's poverty trap, specifically designed for developing nations in need of foreign aid.

Burnside and Dollar (2000) and Hansen and Tarp (2001) argue about the role of foreign aid in initiating economic growth. It appears that in times of political instability the best option is to keep the government as distant from the economy as possible. The reason might be that political turmoil in no way contributes to economic stability and even less so, to dynamic development. Accordingly, the reduction of the public sector and restrictions on the governmental regulatory powers may prove helpful in Ukraine especially taking into account its vivid political life. Political life in modern Ukraine appears to be more of a struggle than a constructive dialog. According to Boon (1996), foreign aid does not bring immediate economic growth because poverty is not caused by the lack of capital and because politicians are not interested in improving economic policies if the flow of external aid continues.

1.11.2 Economic Growth in the Works of Ukrainian and Russian Economists

Some work on the issues of economic growth was done by economists in Ukraine, but the volume of this work remains insufficient. It is also notable that all the publications on growth appear after 2001. Apparently, the topic was very unpopular in the period of economic decline of 1990s. The major directions of research on economic growth conducted by the Ukrainian and Russian economists may be formulated as given in the following paragraphs.

The role of innovations, intellectual capital, and human resources have been presented in the works of Aleksandrova (2003a and b), Bazhal (2002), Bazhal and Odotjuk (2003), Bridun (2003), Chechelev et al. (2001), Cherevko and Lukash (1998), Danilishin and Kucenko (2006), Dem'janenko (2003a and b), Dubjanskaja (2005), Garipova et al. (2004), Golikova (2003), Heyets (2000, 2001, 2003a–e), Hristenko et al. (2002), Ivlev (2004), Kendjuhov (2005), Kireev and Shnipko (2003a, and b), Lapko and Aleksandrova (2003), Olijnik (2003), Onishko (2003), Pavlova (2001), Perminov et al. (2004), Revenko (2003), Shchedrina (2003), Simkina (2002), Suhorukov (2006), Vovkanich (2005), Zhits (2000).

Investment and investment resources for growth have been reflected in the works of Bolhovitinova (2003), Bolhovitinova and Mar'enko (2003), Gal'chinskij and Levochkin (2004), Kvashnina (2004), Ovchinnikova (2004), Romanova (2002).

Institutions, institutional reforms, and institutional environment have been included in the works of Chechelev et al. (2001), Dan'ko (2003), Golikov and Fedorenko (2003), Grushevskaja (2004), Hrytsenko (1997, 2003), Koshkin and Shabaev (2004), Novitskij (2005), Shnipko (2003), Tarasevich et al. (2003), Ungaeva (2005), Yaremenko (2003).

Macroeconomic modeling, economic growth models, measurements and estimations, macroeconomic dynamics, and economic forecasting have been included in the works of Heyets (1999, 2000, 2001, 2003), Ivanter (2004, 2006), Kosenkov (2005), Krjuchkova (2000), Ovchinnikova (2004), Samojlov (2005), and Zverev (2005).

Finance, stock market, and monetary policy have been presented in Fedorenko (2003), Golub (2006), Krichevs'ka (2003), Kvasnjuk (2000, 2003a and b), Lunina (2000, 2003), Prihod'ko (2003a), Snigir and Shums'ka (2003), and Vozhzhov (2004).

The role of the state, state regulations, governance, fiscal policy, and the state budget are presented by Balabanova (2004), Bazhal (2002), Fridman et al. (1998), Kalinina (2005), Kvasnjuk (2000, 2003a and b), Prihod'ko (2003b–f), Perepelkin (2001), and Vahnenko (2000, 2003).

Theories of transformation and economic growth are presented in the works of Cherednichenko (2004), Chukhno (1996), Evstigneeva and Evstigneev (2005), Heyets (2000, 2001), Hrytsenko (1997, 2003), Kuznetsova (2000), Kvasnjuk (2000, 2003a and b), L'vov (2004), Lavrov and Kapoguzov (2006), Perepelkin (2001), Petkova (2005), Pokrytan (1997), Ponomarev (2004), Rokochaja and Moroz (1998), Saktoev (1999), Salijchuk (2004), Savchenko (2005), Seleznev (2001), Shubravskaja (2005), Sokolovskij (2001), Solovejkina (2002), Spirjagin (2005), Tjurina (2005), Tochilin (2001), Veretennikova (2005), Vilenskij et al. (2002), Yatskevich (2006), and Zemskova (2005),

Economic integration, competitiveness of the national products in the open market, and growth have been presented by Heyets and Shums'ka (2003), Kireev (2003), Kireev and Shnipko (2003), Krjuchkova (2000), Lavshov and Spizharskaja (2004), Lir and Podolets (2003), Shnipko (2003), Sidenko (2003a and b), Tolmachev (2005), and Zas'ko (2004).

The strong features of the research on economic growth, conducted by the Ukrainian economists, lie primarily in the domains of the theory of transformation, vision of economic growth in line with transition from predominantly exogenous to endogenous forms of growth, institutional aspects of growth, and the role of innovations and intellectual capital in economic growth. Works of the Russian economists, devoted to economic growth, are presented first of all in such subfields as theories of transformation, analysis of the basic Western concepts, and theories of economic growth, including issues of the macroeconomic dynamics and general equilibrium, models of economic growth, and impact of macroeconomic variables on economic growth.

The common feature of the research done by both the Ukrainian and the Russian economists is the popularity of studying the role of investment and finance for economic growth. For us, the structuralist approach has certain advantages along with the neo-liberal approach. It might be beneficial to pay more attention to such aspects of economic growth as methodology and categorization, structural reorganization of the national economies in the post-transition societies, national accounts and macroeconomic balance, macroeconomic modeling, and long-run economic forecasting, rather than to the issues of foreign direct investments, currency exchange rate fluctuations, and the like.

This study considers transition only to the extent necessary to highlight and explain growth, its possibility, and place in the flows of economic transition. It is not intended to design a new system of economic incentives or explain the political economy of transition. This research is focused on economic analysis of growth. It points to the increasing well-being of Ukrainian society as a result of growth as well as an indication of economic development. But the focus is on the fact of positive and significant growth, possible causes of growth, the need for endogenous growth, and the role of human capital in growth. Issues of poverty, inflation, exchange rate, tax policy, and such are all secondary, if at all addressed in this analysis.

1.12 Concluding Remarks

Theories of transition were loosely tied to the theories of growth. While the Western theorists of economic transition focus on such neoliberal concepts and aspects of transition as privatization, inflation, free pricing, and supply and demand, economists in the Russian Federation and Ukraine continue using Marxist and post-Marxist conceptual frameworks for analysis of transition. In their view these frames seem to be more appropriate for understanding of the current events and phenomena that take place in the former Soviet Bloc.

Different approaches highlight different aspects of transition and post-transition development. In this sense all variety of approaches and positions may be considered as beneficial. At the same time exogenous models of growth often specifically designed for the developing economies in the Third World countries are not sufficient in theorizing growth and development in transition economies. Nor are aging concepts borrowed from Marxism up to this task. The economists in transition economies have to familiarize themselves with the different concepts of growth, including both exogenous and endogenous models of growth and learn to synthesize ideas of neoliberalism and post-structuralism.

In our view, the prioritization of the structuralists' approach to the post-transition economies and structuralism overall has an objective ground. Economic growth in the post-transition societies is based on the development of the domestic market. Accordingly, sustainability and rate of growth will be based on the total volume of the domestic market and dynamics of its development. Structuralism as applied to post-transition societies can accommodate institutionalism and studies of institutional transformation, and contain macroeconomic modeling, statistical analysis, stability of the national economies, and points of equilibrium, as well as economic cycle and the theory of long waves.

PART II

ENDOGENOUS ECONOMIC GROWTH IN UKRAINE

We will continue our discussion of growth and move to the events and phenomena directly related to growth in Ukraine. In this chapter, we intend to consider economic growth in Ukraine in the broader context of socioeconomic transformations. Such a contextualization will allow us to discover the possibility of economic growth in Ukraine, and its place in the streams of economic transition. This setting of growth in transition serves as a background to investigate the possible transition of the national economy to endogenous forms of growth. This chapter presents an analysis of the process of economic transition and points to the exogenous and endogenous components of current economic growth in Ukraine. It argues for the need to move from predominantly exogenous to endogenous type of growth.

The logic of this chapter is as follows. First, it considers some earlier projections about economic growth in Ukraine, made in late 1990s and offers a suggestion about possible causes of the delay in this process. Second, it investigates the possibility of endogenous economic growth in Ukraine. It then moves to the process of identification of the place of growth in the transition economy of Ukraine. Growth forecasts and their explanations are offered to develop some ideas about future economic cycles in the national economy. Transition from exogenous to endogenous forms of growth indicates future perspectives and targets for Ukraine.

2.1 Possibility of Endogenous Growth in Ukraine

Sustainable GDP growth in Ukraine of 5.9 percent in 2000, 9.4 percent in 2003, and 12.1 percent in 2004 with predicted growth of around

6 percent for 2008 is impressive, indeed, especially as it happens along with the stable and continuing decline in population. While in the year 2000 Gross National Income per capita was only $690, it constituted $970 in 2003, and has risen to $1,260 in 2004 and $2,555 in 2007, with predicted further increase in 2008. These numbers are in nominal U.S. dollars and the real values are much higher. Economic growth in the former Soviet Union was mostly extensive, and always required new injections of capital and labor. Volume of capital and labor increased over time. Human capital development as expressed by the level of educational attainment of population was among the highest in the world for the last five decades. Technical progress was also very impressive. At the same time, capacity utilization was very poor for all factors of production. For instance, products of research were utilized mostly in the military industry. In addition, allocative efficiency was low because the allocation mechanisms were based on plan and directives or orders.

Retrospective analysis shows that by the year 1999 Ukraine was in the deep transition. This transition was multidimensional and had deep roots. It was a change in economic, social, and political life, ideology, religion, and so forth. Indeed, by 1999 Ukraine was undergoing a deep socioeconomic transformation. This transformation found its reflection not only in the economy, but in changing ideology, religion, culture, and other noneconomic spheres of human activities. At the same time problems that appeared during the transition period were not caused by transition. Nor were they creations of the reform. These problems accumulated well before the reform and made the transition more complex than it would be otherwise.

According to the official statistics that does not take into account shadow economy, GDP per capita in Ukraine was only $850 in 1998 and $750 in 1999. It had a 50 percent decline from 1991 to 1997. Industrial production declined 63 percent while output in agriculture decreased 40 percent. Depreciation rates of fixed capital stock in the manufacturing industries were around 35–40 percent during 1991–1995. Many plants did not invest in fixed capital. Machinery, equipment, and other facilities were deteriorating. This caused decline in productivity and manufacturing capacities. National income per worker decreased 50 percent during 1990–1995. The average rate of decline in productivity was calculated at 8.6 percent per annum.

Social and living conditions of population were deteriorating as well. Approximately 40 percent of the population were below the poverty line. Food expenses were around 78 percent of the family budget in Ukraine, around 54 percent in the Russian Federation, and 34 percent in Poland.

Minimum wage in Ukraine in 1990 was twice as high as the living wage. Minimum wage declined to the level of living wage in 1992 and was five times less than living wage by 1995. The official statistics does not reflect two major things: undeclared incomes from the shadow economy and illegal activities and housing cost. While food expenses in Ukraine and the Russian Federation were above 50 percent of the family budget, housing expenses were minimal. Many families did not pay for housing and utilities for months and even years. The payments themselves were incredibly small as compared to Eastern European countries and even more so when compared to Western Europe.

Inequality in income distribution increased during the 1990s. In Ukraine in 1995, income of the richest decile was equal to 30 percent of the total income of population while income of the poorest decile was equal to 2.3 percent only, that is, income of the richest decile was 14 times higher than that of the poorest decile. The minimum wage in the Russian Federation in 1990 exceeded twice the living wage, but in 1992 they were equal, and in 1995 the living wage was 5 times larger than the minimum wage. The minimum wage situation in Ukraine was similar to the situation in the Russian Federation. The richest 10 percent of the population in Ukraine in 1995 received 30 percent of aggregate income, and the poorest 10 percent received 2.3 percent. The Gini coefficient in 1996 was 0.382 for Russia, and 0.386 for Ukraine. In 1997, there was little change in the Gini coefficient in either country (Osipian, 2001). Assuming that access to undeclared income was much higher among the families that belonged to the richest decile, we can think that the real difference was even higher than 14 times. Inequality in income distribution increased 1.6 times from 1991 to 1997. The Gini coefficient was calculated from data on the declared income only, and thus the measure of inequality likely increased more than 1.6 times during the six-year period of 1991–1997.

Such a sharp increase in inequalities and deterioration of living conditions, reported based on the official statistics, necessitates an explanation regarding the presence of potential resources for future sustainable growth. Indeed, change of sharp decline with sharp increase in GDP requires a conceptual explanation. This worsening in socioeconomic conditions of the population in Ukraine motivates research on the causes and consequences of this disruption so that effective policy can be developed and implemented to assist those most in need, to maintain economic stability and sustainable growth. The question one should address is to what extent was it possible to predict the growth of 2000s in the mid- and late 1990s? Did it seem possible to have economic growth in

Ukraine at that time? The (IMF) addressed this issue in 1995 in the IMF Staff Country Report #96/21, and its analysis and proposed forecasts were based on discussions with the Ukrainian authorities. Average wage per month was expected to grow from $49 in 1995 to $155 in 2000. Consumer price growth was expected to stabilize at 10 percent. Positive growth in real GDP was projected to be 3 percent in 1997 and increased to 6 percent in 2000. The projected average wage per month, expressed in U.S. dollars, increased threefold during the period of 1995–2000. The percentage changes in both consumer prices and producer prices were projected to decrease from 182 and 172 in 1995, respectively, to 10 percent in 2000. Domestic saving was projected to slightly increase from 16.6 percent of GDP in 1995 to 19.3 percent in 2000. Finally, projected total external liabilities decreased from 22.6 percent of GDP in 1995 to 15.4 percent of GDP in 2000. These projections were too optimistic, and some of them were not realized.

Real GDP growth in 2000 was 4.2 percent, which was below the 6 percent growth rate projected. In addition, as mentioned in the IMF report of 2001:

> The economic situation in 2000 has been encouraging. Following the gradual stabilization of the economy in 1999 in the aftermath of the Russia crisis, real GDP growth in 2000 turned positive for the first time since independence, and was expected under the program to reach some 4 percent for the year as a whole. The nominal exchange rate remained broadly stable in 2000. Arrears in the social sectors were reduced by 1.1 percent of GDP, with pension fund arrears eliminated by end-September. Some payments arrears, however, were accumulated in the energy and utility sectors. Some progress has been made on structural reform. Executive Directors welcomed the recent improvements in economic policy implementation, and endorsed Ukraine's overall economic strategy based on a sound budget, tight monetary policy, and supportive structural reforms. Directors were encouraged by the recent economic performance, noting that real GDP growth in 2000 is expected to be positive . . . and approach 5 percent. (p. 7)

In Ukraine and the Russian Federation of 1990s output growth was negative. In Ukraine, the decline was 11.9 percent in 1991, 22.9 percent in 1994, and 3.2 percent in 1997 (Havrylyshyn et al., 1999).

There was always a large amount of available labor force present in the economy, because of high real and hidden unemployment in the country. At the same time Ukraine had a very high rate of capital accumulation, possibly even higher than during the Soviet times. However, accumulated capital has been leaving the country. It came to the point when wages and social payments, including stipends and pensions, were suffering of arrears lasting for several months and even years. There was no process of reinvestment taking place. Low capacity utilization (underemployment, for instance), low allocative efficiency as a consequence of the corporate-monopolistic type of allocation, depreciation of principal capital, human capital outflow, slowdown in technical progress, and the lost time and missed opportunities for timely changes made the problem of initiating growth even more difficult. At the same time, the authorities in Ukraine emphasized the development of the domestic market rather than steering the economy toward export orientation at the beginning of transition. They requested more foreign credits and foreign direct investments (FDI) without creating welcoming conditions for businesses in the country.

Unemployment was around 1 million in 1998, with the official rate of unemployment of around 5 percent for the year 2000 (Kravchuk, 2002). These indicators did not account for latent unemployment, underemployment, long-term leaves, and arrears in salaries and other compensatory payments. As Kravchuk (2002) points out: "Wages tend to bear little relationship to labor productivity level, which vary broadly. In any case, labor productivity rates in Ukrainian industry have been falling since 1991, and by 1997 were but 70–75 percent of their 1990 levels. As such, Ukraine has not been able to take advantage of its relatively low-cost, well-educated work force" (p. 28). Intensive human capital outflow, the so-called brain drain, along with intensive "capital flight" that took place in Ukraine, Russia, and other CIS countries, was especially significant during the period of 1993–1999. The primary venue for capital outsourcing was import-export operations, when profits were deposited in foreign banks instead of being returned to the country and reinvested. By some estimates, the amount of Ukrainian capital abroad constituted somewhere around $25–50 billion in 1996 (p. 32). This outflow of capital had a negative economic impact on growth.

The implication for Ukraine was that a very large inflow of foreign capital was needed to compensate for this drain of the nation's own capital resources, but this was not likely to happen soon. Ukraine had "to live above its means" and depend upon the foreign credit it received. Alesina and Rodrik (1994) conclude that foreign aid is, at best, only partially successful at promoting growth and reducing poverty. The reasons are poor institutional development, corruption, inefficiency, and bureaucratic failures in developing countries (Alesina and Rodrik, 1994). Moreover, the situation becomes more difficult with the necessity to service foreign debt, which, in contrast to domestic debt in wages and social payments (pensions, stipends), is always serviced on time. Some of the chief vehicles for debt reduction are debt-equity swaps and debt-debt swaps, which are going to take place particularly between the Russian Federation and Germany and are described by Dornbush (1996). Dornbush concludes that these swaps rarely serve the interests of the creditor. In addition, Brazil and other countries recognized in the 1990s that their interests were poorly served by swaps.

Ukraine's positions on the international credit markets were very favorable at the beginning of the reform. As the Russian Federation took over all financial obligations of the USSR, Ukraine was considered quite credible by potential creditors and at the same time did not have any foreign debt. In this regard Kravchuk (2002) notes the following:

> In 1992, Ukraine had no foreign debt outstanding. This provided the country's most significant inherited economic resource: an enormous amount of debt capacity. As might be expected, Ukraine's foreign debts steadily increased over the 1990s. From an estimated $1.4 billion in late 1992, Ukraine's indebtedness grew to over $12.1 billion by early 2000. The debt-to-GDP ratio stood at between 15 to 20 percent in 1998 but rose to over 40 percent in 1999. (p. 33)

Servicing foreign debt becomes more and more of a burden. The financial system in Ukraine was supposed to accumulate savings and convert them into investments, but it was not up to this task: it was poorly developed and mismanaged. According to the research on the role of financial development in growth and investment by Benhabib and Spiegel (2000), such a financial system could not support economic growth.

The detailed studies of particular areas of economic activities and industries in Ukraine, including foreign trade, institutional reform, modern growth trends, finance, fiscal regulation, investment, infrastructure, state regulation, restructuring, role of natural resources, and regional aspects of development are presented in works of Dabrowski (2002), Dodonov et al. (2002), Eremenko (2002), Gavrilenkov (2002), Gylfason (2002), Havrylyshyn et al. (2002), Heyets (2002), Jahnke (2002), Kravchuk (2002), Mankovska and Dean (2002), Scherbakov (2002), Thiel (2002), and others.

In Ukraine, in 1998, all the indicators showed that the initiation of economic growth was quite problematic. I would like to point out the following:

1. In Ukraine, in 1997, per capita GDP was $1,040, and per capita GNP calculated based on the basis of purchasing power parity (PPP)

was $2,170. According to the estimates, presented by the World Bank, per capita GDP in 1997 was $850 and in 1998 it was about $750, and income inequality, indicated by the Gini coefficient, was equal to 0.38672 in 1996 and continued to grow. Productivity of labor was only 60–70 percent of 1991, caused not only by dequalification of the workforce, but by the high level of depreciation of principal capital. Production facilities, equipment, and machinery were aging. While foreign credits constituted $12.5 billion as for 1998, foreign credits per capita were only $250. At the same time, total debt services were $2 billion, with debt services per capita of $40. FDI net inflow was equal to $743 million, with FDI per capita of only $15.5 and aid per capita of $7.6. The estimates for national capital outflow varied from $20 to 60 billion. Savings of population were around $12 billion by 1996, but most of this money was never invested in production.

2. According to some commonly accepted estimates, Ukraine needed approximately $60 billion in long-term investments and credits for restructuring. During the period from 1992 to 2000 it received only $12.5 billion in the form of credits, less than $1 billion in FDI, and a small amount of portfolio investments. For comparison, Mexico received $40 billion in 1989 during its crisis; Republic of Korea received approximately $50 billion in 1998 to support its national currency. These were short-term credits from the currency stabilization funds. Poland received $60 billion in foreign credits and FDI at the beginning of transition in the early 1990s for restructuring and renewal of its principal capital in the industry.
3. The significant capital outflow along with the personal savings not being converted into investment caused negative economic growth in Ukraine. Diminishing population, depletion of resources, depreciation of principal capital, low productivity of labor, structural problems, poor management, and absence of a well-developed state economic policy, all contributed to the long-run negative economic growth in Ukraine.

Barro (2000) suggests that inequality retards growth in poor countries but encourages growth in richer places. Growth tends to fall with greater inequality when per capita GDP is below around $2,000 in 1985 U.S. dollars and to rise with inequality when per capita GNP is above $2,000. Inequality is likely to have a negative impact on growth in low-income countries (Barro, 2000). The low level of foreign capital can keep growth at a low rate (Leontief, 1958). From this discussion, one might conclude that Ukraine would not grow rapidly without large initial infusions of capital. We, therefore, seek some other "engine of growth"—in addition to the accumulation of capital. Solow (1957, 1960) proposed technological change, a steady flow of new ideas. The neoclassical growth model focuses on the capital accumulation decision, but it is growth in ideas—not merely in capital—that drives the system. A shift in emphasis from physical to human capital accumulation is needed, as well as a focus on decisions—such as the allocation of time among activities—that affect the rate of learning and the rate of accumulation of skills and ideas. In Ukraine, human capital constitutes 6 percent of the overall world potential, with population 0.1 percent in 1993. Nevertheless, this capital was used in the system of the planned economy, and now the new system does not use this capital effectively in production.

Dabrowski (2002) points out two groups of hypotheses of the recent economic growth in Ukraine:

> The first one refers to various temporary factors such as the low statistical base and presence of free production capacities after many years of output decline. Other "windfall" factor can be connected with effects of 1998–1999 devaluation of Hryvnia, and strong external demand, particularly for the metallurgy products in year 2000. The second approach believes that long-term structural factors such as effects of privatization and restructuring carried out so far, and moving a part from the shadow sector into the official one created a favorable environment for economic growth. While the latter leads to conclusion that the current growth may be sustainable in longer term, the former suggests a gradually decreasing growth trend. (p. 77)

Blanchard (1997), Fisher et al. (1996), Havrylyshyn (1999), and Shen (1996) examined the following key measures of the reform in transition economies: macroeconomic stabilization; price and market liberalization; liberalization of the exchange and trade system; privatization of state-owned firms; establishing a competitive environment with few obstacles to market entry and exit; redefining the role of the state as the provider of macro stability, a stable legal framework, enforceable property rights, and occasionally as a corrector of market imperfections. Based on such concepts, the authors anticipate the following implications for growth that differentiate the transition economies from developed market economies: "First, output will necessarily decline initially. Second, growth of the new will not occur until the new incentives are in place and made credible. Third, the proximate mechanisms in the early recovery period are most likely a variety of efficiency improvements rather than expansion of factor inputs such as investment and labor" (Blanchard, 1997).

As Mankiw et al. (1992) point out, future research should be directed at explaining why the variables taken to be exogenous in the Solow model vary so much from country to country. They expect that differences in tax policies, education policies, choice of having children or otherwise, and political stability will end up among the ultimate determinants of cross-country differences. By 2004, Ukraine achieved pre-reform level of per capita income. This indicates that the economic crisis is over. Nevertheless, overcoming the crisis alone does not present necessary grounds for a suggestion that the national economy is now a pure market economy. Ukraine can rather be characterized as a predominantly market-type mixed economy, where a substantial public sector coexists with the dominating private sector. The private sector functions based on the market mechanisms, while there are also transitional forms and mechanisms of economic organization present in the country. These transitional forms continue to exist since early 1990s and slowly disappear, giving way to the market ones. Further structural reforms are needed in the publics sector, including comprehensive pension reform (Osipian, 2001). While the need for reform was obvious since early 1990s (Osipian, 1997c, 1998b), the introduction of the three-tier pension system with accumulative options is slow.

Economy of Ukraine in 2007 can still be characterized with a certain level of mosaics. This level of mosaics, or mixed forms of economic activities and mechanisms, is less significant and not as noticeable as it was during the transition of 1990s. Characterization of Ukraine's economy as a predominantly market-type mixed economy should not be considered as an indicator of the economy's insufficiency for at least three reasons. First, pure market economy is nonexistent and cannot be found anywhere in the world. Even in the U.S. economy, probably the nearest approximation to what is known as a pure market economy, there are such features as the high degree of monopolization of the national economy, the large state sector, the growing public sector, including nongovernmental organizations, and numerous noneconomic restrictions and regulations. All of those utilize nonmarket mechanisms and prevent from achieving a highest possible degree of economic effectiveness and efficiency. Second, Ukraine's economy still encounters a presence of some elements of transition economy, distinct from both planned economy and market economy. Third, Ukraine will likely preserve a substantial public sector, including health care, education, transport, and infrastructure. Ukraine has the European mentality with its welfare state, rather than the U.S. mentality. This anticipates broad access to medical services and quality education.

In order to identify the nature of economic growth and the role of human capital in the initiation of sustainable growth in the post-transition economies of market type, it is necessary to use the following estimation criteria: volume, density, and structure of external inflows to the national economy, including foreign direct and portfolio investments, capital outflow, external debt volume and service; level of socialization of the economy, and presence or absence of the social trajectory in the current development; level of socioeconomic development and presence of economic environment that favors involvement of human capital in production, including development of the labor market and the stock market; level of involvement of human capital in the national production for each national economy; scale of reproduction of human capital (increased, stable, reduced); forms of connecting workers with the means of production, the system of production relations, and the trajectory of its development; vectors of economic transition; level of development of socioeconomic and organization-economic relations in the system; rate of economic growth and macroeconomic dynamics overall; degree of prioritization of innovative development and its structure; presence of positive correlation between human capital and economic growth and its estimates; presence of the necessary conditions for an increased scale reproduction of human capital; presence of the conditions necessary for transition from predominantly exogenous to endogenous economic growth and socioeconomic development.

2.2 Place of Growth in the Transition Economy of Ukraine

The recent calls for innovative development are numerous. The new terms and economic categories are being developed in support of the claims for innovations in the economy. Unfortunately, modern economic thought in Ukraine does not go far beyond the general discussion of the advantages of innovative path of economic development. It remains within the limits of pseudo-theorization and rarely attempts empirical research. The necessity of creation of the conditions favorable for the innovation-based economic development requires determining whether such process is possible and the degree of such possibility. This can be done based on the study of the major determinants of transformation and finding the place of such a process within the market transition and development of the post-transition economy.

After the disintegration of the USSR, Ukraine and other Newly Independent States (NIS) were in the process of deep socioeconomic transformation. The transition of the national systems from one major condition to another was not linear, smooth, and gradual. While the general vector of transition was defined as moving toward the market, the reality presented former republics with a mixture of forms and mechanisms of economic development, including recession, crises, and social and economic disintegration. Local crises turned into simplification of the economic mechanism and led to shortages in entire industries. Well-developed market mechanisms coexisted with the primitive form of economic organization in countryside. There was a rapid increase in the differential between the center and the periphery. The system was initially reformed from the emerging market economy with agriculture dominating the entire economy into the centralized and bureaucratized system of planned economy with the substantial process of militarization. Domination of the defense industry and a large military complex are characteristics of centralized systems.

The transition received an immense attention from the economists. We will briefly characterize major points of the scholarly discussion of economic transition that took place in 1990s and continues today. Lisovitsky (1992) points out that the reform of 1990 led to the inversion of the previous system, while the degree of inversion was predetermined by the degree of its involution (p. 20). Pokrytan (1997) characterizes market transition in Ukraine as a move to capitalism (p. 18). Buzgalin (1995) says that the transition is a change of economic relations, including allocation of the resources, property rights, mode of production, incentives, goals and means of economic development, institutions, and legal conditions (p. 40). Buzgalin sees noneconomic determinants as dominant in transition and points out the mosaics of the transition economy that consists of many pieces of the new and the old. Economic development is influenced by noneconomic processes and events, including political, geopolitical, sociocultural, ideological, military, and other factors. Accordingly, the transition economy is predetermined to be unstable.

Market transition faces harsh critiques as well. Gosh (1998) sees process of transition as a process of emerging financial oligarchy and its alliance with the state (p. 59). Both political events and inertia of the past system influenced the process of market transition. Gosh supports gradual transition as the only possible productive form of market transition and relies on the examples of China and Vietnam. He also points out that the destructive character of the reform is directly connected to the degree of the reform. In his view, the Ukrainian economy suffered much more than did the economy of Belarus, because economic and political reforms in Belarus were less significant and more gradual than in Ukraine (p. 22).

Buzgalin (1995) marks three major trends in the transition economies, including the gradual death of the mutant socialism, the emergence of the modern capitalism, and the humanization and socialization of socioeconomic life (p. 41). He gives priority to the last trend that includes innovative development and priority of human capital (p. 43). Chukhno (1996) delineates two major possible models of the economic transition and the future system. The first one is the way of classic capitalism that slowly evolves to the developed forms. It includes unavoidable formation of the army of workforce, alienation of workers from the means of production, high level of economic exploitation along with some elements of noneconomic methods or forced labor, slow development of social partnership and humanization of labor (p. 18). The second model is way more idealistic and relies on plurality of property rights, profit-sharing, worker participation, social partnership, and the move toward postindustrial society (p. 19).

Kolganov (1995) makes emphasis on institutional diffusion a characteristic of the transition economy (p. 57). This includes legal vacuum, unclear and changing property rights, and broken connections between different civil, economic, and regulatory institutions. The continuous redistribution of property rights takes place along with the process of legalization of criminal capital and shadow or unofficial economy, and money laundering. Redistribution of property rights during the exogenous transformation is influenced by the local and corporate regulation and noneconomic determinants. Forms of property and property rights embedded in the legislation are often inadequate to the realities of transition. Around 70 percent of large privatized enterprises were open-membership joint-stock companies under the control of the state and the workers. This meant de facto concentration of the property rights in the hands of the plant administration and the state bureaucrats. Zadorozhny (1996) points out that the existing forms of property are not supported by the necessary legal mechanisms (p. 134). The process of distribution and redistribution of property rights is often oversimplified and viewed as a development of private property. For instance, Temchuk and Palamarchuk (1994), referring to Sachs, say that former state property is distributed for free among workers and population (p. 48). This view is based exclusively on the legislation and does not take into account real processes in the economy.

In the Soviet times, alienation of workers from the means of production was hidden behind the fact of virtually absent unemployment and so-called state and collective forms of property. Private property did not exist, at least in legal terms. Economic transition included the process of conversion of the state property into monopolistic property of newly emerged corporations, where private capital shared property rights with the state *nomenklatura*, that is, former and present state bureaucrats. Alienation of workers from the means of productions on both levels—process of production and property rights—led to a dramatic increase in unemployment. Gritsenko (1997) points out that under the inversion-type transition alienation of workers from the means of production was formalized in legal terms (p. 7).

The state started introducing the new system of economic relations and mechanisms of functioning in the old Soviet system that had yet to use all of its resources and potential for the development. This process defined economic transformation as exogenous, made under the influence of external noneconomic forces, such as the state (Hrytsenko, 1997). Exogenous transition led to the mixture of different forms and mechanisms of economic activities in the newly independent states, including the remnants of the soviet economy and the new emerging elements of the market economy. Mixed character of the market transition is different from the mixed economy. The mixed economy is a stable form of the national production that exists in all developed societies.

In distinction of the classic historical way of development where market relations preceded industrial revolution and later industrialization, in the former USSR market relations were introduced in the industrialized system of production. As a result, the state property was transformed into the private property, planned prices were replaced with the free pricing mechanisms, and full obligatory employment gave way to the slowly emerging labor market. Under the classical type of transition from nonmarket to market economy, workers are alienated from land. At that time land along with labor was a major factor of production. A good historical example would be the primary capital accumulation and early stages of capitalism in England. Under the inversion-type transition from the centralized system to the market system workers are alienated from the means of production, created by the previous generations of workers. These are primarily machinery, equipment, and buildings, that is, products of industrialization. This process is described by Gritsenko (1997) along with the processes of socialization of primary capital accumulation during the transition toward market (p. 6).

The dilemma of what comes first, institutions or economic growth that leads to higher level of material production, points to a classical "chicken and egg" problem. Institutions are needed to set or change the rules of the game and regulate the incentive structure that will lead to growth, and at the same time a certain level of material well-being maintained by the continuous economic growth is needed to back up the institutions. Naturally, economic development comes first, supported by the technological progress, and institutions emerge in order to regulate the system and minimize transaction costs. The inversion-type transition anticipates the reverse sequence. Institutions are set by the state and are supposed to facilitate growth. Some institutions mutate, others perform functions different from the intended, and some can disappear or dissolve, even though they can reemerge later. For instance, the idea of commodity exchanges was transformed into the establishment of numerous real estate exchanges. Such a mutation was explained by the fact that according to newly developed legislation, it was cheaper for buyers and sellers to register transaction with real estate through exchanges than through the notary services. It is hard to imagine how an apartment or a house may become a commodity traded on a commodity exchange. Employment centers, established to help people find jobs, turned into social welfare centers, competing with those already set by the state. They were unable to perform their intended functions. Private secondary schools emerged in early and mid-1990s and soon disappeared due to the traditionally high quality of secondary education. Later, few schools reemerged again, but only in large cites where parents with high income look to place their children in specialized schools.

The economic transition influenced forms of socialization as well. In the planned economy people were guaranteed workplace, certain level of consumption, free access to elementary, secondary, higher, and graduate education, free access to health care, distribution of housing, and a well-developed social security system. This system is to be replaced with the new system of social guarantees, typical for a market economy. However, the market system is only at the stage of its formation and not development. Such a mismatch led to the weakening of the system of social guarantees without its immediate replacement by the new system.

Vorobyev et al. (1997) see the contradiction between the old and the new system of social guarantees as one of the major characteristics of the inversion-type transition. The growing income inequality and distribution of property create incentives for economic growth (p. 70). Gosh (1997) suggests that the total volume of production in Ukraine declined 58.9 percent over the 1990s and that this proves the destructive character of market transition (p. 59). Rokochaja and Moroz (1998) argue the opposite, suggesting that economic transformation in which exogenous factors dominate is an effective way of evolutionary development (p. 59). The disintegration of the USSR led to the partial disintegration of the unified monolithic national economy with all of its ties. Only 20 percent of all the production in Ukraine was so-called full-cycle production. In most of the instances resources and parts were brought from the other republics and the final product was exported outside the republic. Despite the process of disintegration and other negative processes for the economy, the decline in production never reached 59 percent and was less significant.

The capitalization of the economy is also a positive process. The national economy will likely preserve a substantial public sector with guaranteed access to health care and education. This will be to a certain extent a product of the Ukrainian mentality. In Ukraine, as well as in Russia, access to medical services and quality education is traditionally considered as a human right. This is not typical for many countries. In the United States in 2006 over 50 million people did not have health insurance and hence did not have access to health care. The share of workers who have health coverage through their employers declined from 73 percent in 1975 to 60 percent in 2006. This means that one out of every six people in the United States effectively does not have access to medical services. And this is in the most advanced nation where health care industry constituted in 2006 16 percent of the GDP. It seems necessary for every developed nation to have universally accessible health care. In fact, the United States might be the only exception in this sense. All of the developed countries, including Western Europe, Canada, Japan, Australia, Eastern Europe, and the Russian Federation, have systems of universal health coverage.

A successful process of socialization is characterized by the sustainable and increased reproduction of human capital. Continuous process of reproduction of human capital necessitated a significant presence of the state in the national economy during the market transition. The leading role of the state for the initial stage of the transition was clear from the very beginning. Mocherny (1993) pointed out the necessary evolution of the state's functions due to the fact that so-called market failures will be unavoidable (p. 18). We can name the following major characteristics of the process of market transition in Ukraine: property redistribution and alienation of workers from the means of production; economic restructuring; creation of market institutions; integration of the national economy into the world economy; partial dismantling of the socialist system of social guarantees and creation of the new system, based on the predominantly market economy.

In 1990s the economists expressed both pessimistic and optimistic views on the transition and the future of the nation. Gosh (1998) pointed out that there are no technologies, natural resources, human resources, and other socioeconomic factors in Ukraine that would allow for transition from industrial to postindustrial production (p. 57). This opinion appears to be quite pessimistic. Ukraine as well as the Russian Federation is an industrially developed society with a significant amount of human capital. It needs structural and institutional changes in order to sustain technological advancements and increase productivity. Abalkin (1997) sees the opportunity for a significant technological advancement during the transition (p. 622).

A specific feature of human capital as a factor of production is that its total amount can increase even when the total population declines. While such factors of productions as labor and capital can increase thanks to an increase in the total labor force and capital accumulation, respectively, human capital can reproduce on an increasing scale even when the total workforce declines and the productive capital is constant. This lays down the first principle that establishes possibility of future sustainable growth and socioeconomic development in Ukraine even under the conditions of relatively slow capital accumulation and negative growth in population in the long run. This principle points to insufficiency of the exogenous theories of growth as applied to Ukraine. The second principle that comes out of the first one is that the endogenous growth model connected to human capital may be the only perspective option for the future development in Ukraine in the long run, especially when the resources of the exogenous growth will be depleted. The third principle establishes that human capital is capable of growing based on its internal potential and already accumulated human capital. Such a process is based on the human nature to produce and accumulate new knowledge. The fourth principle says that the process of human capital reproduction on an increased scale expressed in the usage of human capital in the societal production as a major factor of production lies in the basis of the total factor productivity increase. Human capital as a factor of production makes service industry specific. If earlier consumption was traditionally divided on personal consumption and production consumption, now a certain part of consumption becomes personal and at the same time productive. Consumption facilitates reproduction of workforce and accumulation of human capital. The process of development of each individual is of value to the society because it means accumulation of human capital, development of certain characteristics and skills that are in demand in the economy. A substantial part of the basis for an increased reproduction of human capital consists of the systems of health care and education.

Health care and education industries in Ukraine as well as in the Russian Federation and countries of Eastern Europe in many instances continue to operate on the same basis and with the same mechanisms as they did during the Soviet times. The national systems of higher education experience slow but significant changes, while secondary education and health care preserved most of their old features. Until recently, the high level of medical services and education in the countries of the former Soviet Bloc allowed them a luxury of not changing much in these industries. One might expect that universal access to health care will be preserved as it is in the Western European welfare states. The same will be true for the secondary education, as the access to it will likely remain universal, compulsory, and free for immediate consumers. However, higher education industry faces dramatic changes in the near future, including its further decentralization, deregulation, privatization, marketization, and commercialization. Such changes will make the industry more effective and efficient in creation of new knowledge and human capital accumulation. This includes higher level of flexibility and responsiveness to the market demand. Some of the industries that traditionally belonged to the public sector should be rebuilt on the basis of shared responsibility between the state and the public, including businesses and individuals. In higher education this will include introduction of the concepts of plurality of forms of organization and property rights, and cost-sharing in education funding.

In addition to the essence of transition, it is important to consider views about the major stages of the process. Chukhno (1996) sees three major stages in transition. The first stage includes an overcoming of the crisis, economic stabilization, and initiation of growth. The second stage includes privatization, demonopolization, and effective functioning of the enterprises. The third stage includes restructuring of the national economy and technological advancements. Chukhno anticipates the third stage to take at least two–three decades (p. 20).

The major stages of transition according to Sachs and Pivovarsky (1996) include: stabilization or critical phase, when the government fights inflation and other negative consequences of the disintegration; phase of market-building, when market institutions are developed; and phase of the structural adjustments, when the character of production and employment change (p. 54). Major stages of social transition include a compensatory socialization during the privatization and restructuring; a reduction of unemployment; socialization of property through joint-stock companies; and technological innovations. Economists discuss the opportunities for socially oriented transition and see social stability and increasing social welfare among the major characteristics of the socially oriented mixed economy (Cherevko and Lukash, 1998, pp. 48–49; Sidorovich, 1997, p. 594).

2.3 Growth Forecasts and their Explanation

Long-run forecasts of economic growth in Ukraine and their interpretation will be presented in addition to the macroeconomic indicators considered earlier in this chapter. Long-run forecasts for the key macroeconomic indicators for the period of 1989–2030 include a variety of indicators for GDP, GDP growth, contribution to GDP by expenditures, demographics, labor, and productivity. The forecasts are based on Economist Intelligence Unit (EIU) calculations, the data from the Ministry of Economy and European Integration, and the State Committee of Statistics. The data indicate that GDP per head (USD at PPP) will reach $10,720 in 2010 and $41,280 in 2030. Real GDP growth per head (percent per annum) has reached its peak of 13 percent in 2004, and then slowly declines to 4 percent in 2018. Real GDP (PPP billion USD at 1996 prices) will increase from $338.601 billion in 2009 to $758.555 billion in 2030.

There is a significant difference between the values of GDP in billions of dollars expressed in constant 1996 prices and GDP in billions of dollars expressed in constant 1996 prices in PPP. Such a significant and consistent difference of almost four times cannot be attributed exclusively to the deviations of exchange rates from the PPP or volatility in the national currencies. The Ukrainian national currency always was and still is much stronger with respect to the U.S. dollar than expressed in the currency exchange rates. This bias affects statistics as well as the technical and country reports.

Another significant characteristic of the data used in the statistical analysis is that the dynamics of GDP in Ukraine are presented in billions of dollars expressed in constant 1996 prices while it is a well-known fact that the Ukrainian national currency was relatively strong in relation to the U.S. dollar at that time. This preceded the currency crisis of 1998 when exchange rate of the Ukrainian national currency in relation to the U.S. dollar declined from around 2 : 1 to 4 : 1 within a six-month period. Accordingly, if the dynamics of GDP in Ukraine were presented in billion dollars expressed in constant 1998 prices, then the difference between the values of GDP and GDP in PPP would be even more significant.

Dynamics of the components of GDP in Ukraine for the period of 1989–2006 and in the forecasts till 2030 point to the growing role of private consumption in real per capita GDP growth. Real government consumption is predicted to grow from $4.252 billion in 2008 to $10.307 billion in 2030. Real gross fixed investment (billion USD at 1996 prices) is predicted to increase from $19.5 billion to $51.4 billion. Real private consumption (billion USD at 1996 prices) is predicted to grow from $72 billion in 2008 to $241 billion in 2030. Real imports of goods and services are expected to grow from $44 billion to $201 billion. Real exports of goods and services are expected to grow from $34 billion to $129 billion. The figures are presented in constant 1996 prices. The rate of growth of real capital stock is expected to increase from 3.6 percent in 2008 to 6.4 percent in 2030. Dynamics of the demographics, labor, and productivity in Ukraine for the period of 1989–2006 and in the forecasts till 2030 point toward the continuing decline in the total population and active labor force and a steady increase in productivity. The population is expected to be around 42 million people in 2030, labor force of around 18.5 million as compared to 22 million in 2008, and unemployment of around 5 percent. Labor productivity growth will decline from the record high of 11.4 percent in 2004 to 4.9 percent in 2022 and then to around 3 percent in 2030. Total factor productivity growth is expected to decline to 1 percent by 2030.

The EIU utilizes a supply side framework for long-term forecasting. In this framework, output is determined by the availability of labor and capital equipment, and the growth in productivity. The forecasts completed by the EIU and presented earlier are not perfect, as would be the case with any other economic forecasts. One of the major problems with such forecasts is that they do not account for economic cycles. A business cycle is the predominant form of economic development in market economies in the long run. It would be reasonable to expect that the economy of Ukraine, as well as those of the Russian Federation and countries of CEE, will reach the stage of cyclical development in a decade or so.

The process of economic changes can be divided into stages depending on the rate of growth of real GDP. The data presented earlier indicate an initial decline in the rate of growth of real GDP in Ukraine in 1989 that later turned into the negative rate of growth. This negative growth continued according to the most pessimistic estimates from 1990 to 1999. The period of 2000–2004 is characterized by a significant increase in business activities and positive economic growth that reached 12.1 percent in 2004. The period of 2005–2010 will most likely be characterized as a period of slowdown in the rate of GDP growth, fluctuating around 6 percent per annum. Further slowdown in economic growth is expected in 2011–2015 with the rate of growth declining from 6 to 4 percent. Real GDP in Ukraine during the period of 2015–2030 is expected to increase at the rate of around 3.6 percent annually.

Based on the forecasts, the stages of GDP growth can be presented as follows: decline in the rate of growth (till 1989); negative economic growth (from 1990 to 1999); significant economic growth along with a significant increase in business activities in the country (from 2000 to 2004); slowdown in the rate of growth (from 2005 to 2010); further decline in the rate of growth (from 2011 to 2015); stabilization of the rate of growth at the moderate level (from 2015 to 2030). These stages can be presented as follows: low rate of economic growth; negative rate of growth; significant growth; significant but declining rate of growth; average and declining rate of growth; moderate economic growth. The prognoses are based on average and moderate values. This strategy is normally used to ensure that possible significant deviations will not occur. At the same time such a strategy is not necessarily the best at reflecting the economic future and thus it is not always appropriate.

The stages of economic growth presented earlier are not the phases of economic cycle. First of all, economic cycle is typical for market economies, while the presented stages of growth were initiated by the exogenous impact and were stages of the process of transition. Second, the phases of growth characterize the transition economy. Third, economic growth that takes place in Ukraine is sustainable growth, not a part of the economic cycle. Finally, the very understanding of the economic cycles and possible future cyclic development of the nation's economy is missing in the presented forecasts. Another problem of long-run forecasts is that they freely interpret the term "long run." In economics, long run is a period sufficient enough to renovate principal capital, if such necessity exists and is supported by the major structural changes in a particular firm, industry, or national economy. The reaction of the businesses on the major shifts in demand in the long run is expressed in the changing capital structure or an increase in production capacities. In macroeconomics, long run should be interpreted as a period of time sufficient for a substantial renovation of principal capital in the national economy. Such a renovation would be quite normal in a post-transition economy. Nevertheless, in the forecasts, the term long run normally means a significant period of time and very often a period of twenty years, yet unrelated to its economic meaning.

The two comments on the long-run forecasts presented earlier that address the necessity of taking into consideration economic cycles and considering long run as it is intended in economics are closely linked, because every economic cycle has in its fundament a renovation of principal capital. The long-run forecasts for Ukraine, as well as for the Russian Federation, Poland, Hungary, and other post-transition economies, should be linked to the concepts of economic cycles and cyclic development as well as the time when these economies will reach the stage of cyclic development. It is hard to point an exact date when Ukraine's economy will enter its first economic cycle. Moreover, unclear phases of modern economic cycles make the task even more challenging. Nevertheless, it is possible to present most likely scenarios in the country's development that will eventually lead to the cycle.

Undoubtedly, the first economic cycle will start after the massive renovation of the principal capital. The slowdown in the accumulation of amortization funds during 1990s along with the growing depreciation of principal capital was considered as a time bomb for the industry. Now it becomes obvious that a significant renovation of principal capital is necessary and almost unavoidable. One can say with a high degree of certainty that Ukraine during the next decade, that is, from 2008 to 2018, will have to renovate at least a third of its principal capital. If a massive technical renovation and incremental growth in production capacities will take place right after the period of significant growth of 2004–2006, then the national economy will enter the stage of cyclical development earlier. If, however, the massive renovation of principal capital will be preceded by the period of economic growth slowdown, predicted for 2007–2010, then the nation's economy will enter the cycle later.

We tend to consider the second scenario as more viable and likely to take place in Ukraine. The slowdown in economic growth will indicate stabilization of the system. Later, based on this already achieved stabilization, renovation of principal capital will began. This renovation will start from the most viable, economically effective and profitable industries, which were, nevertheless, utilizing old and morally outdated machinery and equipment. Here, technological changes will be accompanied with the incremental increase in principal capital based on reinvestment of profits, earned in these industries over the last decade.

Economic integration is another argument for the irreversibility of the process of transition to the cyclic development and the necessity to account for it in long-run forecasts. The process of economic integration of Ukraine, the Russian Federation, and countries of Eastern Europe in the world economy, participation in the global socioeconomic processes are to be considered in the forecasts. Economic forecasts presented by the EIU indicate all the significance of exports and imports in Ukraine's economy that will be achieved by 2030. An increase in the openness of the national economy and its integration in the international system of the division of labor are obvious. Certain difficulties faced by Ukraine while entering the World Trade Organization (WTO) appear to be somewhat ungrounded. Same may be fair to say for the Russian Federation. Economic stability and market reforms in Ukraine and the Russian

Federation are obvious while the membership in the WTO is granted to numerous developing nations with unstable economies, unclear paths in socioeconomic development, and unstable political regimes.

While making forecasts for economic growth in Ukraine, one should not be overly optimistic. It might not be a good idea to compare growth rates in China and in Ukraine. Chinese economic miracle becomes a charismatic example of successful rapid economic growth in modern times, as it was earlier with Japan. High rate of growth in Ukraine in the first half of 2000s was at par with the rate of growth in China. However, the essence of growth and its grounds were different in the two cases. The stable and high annual rate of growth of the average of 9.7 percent in China over the last 15 years is nothing but an indication of a fundamental process of industrialization, the transition from preindustrial to industrial mode of production. Also, in China, population growth continues, while in Ukraine there is a stable and continuous population decline. Accordingly, while calculating GDP per capita, this indicator for China decreases, and for Ukraine it increases in time. The continuing boom in the Chinese economy is somewhat analogous to the U.S. roaring twenties at the beginning of the twentieth century, or the period of industrialization and the postwar reconstruction in the USSR. At the same time there are such rudiments of preindustrial mode of production as high but declining illiteracy rate, especially in the rural areas, undeveloped social sphere, lagging behind agriculture that often has a form of primitive production, and state property in the heavy industry, especially mining and machine building. All of these are characteristics of the Chinese economy.

Until recently, over 70 percent of population in China resided in rural areas, while for the developed countries this indicator rarely goes higher than 30 percent. Urban population in Ukraine in 2004 constituted 68 percent, in Russia 72.9, in China 36.7, in Poland 62.5, Hungary 64.8, in France 75.5, in Germany 87.7, and in the United States 77.4 ("World in Figures," Washington, DC, *The Economist*, 2005). Social and economic transformation of the Chinese society occurs along with the process of industrialization and growing inequality in the development of different regions and industries. Economic transition in the post-socialist world occurred on the basis of already formed and sustainable industrialized economy. Therefore, in Ukraine, Russia, and other NIS, capital accumulation was replaced with the processes of concentration and centralization of capital. Such processes found their expression in the active redistribution of property rights, changes of the system of property rights itself, and specifically alienation of workers from the means of production and de facto and de jure concentration of the property rights on principal capital in the hands of few. This served as a ground for the famous postulate that on the post-Soviet territories economic transformation turned into the redistribution of already accumulated wealth and property through the process of privatization, while in China the economic reform has a creative character and takes place under the guidance and oversight of the existing political regime. In China, processes of industrialization and initial capital accumulation meant an increase in production capacities and gradual changes in economic relations, including introduction of market mechanisms, typical for mixed economies. The economic transition in the post-Soviet states took place without an increase in production capacities. It included major changes in the system of economic relations and preservation of production capacities, some of which were even abandoned and did not find new owners.

Realization of the large economic projects, such as construction of hydroelectric power stations as well as the fact that China is now the largest consumer of raw materials in the world confirm the suggestion that China's rapid growth is extensive in its nature. The initial capital accumulation in the Chinese model was based on the export increase. The massive increase in production and export of consumer goods was possible thanks to the significant amount of readily available and cheap labor in the country. The high rate of capital turnover and high rates of profit made it possible to invest in other industries. By the end of the transition to the industrialized economy, the rate of growth in China will decrease significantly. There are already estimates that the Chinese economy is overheated. The official forecasts place the growth rate in 2008 at 8 percent as compared to 10.7 percent for the previous year.

It is obvious that the Ukrainian society and the national economy are at the level of development different from that of China. The processes that take place in China now occurred in Ukraine several decades ago. One would not expect significant construction projects and more so massive import of raw materials in Ukraine. This is a fundamental distinction between the Ukraine's economy and the economies of China and Russia. Ukraine can afford neither the luxury of economic development at the expense of exporting raw materials, as does Russia, nor the significant import of raw materials, as in China.

Similar to China, Ukraine's economy now experiences a more rapid process of regionalization than it did during the Soviet times. A previously vague divide on Eastern and Western Ukraine that started after independence became more obvious during the last decade (Osipian, 1999). An emphasis on centralization and development of the regions through the center that existed in the Soviet system is now being replaced with the strategy of more regional autonomy and independence, but disparity as well. This strategy, however, is contradicted by the continuing and consistent attempts of the center to collect all of the taxes in the central budget and redistribute some of it back to the regions. Unstable political situation and more voices for regional economic autonomy point toward further decentralization and distancing of the politics from the national economy (Osipian and Osipian, 2006). This is especially true for an industrialized Eastern enclave known as Donbass.

The ground for sustainable growth in Ukraine is seen in the development of high-tech industries and, more importantly, in an increasing organizational and economic effectiveness of already existing and well-established industries. These industries include, first of all, metallurgy and heavy machine building. Development of the knowledge based or high-tech industries does not necessarily mean hypothetical attempts to transfer to production of computers, software, and biotechnologies. Rather, as applied to Ukraine, it means introduction of new technologies in already existing industries with the goal of increasing their effectiveness and efficiency. These technologies should guarantee resource-saving and be environmentally friendly. Technological innovations are much needed in the agricultural complex as well. It seems irrational to import agricultural products to the country with the largest stock of rich and fertile soil in the world.

Ukraine, Russia, and China share common problems as well, including those created by the rapid economic growth. China already faces ecological problems, including environmental pollution due to the loosely controlled economic activities and old ecologically unfriendly technologies. Similar problems have been existing in the Russian Federation and Ukraine for decades. The economic decline during 1990s led to the slowdown in environmental pollution and even improvements in ecological situation. The slowdown in economic growth in Ukraine starting in 2006 appears to be logical. Noneconomic factors, including political instability, public distrust in the government, absence of market mentality, pessimism, disbelief in the future success, and corruption also play a certain role. Old production technologies contribute to environmental pollution. Economic forecasts for Ukraine are quite optimistic. The population decline leads to the real DGP per capita growth rate being higher than GDP growth. At the same time the predicted annual growth rate equals to 5–6 percent for the period of 2006–2014 and then continuous real GDP per capita growth of around 4 percent per year. These are very optimistic predictions. Ukraine will not be able to keep the pace of

Chinese growth due to the reasons presented earlier. Even real GDP per capita annual growth of 2–3 percent is a good indicator for Ukraine in the long run. In the countries of the European Union, annual growth rate of 1.2–2 percent is considered as a good indicator.

2.4 Transition from Exogenous to Endogenous Economic Growth

As we pointed out earlier, there was a reproduction of human capital on an increased scale along with the exogenous forms of growth and the extensive model of development of the national economy in the USSR. Human capital accumulation was done through the development of education, science, and health care. The extensive growth was based on utilization of additional resources, including labor, capital, and natural resources. The richness in natural resources allowed for economic expansion, relatively high standards of living, and the large military complex. Finally, the demographic situation was also favorable for extensive growth.

The disintegration of the Soviet Union and fundamental economic transition make extensive forms of growth less viable while urging to turn to intensification of economic development. While in the Russian Federation the unfavorable demographic situation may be partially compensated by the huge natural resources, in Ukraine declining population and limited natural resources necessitate technological changes and an increased reproduction of human capital. The transition from exogenous to endogenous growth will occur while there still is a potential for exogenous growth, mainly thanks to the economic decline of 1990s. When the resources for exogenous growth will be depleted, endogenous growth will become dominant and reproduction of human capital on an increased scale will become of primary importance, especially due to the continuing decline in population. The process is not expected to be linear. It will depend on external impacts as well, including political reforms, formation of civil society, changes in the world economy, globalization, local crises, and such.

The economic transition has been completed by 2006. It will be fair to say that the presence of the mixed and predominantly market-based economy in Ukraine is a fact. Major features of the newly formed market economy in the country include: supply and demand based on the market mechanisms and free pricing. Prices are defined as a result of achieving an equilibrium of supply and demand; the economy of deficit had disappeared. The market has enough goods and services to satisfy consumer demand both in terms of quantity and in terms of quality; the state monopoly in production is gone. The major part of goods and services is produced by the independent producers; the competition is growing. Improvements in the competitive environment make products more competitive in domestic and foreign markets; the process of creation of market institutions is completed; the national economy is characterized with the high degree of openness. This is confirmed by the growing volume of foreign trade. The structure of the national economy is to a certain extent determined by the volume of potential import and export, with the growing demand on the national goods from abroad; hyperinflation of the mid-1990s is tackled and replaced with the regulated inflation with the annual rate of around 10–12 percent; the well-functioning monetary system is characterized by the stabilized national currency and stable exchange rate. The value of the national currency grew from 6 UAH to 5 UAH per $1.

There is a new balance of different forms of property in the transition economies. Heyets (2001) points out that in 1999 only 54 percent of all production facilities were left in the state property in Ukraine, while at the beginning of the reform in 1991 almost all of the principal capital belonged to the state. The share of private businesses in principal capital in 1999 was around 2.2 percent, while the share of collective property was equal to 44 percent. Foreign entities owned only 0.1 percent of the production facilities in Ukraine (p. 9). This indicates little involvement of foreign companies in Ukraine's economy.

Categories of economic growth and economic development are not identical. Economic growth can take place along with the temporary decline in the living standards and weakening of social ties. For instance, the significant temporary and seasonal labor migration from Ukraine abroad, especially intensive in 1990s, can be interpreted as a phenomenon that has a negative impact on the social welfare, social capital, and social ties. It includes breaking or weakening of family ties, social connections, absence of the adequate legislative base, insufficiency of the state regulation, and oversight for the processes of labor migration that already take place, hard working conditions, lack of access to medical services, visa problems, and such. At the same time from the purely economic standpoint, the process of labor migration abroad clearly had a positive impact on the national economy. First, it eased the problem of unemployment. Second, it helped to avoid much of the social payments and dole to unemployed individuals from the state. Third, a significant part of the earnings of the labor migrants came to the national economy through the money remittances, mostly made in hard currencies.

An alternative to the labor migration abroad would be the high level of unemployment, large social payments and subsidies, high taxes, expensive labor, and low efficiency of the national economy. The arguments against the extensive labor migration abroad include rebuilding "other" economy. As a result, there are such stereotypes as "Ukrainian construction worker," "Polish plumber," and so on. Another argument against the migration is the rapidly rising real estate prices. It is assumed that labor migrants return home and buy housing for themselves and their families. However, since not much was built in the country, prices go up. By estimates, share of labor migrants abroad in Ukraine was higher than in Russia, but much lower than in Moldova. The major destinations were member countries of the European Union and Israel. In East Germany, labor migration did not grow to a large scale. As a result, the level of unemployment was equal to 18 percent during the entire period of transition. Of course such situation could be interpreted as socially positive, but it had negative impact on the economy and economic growth.

The earlier examples have been presented in order to delineate terms of economic growth and socioeconomic development. Economic development includes access of population to education, health care, ecological and environmental programs, stable energy supply, well-functioning governmental institutions, and such. All of these may lead to an increase in labor productivity. Success of the economic transition should be measured in terms of all of these factors and indicators, based on the complex strategy of development.

Ukraine needs to redefine its balance between the manufacturing and the services industry. In our view, a hyper-inflated service industry will not do well in the country. Employment in the service industry of around 50 percent of the total employment in the national economy may be a good indicator for Ukraine. This is accounting for the low level of automation in the service industry and the large amount of manual labor needed. As compared to the other developed nations, manufacturing's share in the total GDP in Ukraine is the highest. Statistics on the structure of GDP based on the sources and structure of employment in the industry in Ukraine, the Russian Federation, Poland, Hungary, China, France, Germany, and the United States for 2004 are presented in table 2.1.

Service industry in Ukraine is characterized by the low level of productivity, possibly because of the low labor productivity and traditionally large amount of the manual labor utilized. The share of the employed in the service industry constitutes 48 percent of all the employed in the national economy, while the share of the industry in GDP equals only 35 percent. Intensive use of manual and often low skill labor is common

Table 2.1 Origins of GDP and structure of employment in selected countries, 2004

	Origins of GDP (%)			*Structure of employment (%)*		
Country	*Agriculture*	*Industry*	*Services*	*Agriculture*	*Industry*	*Services*
Ukraine	23.4	41.5	35.1	26	26	48
Russia	7.2	39.4	53.4	12	29	59
Poland	3.8	31.4	64.8	19	31	50
Hungary	4.1	33.8	62.1	6	35	59
China	16.4	51.1	32.5	50	23	27
France	3.3	25.7	71.0	1	25	74
Germany	1.2	30.2	68.6	3	33	65
USA	1.4	20.3	78.3	2	23	75

Source: Composed from the data presented in "World in Figures," Washington, DC, *The Economist*, 2005.

for service industry in every country. Millions of seasonal labor migrants and illegal aliens are employed in agriculture and service industries in all developed countries in Europe. Official statistics do not count this type of workers. Migrant labor helps cover a substantial part of the demand for low skilled labor in such industries as agriculture, hospitality industry, and retail. This means that the actual share of employees occupied in these industries is higher than is normally indicated in statistical reports. The share of workforce employed in agriculture and service industry in the United States, France, and Germany is higher than is presented in table 2.1. The same situation is true for Hungary and Poland. Using the cheap unskilled labor of migrants that come from the outside of the system slows down the process of implementation of latest technological achievements and innovations. It is cheaper for the businesses to hire unskilled laborers, including illegal aliens, than to modernize production process in agriculture, services, and other labor intensive or seasonal industries. The demand on high-tech solutions remains low. This, in turn, slows down technological progress. As a result, labor intensive industries do not transform into capital intensive industries.

Mechanization and automation of manufacturing and agriculture should be followed by the mechanization and introduction of new technologies in the service industry. The structure of the service industry is even more important than its mechanization. The future development of the service industry in Ukraine, Russia, and other NIS is seen in further development of education and health care industries rather than retail sales. If service industry takes up two-thirds of the entire workforce in the country, this can only be justified by the highly developed high-tech industries that provide educational and medical services. In distinction from the traditional service industries, such as tourism and hospitality industry, education and health care industries utilize high-skilled labor and advanced technologies.

In the foreseen future Ukraine will have to learn balancing export promotion with import substitution, structural reforms and development of the domestic market. The initial stages of the reform in China were focused on export increase while now this country's major goal is a development of its domestic market. Foreign investment alone cannot move the system far enough to achieve a new higher level equilibrium. The reliance on the public spending and foreign capital inflow gives way to the emphasis of domestic investment and reinvestment.

Heyets (2001) points out that firms owned by foreign investors in Ukraine have the share of around 0.6–0.8 percent of all the capital investment, while their revenues from owning properties constitute around 2.6 percent. The share of profit of the foreign-owned businesses amounts to 2.1 percent of all the nation's profits. This indicates that the foreign investors are interested first of all not in the principal capital accumulation, but in the exploitation of already exiting production facilities and properties they own. According to the data for the end of 1998 the revenues from property were exceeding volumes of capital investments several times (p. 11).

One of Ukraine's major concerns is the complicated demographics. Despite the slowdown in the population decline, the process of decline in absolute terms continues and appears to be irreversible at least in the near future. It is expected that the total population will decline with the annual rate of 0.5 percent during the period of 2007–2011 and then with the rate of 0.4 percent starting 2012. The low level of birth rate does not make Ukraine an exception. Such a trend is common for all developed nations, including the Russian Federation and European countries. The only exception is the United States. However, even in the United States population growth occurs thanks to two major factors: continuing immigration and high birth rate among the immigrant families. In 2006, when the population of the United States reached the benchmark of 300 million, half of all the population growth was based on the immigration from Mexico and children born in the families of immigrants from Mexico. Population in the countries of Western Europe increases very modestly thanks only to the intensive immigration from the developing countries. Birth rates in such traditionally Catholic societies known for strong family values, such as Italy and Spain, barely reach 1.2 children per family. In France and Germany the situation is not much better, with the birth rate of around 1.58. Even simple scale reproduction with zero increase in population requires the birth rate of 2.1. Demographic situation in the Russian Federation is even more complex than in Ukraine. While the birth rates in both countries are about the same, around 1.14, and are the lowest in Europe, the life expectancy at birth in Russia is lower than in Ukraine.

In distinction from Russia, Ukraine does not have a substantial migration into the country. Instead, it has labor migration abroad. In the future, repatriation of the labor migrants back to the country will become one of the priorities in the state's economic policy. Declining population allows preservation and conservation of natural resources. This might be the only positive characteristic of the process of population decline. The unemployment level of 5 percent per annum offered in the forecasts appears to be quite moderate. Such a low level of unemployment can be found only in such developed countries as the United States and Japan. In the United States it is explained in part by the relatively liberal market model and the low minimum wage while in Japan unemployment traditionally is taken very seriously by the government planning agencies. In the Western European countries the level of unemployment varies within the limits of 8–18 percent depending on the country and the business cycle.

Unemployment forecasts for Ukraine do not account for the business cycle and the possibility of cyclic development. There is no doubt that the level of unemployment in Ukraine will not remain stable at 5 percent. Rather, it will change depending on the stage of the business cycle. Fluctuations in the level of business activities will influence the emerging labor market and lead to fluctuations in the level of unemployment. Types of unemployment are also of great concern. It is preferable to have frictional and cyclical unemployment rather than stable and institutional unemployment. With an increase in labor productivity and the complexity of work in the future, the periods of high unemployment can be used for retraining. Labor productivity forecasts for Ukraine are also quite optimistic. A stable increase in labor productivity was present starting in 1999 and reached 14.4 percent in 2000. Remarkably, a high increase in the rate of labor productivity continued till 2006. According to the forecasts this indicator will be at the level of 6 percent per annum till 2017 and then decline to 5 percent per year.

As was pointed out earlier, the resources for exogenous transition are near their depletion, while the resources for exogenous growth are still significant. Ukraine still has reserves of labor and capital that can move the economy forward if involved in production. The labor reserves exist in the following forms: presence of unemployment, labor migration abroad, and limited working time. Accordingly, the measures that can lead to an increase in the total amount of labor used in production and to the exogenous growth will be reduction of unemployment, return of the labor migrants from abroad back to the national economy, and an increase in the working time. The reduction in unemployment is achieved with the help of standard measures, including stimulating demand based on an increase in the final consumption; reduction in the frictional unemployment through the development of information networks and an improved access to this information for employees and employers; reduction in institutional and structural unemployment through the reorganization of social and welfare programs and professional retraining. Return of the labor migrants back to the national economy can be done through the development of domestic labor market and an increase in wages and salaries, balancing the level of wages with the level of prices. The increase of the working time can be done by an increase in the working day and/or working week. The economy will have to present stimuli for additional employment and working overtime while preserving the same level of labor intensity.

The algorithm of an increase in labor as the factor of exogenous growth is fairly simple and may be presented as follows: reduction in domestic unemployment and achievement of the level of full employment; attracting labor migrants back to the national economy; attracting labor migrants non-citizens from abroad; increasing the working time; increasing the labor intensity. All the measures listed earlier are parts of the process of increase of production and exogenous growth. The capital reserves exist in the following forms: undeveloped stock market, shadow economy, national capital outflow, unused production capacities, and unfinished construction projects. Accordingly, the measures to increase the volume of capital involved in production and to support exogenous growth will include creation and development of the stock market, reversing the capital flight from the country and repatriation of capital, legalization of capital, full production capacity utilization, and completion of the construction projects. The algorithm of an increase in capital as the factor of exogenous growth may be presented as follows: creation of the stock market in order to attract capital and channel it to production; repatriation of national capital back to the national economy; legalization of capital used in the shadow economy, amnesty of capital; full capacity utilization of earlier unused production capacities; completion and exploitation of the production facilities that are currently under construction.

The possible ways of an increase in the rate of exogenous growth with both labor and capital are presented in table 2.2. Potential for exogenous growth in Ukraine is presented in figures 2.1 and 2.2. Creation of the open labor market will facilitate more effective distribution of the workforce within the national economy and create an opportunity for attracting foreign workforce to the country if necessary. Creation of the stock market will facilitate development of the capital market, possible attraction of capital from abroad, more investments in manufacturing and service industries, and an increase in the effectiveness of capital investments.

Heyets (2002) points out that

> As far as the state securities market is concerned, it had in fact been frozen for a while after a failed start. The stock market situation is causing a lot of concern, since this extremely important sphere of the market economy does not meet the needs of today, let alone the future. Everywhere in the world, the stock market is a financial instrument which helps to allocate, distribute, and direct investment capital into various spheres of the economy, primarily into the real sector. The Ukrainian stock market has not compensated for the lack of governmental planning and administrative levers. The underdeveloped stock market is impeding the investment process, thus hampering economic restructuring without which it is impossible to increase competitiveness. There is a lack of transparency and of stock market liquidity; there are high systematic risks. The current system regarding taxation of investment funds and security profits discourages investment. The rights of investors and shareholders (founders, partners) of joint-stock companies and other businesses remain unprotected. (p. 87)

Ukraine faces continuing capital flight and labor migration, while further capital accumulation is needed. The process of continuing exogenous growth may be supported by the following steps: using the present internal resources in the process of production at full capacity; repatriation of labor and capital from abroad back to the national economy; attracting additional resources from abroad. In the future, exogenous resources of growth will be depleted. The limited quantity of labor, working time, and capital along with the continuing population decline predetermine the necessity of moving to the endogenous model of growth. This may be done based on the development of labor market and stock market on one hand and further development of education and health care industries on the other hand.

Table 2.2 Potential for exogenous growth by factor of production

	Resource	*Phenomenon*	*Measure*	*Task*
LABOR	Labor force	Unemployment	Decrease in unemployment	Full employment
		Labor migration	Repatriation	Labor force increase
		Working time	Working time increase	Working time max
CAPITAL	Stock market	Undeveloped stock market	Creation of the stock market	Development of the stock market
	Capital flow	Capital flight	Capital repatriation	Complete capital return
	Shadow economy	Shadow capital	Capital legalization	Complete capital legalization
	Production capacities	Unused production capacities	Increase in capacity utilization	Full capacity utilization
	Facilities	Incomplete construction	Construction completion	Full capacity utilization

Source: Composed by the author.

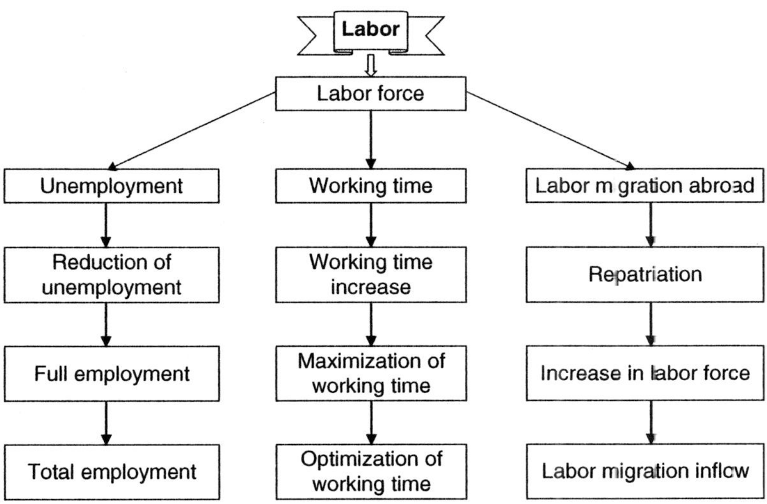

Figure 2.1 Potential for exogenous growth in factors of production: labor.

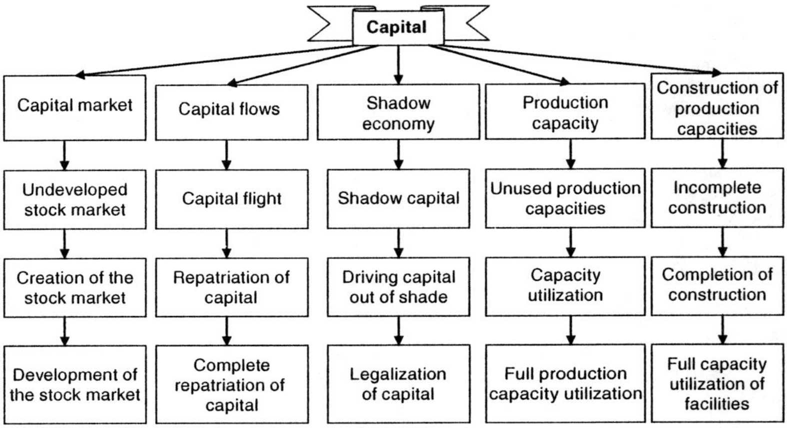

Figure 2.2 Potential for exogenous growth in factors of production: capital.

Labor market, normally underdeveloped even in the well-established market economies with strong traditions of competitiveness, is very weak in Ukraine and other post-transition economies. Personal connections and corruption are still major means of gaining a job placement. In this sense the pseudo-labor market that exists now has even less market features than it had during the Soviet times. As a result, bankers do not know how to do banking, managers do not know how to lead the businesses, and economists have a very vague idea of how to optimize production and maximize profit. This situation becomes even worse when it comes to the state bureaucrats who are still influential in the economy. At the same time highly skilled professionals cannot occupy the work places they are qualified for.

Heyets (2002) notes in this respect the following:

> First of all, we do not have a real labor market since this most important resource has not been truly valued so far. This substantially restricts the effective use of labor, because other resource prices have reached world levels long ago. This fact is a serious obstacle on the way to economic growth, especially taking into account the present skill level of labor. As a result, the motivation to work efficiently diminishes. Moreover, taxation does not provide incentives; on the contrary, it hinders the economic activity of people, thus limiting long-term economic growth. (p. 87)

One of the major misleading assumptions often made about the pace of the reforms, and privatization in particular, is that the sooner the reforms are done, the more successful the process of transition will be. Privatization from this position is seen as a move from one static condition to the other and from one stationary equilibrium to the other. The stationary position is then considered as an absolution, a necessary precondition for a smooth and sustainable development, a goal by itself. The system dynamics in this logic is missing. Transition systems are inherently unstable and characterized by nonlinear dynamics.

Shleifer (2005) points out that

> The need to gain support for reform is the political argument for privatizing rapidly. If privatization is slow, the benefits to the population are by definition small, and hence the political capital they buy the reformers is small as well. Fast privatization is privatization that offers large political benefits from the start, which is exactly what a reformist government needs. Critics of fast privatization have argued that it creates fast unemployment and thus drains the government budget (Aghion and Blanchard, 1993). This can produce both political opposition and economic problems for further privatization. This argument overlooks two essential points First, privatization in Eastern Europe is inherently very slow. Slowing it down further beyond what internal political forces accomplish will stop it altogether. Second, and more important, rapid privatization buys political benefits and thus allows reforms to deepen. (p. 36)

In our view, privatization should be relatively slow. In Ukraine, the process of privatization took longer than it did in Russia. Privatization should be considered not only as a process of property distribution, including the change of ownership of the production facilities, but as a process of investment. Ukraine still has a significant potential for privatization. The state property should no longer be distributed for free or through the fictitious voucher privatization, notorious for its corruption and pointlessness. Instead, it should be sold at market prices to those who are able and willing to pay. This will guarantee at least the effective exploitation of the privatized production facilities in the future.

One of the fundamental problems of the economic mechanisms, incentives for productive labor, and the national economies in general is a rent-seeking behavior. The rent-seeking behavior is best seen in Russia, especially with the ever high energy prices. Other post-Soviet economies can also be characterized as infected with the rent-seeking behavior. Since the resources are controlled territorially and the territories are confined within the national borders, the state is always a major player in the distribution of access to the resources and allocation of the benefits, derived from the resources, if not the major one. In the Russian Federation, one can see the growing involvement of the state in the oil and gas industry. The earlier total privatization of the industry is now reversed with the processes of de facto partial deprivatization, nationalization, and centralization of control over the access to the resources and revenue flows, strengthening the vertical axis of power and increasing participation of the state in the economy.

Ukraine cannot repeat the path of the Russian Federation simply because Russia has the richest natural resources in the world. The Russian economy will always be distinct by the inefficient use of the natural resources and the society will remain under the influence of rent-seeking behavior for quite sometime. In addition, Russia, and Moscow in particular, remains a regional center. In distinction of Ukraine, it did not suffer a significant labor migration abroad that lasted for at least 15 years. Instead, the Russian Federation experiences a significant influx of labor migrants into the country, some of whom come from Ukraine.

The exogenous transition was not very successful not only in Ukraine, but in the Eastern European countries as well, despite the fact that the inflow of foreign capital in these economies was much more significant. Examples of Poland, Hungary, and other countries of the region make it possible to believe that the "honeymoon" of the Eastern European reforms is over. In Hungary, $40 billion in foreign direct investment coexist with the $40 billion foreign debt with the state budget deficit of $10 billion. This in part is a result of the over-reliance on the foreign help during transition. The external help was intended to prevent the significant economic decline, facilitate economic stabilization, and initiate growth. What happened in reality can be characterized as Leontief's "living above the means." Political instability, trade union protests in Poland, violent demonstrations in autumn of 2006 in Hungary, dissatisfaction with the results of the reforms in East Germany prove the insufficiency of the exogenous model of transition, growth, and socioeconomic development.

The rapid economic growth that can be observed in Ukraine in the short run may be explained in part by such factors as statistical errors, legalization of a part of the shadow economy, utilization of already existing production capacities that were not in use during the transition, and reduction in unemployment. However, these factors alone cannot explain the rapid growth in the country that started in 1999 and continues for the last eight years. The presence of the sustainable real per capita GDP growth is unquestionable.

Utilization of unused production capacities and workforce is not enough to achieve sustainable economic growth. Sustainable economic growth can only be based on the continuous technological improvements and innovations, including management and organization of production, as well as accumulation of human capital and an increase in the effectiveness of its utilization in production. Therefore, major tasks for Ukraine become the renovation of principal capital, maintaining a high rate of technical progress, utilization of new technologies in the process of production, human capital accumulation, and organizational innovations.

Human capital exists indivisibly from each individual and from the societal production. Human capital is personified as it is embedded in an individual, and is accumulated, as any other form of capital. Human capital has value only in the process of production. Human capital is created, accumulated, and realized only within the process of societal production. The components of human capital, such as knowledge, special skills, experiences, are utilized in production. Endogeneity of human capital is explained by the fact that human capital is produced within the system, by the system, and for the system.

2.5 Education Corruption, Reform, and Growth

2.5.1 Basis for Corruption

The transition from endogenous to exogenous type of growth may face a few obstacles, including corruption in higher education. This section comes from the idea of combining education corruption and growth. So far, the impact of education corruption on economic growth remains in the realm of speculation and some theorizing. There is a lot of research done on human capital, education, economic development, and growth. There is also a substantial bloc of literature on corruption and economic development and growth. This bloc of scholarly literature, however, is represented mostly by theoretical works. Few empirical works have been produced so far, primarily due to the lack of data. Reliability and validity of the existing scarce data on governance and corruption also remains an issue.

Corruption is a growing problem throughout the world and receives more attention now than ever before. According to some estimates, transition economies are believed to be among the leaders in terms of corruption. The surveys conducted by Transparency International and the World Bank depict Ukraine as a very corrupt country. According to the corruption perceptions index (CPI), developed and calculated annually by Transparency International, Ukraine was 83rd out of 91 countries surveyed in 2001, sharing the ranks with such countries as Russia, Tanzania, and Azerbaijan. In 2008, Ukraine was in 134th place, with the score of 2.5, out of 180 countries (Transparency International, 2008). CPI score relates to perceptions of the degree of corruption as seen by business people and country analysts, and ranges between 10 (highly clean) and 0 (highly corrupt). The lower the numerical value of the country's score, the higher is the level of corruption in the country.

In this section, we target education corruption, human capital, and growth in Ukraine and offer examples from other NIS. More specifically, we look at corruption in education first, and then at its possible implications for economic development and growth in Ukraine. We consider specific aspects of education corruption and its probable impact on growth. These include interactions between education corruption and total factor productivity and interactions between corruption and structure of the national economy. Accordingly, the questions to be addressed are: Does education corruption harm total factor productivity? And does productivity reduce education corruption? The areas include education and labor market. Another set of questions include the following: Does education corruption define or influence the structure of the national economy? Can corruption in the education sector be reduced through the changes in the economic structure? The areas to be touched upon are the level of concentration of property rights and distribution of property rights on production capacities.

What is the basis for corruption? Whatever problem economists might have in explaining corruption is indicated by Rose-Ackerman's definition (1978) of corruption as an "allocative mechanism" for scarce resources. The state monopolizes certain allocative functions, be it permissions and licenses, or access to public services. State officials' profiteering is based on abuse of their discretionary powers and monopolistic positions. Referring to Klitgaard (1988, p. 23) Gong (2002) states that corruption: "than occurs when an agent betrays the principal's interests in pursuit of his/her own or when the client corrupts the agent "if he or she (client) perceives that the likely net benefits from doing so outweigh the likely net costs" (p. 88). Describing collective corruption Gong says that its purpose is "to maximize individual gains and/or minimize the risks associated with corrupt activities" (p. 88). According to the "grease-the-wheels" concept of corruption, it helps overcome bureaucratic obstacles that remain from the previous regime. This may be especially true for Ukraine and other NIS during the transition period of 1990s.

Addressing the question whether higher wages for bureaucrats reduce corruption, Svensson (2005) notes that it might be true, but that there is not enough evidence to support it (pp. 32–33). According to the data analysis, presented by Shleifer and Treisman (2003, pp. 27–28), administrative corruption is very high in poor countries of the former Soviet Union, such as Uzbekistan, Armenia, and Azerbaijan lower in the Russian Federation, Bulgaria, and Lithuania, and even lower in relatively wealthy Hungary and Slovenia. Individuals' perceptions about corruption put Russia lower than Argentina, Brazil, Romania, or Lithuania. Svensson (2005) notes that "All of the countries with the highest levels of corruption are developing or transition countries. Strikingly, many are governed, or have recently been governed, by socialist governments" (p. 24). Referring to the works of Demsetz (1967), Glaeser et al. (2004), and Lipset (1960), the author points out that higher per capita income and higher level of human capital reduce corruption.

The increasing gap between pay rates in private and public sectors of the economy urges public employees to seek other sources of income (Gorodnichenko and Sabirianova, 2006). Along with the health services industry, higher education in Ukraine has become one of the industries most affected by corruption. At the same time rapid development of higher education, its partial privatization, and the increasing flow of financial resources have created a base for corruption. Professors adjust their professional ethics and behavior by accepting bribes and numerous other illicit benefits and utilizing their privileged position and control over the access to higher education.

Economics has advanced significantly in modeling corruption, but is experiencing difficulties in testing the models due to the lack of large and reliable datasets. From anywhere in the world, documented evidence on education corruption is insignificant. The lack of valid and reliable data and evidence on education corruption slows down the process of scholarly investigation into the issue. The sensitivity of the issue explains methodological difficulties faced by the researchers not only in education corruption, but in other spheres affected by corruption as well. Case studies and small scale surveys with a low response rate remain major tools to assess corruption. The reliability of surveys and interviews is undermined by the sensitivity of the topic; corruption remains illegal. There are some methodologies that allow for approaching the issue of corruption and measuring it (see, for instance, Bellver and Kaufmann, 2005; Besançon, 2003; Kaufmann and Kraay, 2003; Osipian, 2007a), including legalistic (Kaufmann and Vicente, 2005; Osipian, 2008f; Zimring and Johnson, 2005) and economic ones (Kaufmann et al., 2000; Rose-Ackerman, 1978, 1999). Nevertheless, issues of conceptualization, theorization, operationalization, and measurement of education corruption remain largely unresolved. Lancaster and Montinola (1997) suggest that studies of corruption "should ultimately incorporate the most central goal of all comparative analyses—the assessment of rival explanations. The advancement of logical explanations, grounded in systematic empirical testing of theoretically-derived hypotheses, facilitates healthy debate about the primacy of one explanation over another" (p. 187).

2.5.2 Education Corruption

What is education corruption? Definition of education corruption includes the abuse of authority for material gain (Anechiarico and Jacobs, 1996). Heyneman (2004) adds to this definition by arguing the following: "But because education is an important public good, its professional standards include more than just material goods; hence the definition of education corruption includes the abuse of authority for personal as well as material gain" (p. 638). Sayed and Bruce (1998) and Waite and Allen (2003) present a broad social approach to define corruption. Petrov and Temple (2004) apply a narrow definition of corruption that regards corruption as such only if it implies illegality. The task of creating a set of well-grounded definitions seems to be a primary methodological task for the problem-focused research in the field of corruption. Corruption in higher education may be defined as a system of informal relations established to regulate unsanctioned access to material and nonmaterial assets through abuse of the office of public or corporate trust (Osipian, 2007a, p. 315).

What is the basis for corruption in higher education? The process of massification of higher education is driven by two fundamentals: development of production and social development (Dye, 1966; Lindeen and Willis, 1975; Volkwein and Malik, 1997). The national economy presents demand on the skilled labor, that is, human capital, produced in higher education institutions (HEIs) (Marshall and Tucker, 1992). State governments represent interests of producers and so their function is to supply skilled labor to businesses by maintaining the system of public education. The mass public higher education may be in place in every developed nation, but it is not the only determinant in the education industry. The economy requires the productive resource "human capital" at the minimum cost. Hence, the task of the government is to maximize the effectiveness and efficiency of public higher education. It is done on the basis of market reforms, dismantling of the vertical axis of subordination, and balancing university autonomy with its accountability to the state.

The essential feature of human capital is that it is indivisible from its bearer, that is, the individual. Therefore, a social dimension is immanent to the governance of public higher education. Individuals consider higher education as a way of involvement in the process of societal production and sustaining and increasing personal well-being. This social dimension is complex and includes such characteristics as access to higher education based upon social and economic characteristics of individuals. Disadvantaged members of the society are interested in the state's function of decreasing inequalities in access to higher education. They advance their interests through the system of democratic representation. Producers are interested in increasing the access of the public to higher education since it generates the needed qualified labor force, and in reducing inequalities in access to higher education as a way of increasing the social effectiveness of the process of accumulating human capital. The government is under pressure from both the producers driven by profit maximization, and from individuals who want to maximize their socioeconomic position. States make structural adjustments to the higher education sector in order to meet economic and public demands. In addition, higher education may be considered a part of mass consumption.

Business needs human capital to generate profit. In order to maximize profit, it requires human capital of a certain quality and quantity at the lowest price. The cost reduction in higher education anticipates massification of this sector. The economy of scale in this sector is obvious and is reinforced by the nature of education as an important public good. The state represents the interests of business. Its task is to build and operate a system of mass public higher education that would be effective and efficient and would satisfy the demands of business. Higher education in all developed industrialized nations is represented either exclusively or dominantly by the public sector. The leading role of the state predetermines large state bureaucracy in the sector. The state owns HEIs, regulates access to higher education, and controls the curriculum. By shaping the structure of higher education, the state determines characteristics of education programs and criteria for admissions. Distribution of state funding, control over the content and quality of educational programs, and access to higher education are eroded by corruption.

In the Ukrainian system of higher education, the corrupt relations become even more complicated, since the government comes into play as the major financier and regulator. The system is highly centralized with both state and private colleges being regulated by the state. This means that a case of embezzlement or misuse of college property by the college administrator constitutes an act of corruption by way of abusing public trust. The public, through the state, entrusts the college administrator with proper management and financial operations. In case of a corrupt professor, the abuse of public trust occurs not only in terms of assigning a higher grade with no academic merit, but in terms of misusing governmental financing, since half of the college students are funded with Ukrainian taxpayers' money. At this stage, there is no need for the leading role of the state in higher education. There are enough places in HEIs to accommodate all those who want to receive higher education and to meet the demand of business for qualified workforce. It is assumed that private HEIs can provide higher education services more effectively and efficiently. This assumption is based on the generally accepted premise that private enterprises in the market system operate more effectively and efficiently than do public ones. There is no need to collect and redistribute values through the tax system, central state budget, and access regulations. Nevertheless, the state continues to own and regulate public HEIs and regulate private HEIs.

Corruption in higher education comes not from the state bureaucracy, but from the state itself. The state distributes publicly funded places in HEIs and guarantees the degrees conferred in state accredited HEIs. These functions are abused by the bureaucrats and educators. They misuse their monopolistic authority over access to higher education services and degrees. These functions are abused by students as well, including those bribing their way to professional careers. There is no doubt that private education also has plenty of misconduct and illicit activities. However, if decentralized, the new system will be a natural part of the market economy. In the present system, the state interferes in the economy and the education sector is exogenous to the production. The task is to make this system endogenous, while moving the state away from economic production. The major concerns in redesigning the education sector are as follows: (1) quality of education, including its content and responsiveness to market demands; and (2) access to higher education, including educational opportunity, affordability, and inequalities. Inequality in access here is expressed in terms of access itself, educational quality, and student satisfaction.

It is assumed that lower state control and higher university autonomy reduce inequality in access to higher education. The rationale behind this assumption is fourfold. First, less supervised and more autonomous universities independently operate on the market, and hence are more effective, efficient, and more flexible in meeting changing market demands. As a result, quality of education in these institutions rises, as does student satisfaction. It leads to higher access and lower inequalities in access to higher education. Second, more autonomous universities that experience less state supervision are more effective and efficient based upon the fact that they spend more time on core activities, such as research and scholarship, and less time on administrative duties, that is, bureaucracy. This makes universities more competitive. Competitiveness lowers tuition and so increases access to higher education and reduces inequalities in access to it. Third, more autonomous universities are free to enlarge, branch out, establish new programs based on market demands rather than central directive, and merge. This creates more places in higher education, and therefore raises access and reduces inequalities in access to it. Fourth, indirect funding from the state leads to competition among public universities, closing programs that are not in demand, and consequently, higher quality, higher student satisfaction, and lower tuition, which means increased access and lower inequalities in access to education.

The higher education sector cannot stay outside the mainstream of development and has to operate in changing socioeconomic conditions. Accordingly, corruption becomes part of the education sector, as it is of other sectors of the economy and the government. The hypothetical evolution of corrupt hierarchies in HEIs points to changing internal structures shaped by external influences of the market and the state (Osipian, 2007b, 2008b). The state may be interested in corrupt HEIs as objects of blackmail, coercion, and control (Darden, 2008; Osipian, 2008e). The nexus of political graft and education corruption that may be observed in the former Soviet republics includes collusion, compliance, and control (Osipian, 2008a). Underpaid educators are more susceptible to corruption. The state uses educators' need for illicit benefits to create the "feed from the service" scheme and to control the agenda in HEIs (Osipian, 2007d). The state might be interested in maintaining corruption in education and preserving its functions of financier and regulator of access.

2.5.3 Education Corruption in Ukraine

Heyd (2008) offers an insider's perspective on the cultural specifics of higher education in Ukraine. Media reports are rich in news about education corruption as well. The problem of corruption in Ukraine is reflected in a number of scholarly publications and its existence is proven on the basis of national surveys. For instance, a poll developed by the Ukrainian Institute for Social Research in 2002 showed that 78 percent of respondents believed that all or most of the government officials have accepted bribes. More than 80 percent stated that corruption was prevalent within the judicial branch of the government, while 71 percent responded in the affirmative to a query about whether they believed that most government officials were tied to the mafia or private family business relations. According to Woronowycz (2003), many Ukrainians accept bribery as a normal part of everyday life. Solomon and Foglesong (2000) point out that the number of reported incidents in Ukraine rose two-and-a-half-fold between 1990 and 1998 to 2,449, and these incidents led to 1,641 convictions (p. 75).

Corruption may be found in many sectors of the national economy, including higher education. Corruption in education is more detrimental than typical bureaucratic corruption. Corruption in higher education is detrimental to the society for at least three major reasons. First, it has a negative impact on the economy and society due to the lowering of the system's efficiency, as does bureaucratic corruption. Second, as distinct from ordinary bureaucratic corruption, corruption in higher education reduces the total social welfare of the society because of its negative effect on the quality of educational programs and qualifications of college graduates. Finally, corruption in education eats away social cohesion, because students learn not only their subject matter, but also pervasive ways and practices of corruption. Corruption in higher education negatively affects access, quality, and equity. Contrary to expectations, development of a substantial private sector in higher education in Ukraine leads to an increase in corruption. Private HEIs are as corrupt as their public counterparts, which proves that public officials are not the only ones susceptible to corruption.

There are 680,000 licensed places for freshmen in around 480 HEIs in Ukraine. Of these, 80 percent are in public HEIs and 20 percent in private ones. In addition, there are numerous public community colleges and vocational schools. The projections point out that the number of places in HEIs in Ukraine, licensed and accredited by the government is already higher than the number of candidates willing to pursue college degrees, including distance learning, correspondence programs, re-training, and so on. Half of all the students in public colleges and universities are funded by the government. The admissions to government-funded places are corrupt. Course grades can also be bought from faculty members.

There is a variety of forms of corruption that may be found in higher education in Ukraine. Forms of corruption include bribery, embezzlement, extortion, fraud, nepotism, cronyism, favoritism, kickbacks, transgressing rules and regulations, bypass of criteria in selection and promotion, ghost teachers, cheating, plagiarism, research misconduct, discrimination, and abuse of public property. They rarely appear on their own. Forms of corruption are often connected in bundles. For instance, assigning a high grade to a student in exchange for a bribe implies fraud.

A form itself can have different origins. A bribe can be offered voluntarily or extorted. It can be in the form of cash, merchandize, service, or a monetary donation. All of these forms of corruption are hard to tackle with the help of just one reform, however comprehensive it may be (Osipian, 2009a). In addition to classical forms of corruption, gross waste, misallocation of public resources, and sexual misconduct take place in HEIs in Ukraine. Presence of such problems in the nation's educational system follows from the media reports (Shadnaya, 2006).

According to the survey conducted by the Millennium Challenge Corporation with the support of the Ukrainian government, corruption riddled all the spheres of the economy and society, not limiting itself to the public sector. The respondents consider HEIs as the most corrupted organizations, followed by hospitals and policlinics, law enforcement agencies, and tax collection offices. Of the citizens, 52 percent consider corruption as the easiest and most reliable way of solving many problems. Moreover, such view is more characteristic of the younger generation that constitutes student body and will eventually define the nation's future.

Many students either create situation for corruption or would not miss a chance of improving their grades in exchange for bribes, if such offer would come from their professor. The survey shows that the share of such students equals to 21 percent in Donetskaya oblast, 29 percent in Kiev, 28 percent in Lviv, 25 percent in Odessa, and 30 percent in Kharkov. Another 15 percent of the respondents said that they would not take advantage of such an offer but would inform their friends of the existing opportunity. Only 21–26 percent of all students, depending on the region, would not advise to do this. Finally, only 3–8 percent would inform the police. At the same time 42 percent of the parents of the prospective students said that instead of wasting time on preparation of their children for college entry examinations they would rather seek other ways and means, including informal payments and connections (Bazhal et al., 2006).

The survey of freshmen conducted by the Ministry of Science and Education of Ukraine in 2006 showed that two-thirds of them did not face bribery, nepotism, or protectionism during entry examinations. According to Shaw (2005), the data from a 2003 survey conducted by A Partnership for a Transparent Society that included 1,588 freshmen and sophomores in 12 cities throughout Ukraine reveal that

> 56 percent of students bribed to enter their educational establishment, 22 percent bribed to pass exams, 18 percent bribed for credit, and 5 percent bribed on term papers. Over 35 percent felt their educational establishment was "very corrupt" or "rather corrupt" while 48 percent of students viewed

> teachers that accept bribes as "corrupt," "criminal," or as "bribe-takers." Finally, 27 percent of students bribed on their final exams during secondary school. (p. 6)

Corruption in admissions to government-funded places in public HEIs and bribery in academic process may be the most explicit, but certainly not the only forms of corruption in academia. Forms of corruption, typical for just about any industry, are characteristic of education industry as well. Facts of embezzlement, fraud, gross waste, misallocation of resources, and other corrupt activities are found in colleges and universities throughout the country. One of the latest investigations reports that former head of the Lugansk branch of the Inter-Regional Academy of Personnel Management embezzled 831,900 UAH (CityNews, 2006). This case serves as a vignette of administrative corruption in the education sector.

Bribery, embezzlement, and fraud are not the only dominating forms of corruption in higher education. Logrolling in academia is a typical form of latent corruption. Logrolling, as a form of corruption, may be widespread in Ukrainian HEIs. Logrolling in admissions to publicly funded places in HEIs can be formulated as "I admit your protégé and you admit mine." Logrolling is based on the principle of reciprocity. The principle of reciprocity in academia anticipates an exchange of favors between professors. The practice of logrolling strengthens not only interdepartmental connections, but interuniversity connections as well. A professor in medical school can guarantee the admission of a protégé from the school of economics, and a professor in the school of economics can admit his/her protégé in exchange. This exchange of favors can be split in time. Placement in a university may be swapped for a job placement. Such an illicit practice in education can be defined as an education swap. Education swap is a form of education corruption that may be more prevalent than monetary transactions.

Diploma mills and low quality educational programs, previously unknown in Ukraine, can now be found in the form of poorly managed branches of public and private HEIs. The Ministry of Science and Education fights diploma mills, producers of fake diplomas, and oversees quality of higher education services through the processes of licensing and accreditation. The State Attestation Commission withdrew licenses of 116 educational programs, branches, affiliates, and colleges only in 2006. The licenses were recalled, among others, from Kiev business-college, educational programs of Kharkov National University of the Ministry of Interior in Smila, Poltava, Melitopol, Yevpatoriya, Kerch, Mariupol, Herson, the educational branch of Kharkov Aeronautical University in Alushta, and a branch of East-Ukrainian University in Feodosiya. According to yet another source in the Ministry of Science and Education, 104 licenses of the different educational branches and programs were suspended by the Ministry in 2006 and 2007, including educational consulting centers, branches, faculties, and departments, which are often created on the basis of vocational and professional two-year colleges and nevertheless manage to produce four-year Baccalaureate degrees and even five-year specialist degrees. Almost half of those educational units, 45, were created by the state HEIs, while the remaining 59 were established by the private HEIs. To summarize, results of surveys and interviews point to a large-scale problem of corruption in higher education in Ukraine. Top government officials acknowledge widespread corruption practices in the nation's education industry. At this point, the presence of corruption in academia is backed by substantial evidence and is undeniable.

The Ukrainian education sector is by no means an exception in terms of high level of corruption. Russian secondary and higher education suffers from corruption as well, as do national educational sectors of other former Soviet republics (Osipian, 2007d). Table 2.3 presents data on everyday corruption market characteristics in the Russian education sector in 2001 and 2005. According to the data, the demand of bribes from the side of educators is growing, as is the average size of a bribe. According to the survey, conducted by the Center for Public Opinion Research in October 2004, diminished accessibility to free education and medical help is pointed out by 23 percent of Russians as the greatest problem whereas 55 percent consider bureaucratic high-handedness and corruption among the present political and economic elite as the major contributing factor that prevents Russia from getting out of its socioeconomic crisis and achieving economic prosperity (Kofanova and Petukhov, 2006, p. 24).

Discussions of the nature and function of Russian education point to such priorities as upbringing (Nikandrov, 2007) and development of civic values and patriotism (Gavriliuk and Malenkov, 2004). Value orientations of contemporary youth include friends, health, interesting work, and money (Semenov, 2007). According to the results of the survey of students conducted in four HEIs in St. Petersburg in 2005,

> when it comes to prestige, the leading professions are *economist* (37 percent) and *lawyer* (36 percent), with the lowest rankings going to *schoolteacher* and *blue-collar worker* (1 percent each). At the same time, when it comes to the social significance of occupations, the ratings are different, with medical specialist (45 percent) and schoolteacher (36 percent) at the top. (Semenov, 2008, p. 42; emphasis in the original)

Table 2.3 Everyday corruption market characteristics in the Russian education sector, 2001 and 2005

	Secondary education		*Higher education*	
Indicator	*2001*	*2005*	*2001*	*2005*
Supply of and demand for corrupt services				
Corruption risk (risk to be subjected to corruption, %)	13.2	41.0	36.0	52.1
Corruption demand (readiness to bribe, %)	76.2	60.8	66.7	63.2
Dynamics of everyday corruption markets' annual volumes				
Market size (million USD)	70.1	92.4	449.4	583.4
Total market share	0.0	0.0	0.2	0.2
Dynamics of the average bribe amount (in rubles) by sector				
Value	1,238.0	2,312.0	4,305.0	3,869.0
Rank*	7.0	8.0	2.0	4.0
Change (%)	—	1.6	—	–0.2
Corruption intensity within corruption markets				
Value	2.2	0.9	0.8	0.9
Rank**	1.0	5.0	10.0	6.0
Change (%)	—	2.2	—	–0.3
Demand on public services in corrupt markets (%)				
Value	6.1	2.9	8.1	7.4
Rank***	9.0	12.0	4.0	6.0
Change (%)	—	–52.5	—	–8.6

School: Corruption needed in order to enter the school and to finish successfully the education process

Higher education institution: corruption needed in order to enter HEI, transfer to another HEI, pass course examinations, midterms, term papers, theses, and so on.

* The rank 1 is assigned to the sector based on the largest average bribe

** The rank 1 is assigned to the market with the most intensified corruption activities

*** The rank 1 is assigned to the segment of the public services market with the highest demand

Source: Composed from Satarov (2006).

This points out a certain differential between the personal and societal orientations on social and human capital.

2.5.4 *Impact of Education Corruption on Growth*

The key question in this section may be formulated as follows: Is education corruption harmful to the economy? If yes, in which ways? So far, there is no direct evidence for Ukraine that corruption in higher education has a significant negative impact on the national economy or the rate of growth. According to Klitgaard (1986), elitism and lack of meritocracy in access to higher education and leadership positions in some developing countries lead to a decrease in GNP. New empirical studies are needed to reflect the modern day realities. Only theory and some comparisons on general developmental trends may point to disadvantages that a national economy experiences due to a high level of corruption in its educational sector. The discussion presented earlier offers a prediction of possible negative impacts in the long run, when those with relatively low level of human capital will occupy places of more capable individuals. But this may be compensated for with years of working experience.

Corruption is often perceived as a form of rent-seeking behavior. Rent in this case is extracted from the monopolistic position, be it a bureaucratic office or a university professorship. The rent-seeking behavior in the Ukrainian society is perceived as a norm. Public officials, bureaucrats, and public servants attempt to transform their access to material and nonmaterial assets into personal benefits. Educators act in a similar manner. Rectors of state HEIs rent out public property, including academic and nonacademic facilities and land, to businesses in which they often have a share. University professors sell academic degrees by abusing their monopolized function of evaluation of academic progress and conferring the degrees.

What can be done about education corruption? In brief, we would suggest more market and less state control in the higher education sector. It can only be done with further restructuring, privatization, plurality of forms of property and economic activities. Unfortunately, all of these changes must be made primarily by the state. The state, however, may not be interested in such changes (Osipian, 2008a,e). The leading role of the state in the education reform should be supplemented by popular support. If explained clearly and without bias to the population, the reform is likely to be supported by the majority of the population. One may suggest more participatory strategies, more public control, more political activism, broader initiatives on transparency and accountability, civil society, participatory decision making in regard of taxes, and so on. Taxes collected from the public are channeled to the funding of higher education sector through the state budget. If higher education will no longer be free for students, this will mean lesser spending from the state budget. Accordingly, the public will have the right to expect tax reduction from the government. Such a change in the pattern of redistribution may be appealing to the public and thus generate its support.

Little can be done to reduce education corruption in the short run. The measures that target corruption on the functional level, such as transparency and code of conduct, are not enough. Structural, organizational, and institutional changes are needed to resist corruption in education. These are, however, unlikely to be implemented from the top. Structural and institutional changes can only evolve naturally, based on technological changes and demands of societal production. Organizational changes may be made voluntarily, but only in the short run. In the long run, if proven irrelevant, they will disappear or transform to a mere formality.

Organizational and structural changes are possible as secondary measures to reduce corruption. Each of the faculty members has a monopolistic power over a certain course. Graduation requires a set of passes and grades on the sequence of courses, taken over five years. Thus, the bureaucratic system that exists in Ukrainian HEIs can be defined as a sequential model. Certain rules apply for maximization of illicit profits in such systems and certain patterns of behavior among dishonest faculty members may be observed. According to Rose-Ackerman (1978),

> The sequential model is identical to the fragmented except that applicants must have the portions of their petition approved in a particular order. No bureaucrat in the sequence, however, ever reviews the choices made by officials who have already acted. These two models, then, best describe procedures in which each functionary behaves like an independent, specialized expert. (p. 169)

The real structure of corrupt relations in academia is much more complex and often involves rigid hierarchical structures (Osipian, 2008b). Rose-Ackerman (1978) addresses the hierarchy as one of the forms of bureaucratic structure, but in Osipian (2008b), hierarchical structures are presented as ones of corruption. Vertical hierarchies, thus, are not one step further, but rather a different, parallel line of investigation.

Secondary organizational reforms aside, first-order fundamental changes are needed to shorten the gaping chasm between the quality and access. Test-based admissions are admissions to HEIs on a competitive basis, based on the results of independently administered computer graded examinations or standardized tests. These are anticipated to become a major tool in fighting corruption in admissions. The Russian Federation was ahead of Ukraine with the reform of admissions policies. However, any impact of the tests on the level of corruption in admissions to HEIs has yet to be found and proven empirically (Osipian, 2009b). The introduction of standardized tests, even if proven successful in reducing corruption in access to higher education, does not represent fundamental changes. The test-based admissions and vouchers as replacement for the HEI-based entry examinations and direct state funding means preservation of the same system when the state retains the distribution function. Under such a system, corruption is unlikely to decline, even in the long run. In order to remove the state as an intermediary and distributor, direct state funding should be replaced almost entirely with consumer payments. Income-based inequality should be compensated for with educational loans. Educational loans should come as a combination of state and private bank credits. The reform of education financing alone will not result in the change of the system. The reform should include privatization or at least a long-term lease of HEIs. Privatization of state HEIs should include privatization of land. This will allow HEIs to raise funds for investment in university facilities, equipment, libraries, faculty salaries, scholarships for most promising students with low income, and research. While the issue of property rights delineation is fundamental, the tests are crucially important for successful reforms (Osipian, 2008d, p. 101).

Property distribution through vouchers, and auction-based sale of state enterprises focused on creation of open joint-stock companies did not bring expected results; property distribution is characterized by high inequalities, not to mention social injustice and the accompanying tensions. The idea of making individuals stock-holders has yet to come to life. Privatization did not work socially, but the development of the stock market may help. The stock market may introduce additional resources, currently held by the population, into production. The well-developed stock market may not be necessarily a win-win outcome. It may be opposed by those who benefit from the system the way it is now and by the state bureaucrats as well. Economic reforms were initiated by the state, but the state bureaucrats seek to strengthen their positions and gain more control and more property rights. Accordingly, the two fundamentals that still need further development are democracy and private property.

Education corruption and growth may be linked through human capital, and placing value on human capital under different conditions. Transition from the Soviet to post-Soviet reality touches on the higher education sector. During the Soviet times, the major stake for individuals was gaining higher education. Jobs were available for everyone, and higher education was not a "must" for those seeking placement. There was no unemployment in the country and in fact people were not allowed to be unemployed. There was criminal persecution of idle people predetermined in the laws. There were some disincentives embedded in the system of education and employment that worked as regulators or stabilizers: low salaries for educated people kept many away from HEIs and lowered the demand on higher education. State monopoly on all the sectors of the economy led to the fact that wages were set by the state. As a result of low wages for educated professionals, many engineers worked as skilled workers and earned twice as much plus had better benefits, including faster queue for housing and cars, distributed exclusively by the state. There was no labor market in the country in its classical understanding.

In the post-transition economy, massive renovation of production capacities requires investment in principal capital and human capital that would be able to invent and use new technologies, operate the machines, and manage complex technological processes. It is misleading to assume that since the Soviet times, there has been plenty of human capital starting from the 1970s. But this assumption is still being made as a result of high unemployment, especially technical cadres, during the 1990s. As a consequence, the major focus now is on the future investment in principal capital. However, human capital can soon become a limited resource, with qualified specialists being in short supply. Market economies are socially complex systems. Socially complex societies are naturally less productive. In order to realize their potential advantage over the more simple planned economies, complex societies need a sufficient quantity of human capital not only of technical, but of social expertise as well. This will include economists, lawyers, managers, accountants, and such.

In micro-perspective, the major stake in contemporary Ukraine is not higher education, but the job. More and more often, education becomes a necessary formality, such as a diploma to occupy a certain job place, that can be bought. Corruption in higher education allows for circumventing formal requirements for gaining a degree. This situation may change only in one case: if a growing competition between producers makes the need for higher effectiveness stronger, and employers start seeking human capital. In the current situation, the existing level of nepotism, cronyism, preferential treatment, and sometimes outright bribery dictate, in part, employment decisions. Such practices result in an undeveloped labor market. In many instances, high-level human capital is undervalued and its bearers, that is, highly skilled and motivated professionals, are underpriced or artificially made low-competitive. Meritocracy and talent suffer, while low professionalism gains way.

Massive education offers plenty of high quality, affordable, and accessible education. But in addition to honest ways, one can obtain diplomas in exchange for bribes. With broader introduction of tuition programs, when payments for education are made legally, corruption in admissions will inevitably decline. Corruption, however, is not limited to admissions to state-funded places, but continues in the academic process through the program of study. One of the real solutions to academic corruption will be further development of the labor market, when knowledge obtained in HEIs, whether paid for by the state or by tuition, will be valued more highly than personal connections, bribes, and other illicit benefits. A weak undeveloped labor market pools back the nation's otherwise dynamically developing economy.

The process of economic transformation from planned to market economy is characterized by the transition from full employment to unemployment. In the Soviet times, planned economy employed the entire available workforce. The predominantly extensive nature of economic growth explained full employment at that period. In the market economies, full employment is rather a continuing goal to be achieved than a reality. Accordingly, market reforms and a decline in production led to economic restructuring and unemployment.

The illicit ways to receive jobs include nepotism, cronyism, personal connections, and bribes. They are similar to the illicit forms of gaining access to publicly funded higher education. There are two consequences of such realities: a significant portion of human capital is of unclear value, and the high quality human capital is often undervalued and not utilized in societal production at full capacity. Distribution of property rights on production capacities, including plants and mines, is skewed and concentrated in the hands of few. This is a result of corrupt privatization of state enterprises of 1990s. This is especially important since Ukrainian economy remains industry oriented, rather than predominantly service oriented, and rightly so. We argued earlier that this is a better structure for the national economy. Low competition between the producers means no need for the best and brightest. Unequal distribution of property rights on production capacities eventually results in undervalued human capital.

Even competition between the employers does not place the real value and the accent on human capital. Employers need a diploma holder who can do the job for the lowest possible wage. The diploma is needed as a part of the risk aversion strategy, typical for the job market, or in order to satisfy some formal requirements. The result is that employees cannot do the job properly. They are ineffective. Employers no longer rely on diplomas; in addition to degree certificates, they prefer working experience as a guaranty of qualifications. Preferential treatment in higher education and employment may correlate positively. Those with means to buy places in prestigious public HEIs are likely to obtain better job placements by the same way of bribing and using kinship and personal connection. At this stage, these are no longer speculations but rather hypotheses that will have to be tested in future research.

The property rights on the principal capital are in the hands of few. These few are rich enough to profit from the size of the enterprise rather than from its effective organization and high level of productivity. They do not run for the highest effectiveness and efficiency possible. They accumulate large profits thanks to their size, not to the effectiveness of their work. They can afford lavish lifestyles now. Initial state monopolistic structure of the economy inherited from the Soviet times, emphasis on machine building and heavy industry, and poorly designed and implemented de-nationalization and privatization resulted in the high degree of monopolization, oligopolies, and low competition. A weak need for being competitive, as well as the strong tradition of noneconomic solutions for economic problems including mafia, collusions, and illicit business-state relations, lead to low effectiveness and efficiency.

As can be seen from the discussion, high levels of education corruption may harm total factor productivity in the long run, primarily through lowering the level of human capital and slowing down the pace of its accumulation. Ethical standards learned in the process of training in HEIs can also affect the standards of practice in different professions. The growing level of productivity is not likely to reduce education corruption in the short run, but can eventually lead to implementation of higher ethical standards in the education sector. This may happen through the chain of incentives emerging at every stage of the process of creation and utilization of human capital. To simplify, the growing complexity of technological processes will demand higher amounts of human capital, including human capital per capita. This will change the characteristics of the labor force in demand. The labor market will transmit the signal to the education sector and to the future employees. As a result, both producers of educational services, that is, HEIs, and those investing in their human capital, that is, students as customers of HEIs, will demand high quality education rather than bribe their way to educational certificates. It is unlikely that education corruption defines or influences the structure of the national economy. Such explicit manifestations of corruption in the higher education sector as diploma mills are presented in the form of distant branches of colleges and universities. Their total revenue is insignificant as are their enrollments, and they do not occupy a significant niche in the sector. Changes in the structure of the national economy can reduce corruption in the higher education sector due to the reasons presented earlier. These include the demand on qualified personnel and competitiveness of firms. An increase in competition due to the decreasing concentration of property rights and more even distribution of property rights on production capacities will eventually accentuate human capital over state-supported educational certificates.

The prognoses of possible high unemployment in Ukraine are problematic for a very simple reason. Starting in 2009, the labor force will not account for those who were not born due to the birth rate decline of 1991 and onward. Today, these unborn would turn 18 and some of them would enter HEIs while others would join the labor force. Ukraine today is one of the leading countries by the percentage of population in the labor force. It constitutes 52 percent, that is, one of the highest in the world. Similar to China, where the percentage of population in the labor force is exceptionally high but will decline steadily due to this country's demographic policy, in Ukraine aging and massive retirement will eventually leave labor-intensive industries to seek workers more actively. With the continuing decline in total labor force starting in 2009, a high unemployment rate in the long run seems to be impossible. Thus, further development of human capital is the key strategy for the long-run economic stability and growth.

Decentralization and restructuring of the Ukrainian higher education sector diminishes the role of the state. University autonomy may be needed to replace weakening state control. Meritocracy and high social prestige of academic profession and university degrees slowly weakens. This indicates the process of erosion of values, common for the transition society overall. Forgeries will eventually be annihilated by their overwhelming number. If the situation will develop in an unregulated, unorganized way, the university degree will become absurdist. Nevertheless, the process of debasement of the old system creates a ground for the new, three-tier system of academic degrees, including Baccalaureate, Magisterium, and PhDs. In the new system, a doctoral degree will serve as an indicator of the holder's ability to perform independent scholarly research and teaching. Reputation of each degree and degree holder will be based on his/her academic merits and reputation of the granting university. Competitive labor market will place accents on values of academic degrees and human capital.

2.6 Concluding Remarks

The ideas of public spending and foreign investment as the major engines for potential growth, especially in developing nations, are replaced with the ideas about the importance of reinvestment and domestic market development. The theories of growth based on the fundamental assumption that a significant influx of the resources is necessary to initiate sustainable growth do not hold. They might work to a certain degree in the developing world, but appear to be insufficient to explain rapid economic growth in Ukraine.

Despite the difficulties and local crises, the socioeconomic transition in Ukraine may be considered as successful. Political and economic reforms lead to the creation of predominantly market economy. By 2004 Ukraine achieved pre-transition level of GDP per capita. The positive economic growth takes place since 1999. Based on the data available and long-run forecasts, the stages of GDP growth can be presented as follows: the decline in the rate of growth (till 1989); the negative economic growth (from 1990 to 1999); the significant economic growth along with a significant increase in business activities in the country (from 2000 to 2004); the slowdown in the rate of growth (from 2005 to 2010); further decline in the rate of growth (from 2011 to 2015); and stabilization of the rate of growth at the moderate level.

While the exogenous resource of economic transition is depleted and the exogenous-type forms of transition are no longer effective, the exogenous growth still has a certain potential in Ukraine. This is explained by the fact that there are still unused labor resources as well as labor migration abroad and capital flight. Repatriation and legalization of capital, the return of the labor migrants, and full employment will support economic growth in the short run. However, the sustainable growth will only be possible thanks to technological advancements and innovations. This anticipates endogenous growth. Among the major tasks of post-transition development in Ukraine are strengthening of the labor market and creation of the stock market. Such developments will facilitate better distribution of property and lead to an increase in labor productivity. This will eventually bring higher rate of GDP per capita growth and higher living standards of the population.

PART III

ECONOMIC GROWTH IN UKRAINE AND OTHER NIS

Successful transition to the mixed market oriented economy in Ukraine does not remove completely the argument that the period of transition was characterized by the economic crisis. With the different pace of the reforms in countries of the former Soviet Bloc, Ukraine is considered as having a long-term economic decline during the entire decade of 1990s. Furthermore, economic slowdown and negative economic growth are often associated and directly attributed to the process of transition. Simply put, reforms are blamed for the crisis. Finally, growing well-being of Ukrainian population and the rapid growth of 2000s need explanations, supported not only by theoretical, but empirical analysis. In order to address these issues, we offer a comprehensive systematic analysis of the statistical data for Ukraine and other post-Soviet economies.

The logic of this chapter can be presented as follows. First, statistical data is introduced for the transition economies. The data was previously used to substantiate claims about significant economic decline and the existence of a crisis situation in the national economies of the countries of the former Soviet Bloc during the period of 1990–2000. We consider the scale and the continuity of economic decline in transition economies, the level of corruption, the influence of corruption on GDP growth, the shadow sector or unofficial economy and its size in transition economies, energy consumption as a measurement of real volume of production, and the structure of energy production as a measurement of the level of economic development. An attempt is made to determine the extent to which the alleged existence of significant economic decline or an economic crisis was real or mythical. Second, we present and analyze macroeconomic indicators of the national economies of the former Soviet

Bloc, including member countries of the Commonwealth of Independent States (CIS). GDP growth rates in the countries of Eastern Europe and the former USSR are considered here along with the structure of GDP growth by expenditures in Ukraine. The fact of sustainable economic growth in Ukraine is supported by the statistical findings. Third, we further analyze statistical data used to determine whether economic growth in Ukraine was initiated by external forces or by an external shock. For this we consider in detail such processes and indicators as volume of foreign direct investments (FDIs) and portfolio investments as well as capital flight from Ukraine, the Russian Federation, Poland, and Hungary. We also consider indicators of foreign debt and debt service in Ukraine and the Russian Federation. In this chapter such characteristics as unemployment and the labor market in Ukraine and other CIS countries are considered not as social indicators, but as factors that could possibly influence the initiation of economic growth.

Macroeconomic indicators that confirm growth and indicators of external influence on the national economies are followed by selected macroeconomic and social indicators of the countries of the former Soviet Bloc. This is done for the purpose of substantiating the argument about the presence of sustainable economic growth in these countries. In this part of the chapter we analyze such indicators as income and the dynamics of private consumption and prices in Ukraine, the Russian Federation, Poland, and Hungary, and productivity and wages in Ukraine. Examination of the indicators of labor productivity and the average wage will serve as a transition to the analysis of the factors that made possible initiation of sustainable economic growth. Specifically, we consider such internal systemic factors as human capital and conditions for its accumulation and use. We analyze data on the population's access to higher education and medical services, living conditions, life expectancy at birth in the CIS countries, as well as numerous indicators of socioeconomic progress of the Ukrainian society, including its openness and well-being. R&D is considered as one of the moving forces of growth in the future. Concluding remarks are focused on generalization of the results of the statistical analysis and confirmation of theoretical statements and hypotheses presented in part II.

3.1 Recession: Myth and Reality

3.1.1 Cumulative Output Decline and Period of Recovery

The period of economic transition is normally associated with the rapid decline in output and characterized by worsening socioeconomic conditions. Such a decline had different lengths in each of the transition economies. According to the data presented in Dabrowski (2002), the average period of continuous output decline in the countries of Central and Eastern Europe and Baltic states, including Albania, Bulgaria, Croatia, Czech Republic, Estonia, Hungary, Latvia, Lithuania, Poland, Romania, Slovakia, and Slovenia, is equal to 3.8 years. The average period of continuous output decline in the CIS countries, including Armenia, Azerbaijan, Belarus, Georgia, Kazakhstan, Kyrgyzstan, Moldova, the Russian Federation, Tajikistan, Turkmenistan, Ukraine, and Uzbekistan, is equal to 6.5 years, and hence lasted much longer than in the countries of Central and Eastern Europe and Baltic states. The total volume of output decline in the CIS countries is also significantly larger than in the countries of Central and Eastern Europe and Baltic states—50.5 and 22.6 percent, respectively. Moreover, total volume of output decline in the Baltic states was highest in the group, with 51 percent in Latvia, 44 in Lithuania, and 35 in Estonia. Unlike other countries in the group, Baltic states were part of the USSR.

According to the data, the longest period of continuous output decline occurred in Ukraine, where it lasted 10 years. Nevertheless, the output decline was not the most significant among the countries examined. The official output decline in Ukraine was equal to 59 percent, but in Azerbaijan it was 60 percent, in Armenia and in Moldova it was 63 percent, and in Georgia it was 59 percent. Based on its continuous output decline and the slow pace of the reforms, Ukraine has often been referred to in the economic literature as a "national park" of transition, by which is meant a site of preservation, a place where transition takes place very slowly. Cumulative output decline does not correlate with the period of decline. In Georgia, total output decline was equal to 78 percent during a period of decline that lasted for 5 years, whereas in the Russian Federation output decline was equal to 40 percent with the period of decline being 7 years. The correlation of cumulative output decline and the total number of consecutive years of output decline in the NIS in 1990–1999 is presented in figure 3.1.

Figure 3.1 points to the absence of a positive correlation between cumulative output decline and the number of consecutive years of output decline in the NIS. Official data about cumulative output decline and its continuity should be approached critically. In our view, consecutive output decline in Ukraine continued for no more than six years and the decline itself was significantly smaller than 59 percent of GDP. This statement will be proven statistically further in the chapter. The output decline of 59 percent during the period of 1990–1999 can be combined with the

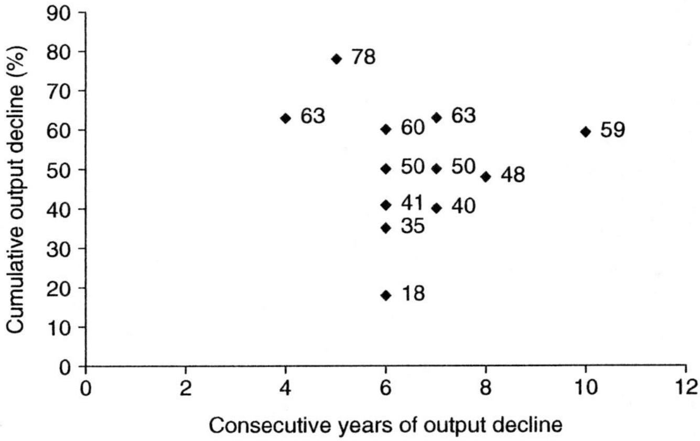

Figure 3.1 Correlation of cumulative output decline and total number of consecutive years of output decline in the NIS, 1990–1999.

reported share of the unofficial economy, which constituted 48.9 percent in 1995. Accordingly, the claimed output decline of 59 percent is the product of narrowly considering only the dynamics of official GDP. The decline started in 1992 and continued to 1998, making the whole period of continuous decline equal to seven years or so.

Economic transition in the Russian Federation has similar characteristics. The output decline of 40 percent during the period of 1990–1999 can be combined with the reported share of the unofficial economy, which constituted 41.6 percent in 1995. Accordingly, the claimed output decline of 59 percent is again the product of narrowly focusing only on the dynamics of official GDP. The decline started in 1992 and continued till 1998, being significantly less than the officially registered 40 percent. Correlation of cumulative output decline and total number of consecutive years of output decline in the Central and Eastern Europe and the Baltic states in 1990–1999 is depicted in figure 3.2.

As follows from the correlation diagram presented in figure 3.2, there was a certain correlation between the cumulative output decline and the total number of consecutive years of output decline in Central and Eastern Europe and in the Baltic states during the period of 1990–1999. The presence of a positive correlation in this group of countries makes it distinct from the NIS. However, even here deviations from the correlation line are quite significant. The value of output decline for the countries with the three-year period of decline varies within the limits of 12–33 percent,

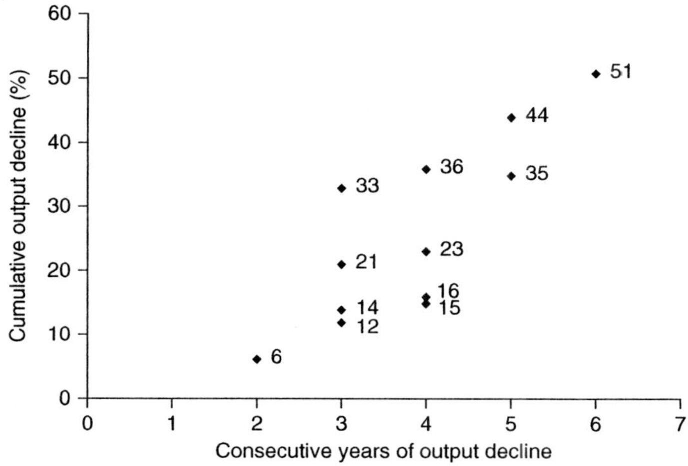

Figure 3.2 Correlation of cumulative output decline and total number of consecutive years of output decline in the Central and Eastern Europe and the Baltic states, 1990–1999.

while for the countries with the four-year period of decline it varies within the limits of 15–36 percent.

3.1.2 Corruption and its Impact on Economic Growth

One of the arguments used to support the idea of sharp and significant output decline in the countries of the former Soviet Bloc is that the high level of corruption in transition economies has a negative impact on production. We will turn to statistical data to test such a statement. The level of business-related corruption in the Commonwealth of Independent States and Central and Eastern Europe in 2002 is presented in table 3.1. The percentage of managers who consider corruption the major obstacle for the business and entrepreneurial activities is considered an indicator of the negative impact of corruption on production. The data was obtained during the survey conducted in the NIS and CEE in 2003.

According to the data presented in table 3.1, the level of corruption in business and the relationship between business and state in Ukraine is average for the region overall, while in the Russian Federation the level of corruption is at the lower end of the scale. Moldova is a leader in corruption, while in Estonia, Slovenia, and Hungary the level of corruption is relatively low as compared to the region's average. Needless to say, data

Table 3.1 Business-related corruption (% of managers surveyed ranking this as a major business constraint) in NIS and CEE, 2002*

Country	*Indicator*	*Country*	*Indicator*	*Country*	*Indicator*
Armenia	13.5	Hungary	8.8	Russia	13.7
Azerbaijan	19.5	Kazakhstan	14.2	Serbia	16.3
Belarus	17.9	Kyrgyz Republic	31.4	Slovak Republic	27.5
Bulgaria	25.4				
Croatia	22.5	Latvia	11.7	Slovenia	6.1
Czech Republic	12.5	Lithuania	15.6	Tajikistan	21.0
		Moldova	40.2	Ukraine	27.8
Estonia	5.4	Poland	27.6	Uzbekistan	8.7
Georgia	35.1	Romania	34.9		

* Data for Kyrgyz Republic, Moldova, Poland, Tajikistan, and Uzbekistan are for 2003.

Source: World Development Indicators. Retrieved from the database on August 10, 2006.

on corruption are always to a large extent subjective, partial, and biased. Nevertheless, they should be taken into consideration when there is a lack of better sources of information.

The issue of slowing down economic growth due to an increase in corruption is still open. While a positive correlation between the high level of corruption and output decline has been proven theoretically, strong systematic empirical evidence has yet to be shown. Correlation of the GDP per capita growth and estimates of corruption made by the businessmen in the NIS and CEE countries of the former socialist bloc in 2002 is presented as a diagram in figure 3.3.

Figure 3.3 shows that there is no clear evidence of a positive correlation between the level of corruption and output decline or GDP growth slowdown. In Moldova, GDP per capita growth of 8 percent in 2002 was possible, with the level of corruption marked at 40.2. In Slovenia during the same year GDP per capita growth was only 3 percent, with the level of corruption at 6.1. In Ukraine GDP per capita growth of around 5 percent in 2002 coexisted, with the level of corruption of 27.5 on the offered scale. Jacob Swensson (2005) points out the puzzle of corruption's impact on economic development and on growth. He suggests that this impact may differ not only in size and significance, but in sign and direction as well:

> Most of the theoretical literature as well as case study and micro evidence suggest that corruption severely retards development. However, to the extent we can measure corruption in a cross-country setting, it does not affect growth. The puzzle may arise from econometric problems involved

in estimating the effects of corruption on growth using cross-country data. For example, the difficulties of measuring corruption may include omitted variables, like the extent of market regulation, and reverse causality, like whether modernization and rapid growth may increase corruption, as Huntington (1968) argued. Another plausible explanation for the mismatch between the micro and macro evidence is that corruption takes many forms, and there is no reason to believe that all types of corruption are equally harmful for growth. Existing data, however, are by and large too coarse to examine different types of corruption in a cross-section of countries. (p. 39)

Figure 3.3 is but a one-year snapshot of the correlation between corruption and GDP growth. We could expect that this correlation would change over time and for that reason we should consider possible links between corruption and growth should be considered in dynamics over time. Further consideration of a possible negative correlation between the level of corruption and GDP growth should be based on time-series data.

3.1.3 Shadow Sector, Unofficial Economy, and its Size

Shadow sector, or unofficial economy, is normally associated with corruption. Accordingly, the size of unofficial economy correlates with

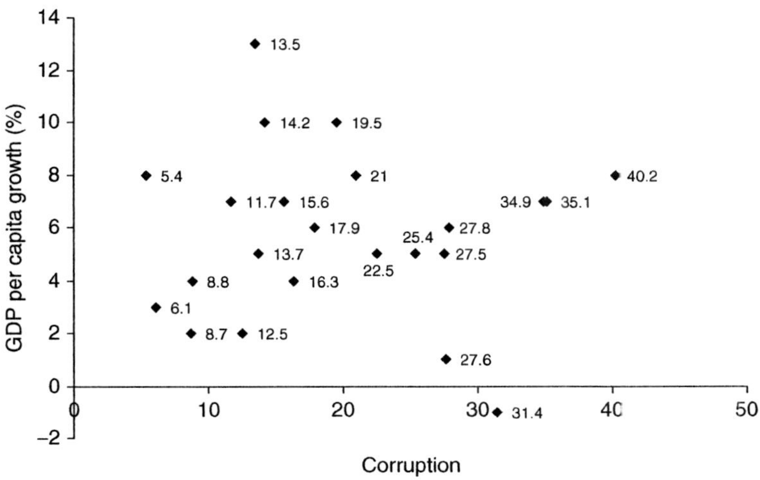

Figure 3.3 Correlation of the GDP per capita growth and estimates of corruption made by the businessmen in the NIS and CEE countries of the former Socialist Bloc, 2002.

the level of corruption in the country. Data for unofficial GDP in Eastern Europe and former USSR for the period of 1989–1995 are presented in table 3.2. A sharp increase in growth of the shadow economy in the early 1990s was observed in all the countries of the former USSR, except Estonia and Uzbekistan. A critical approach to such data should acknowledge that the controlling, estimating, and reporting bases in these countries are insufficient for reflecting the size of the shadow economy. The accuracy of reports on national levels of corruption is always a matter of some concern.

Azerbaijan and Georgia were leaders in the share of shadow economy in the national economies, and, accordingly, in the share of unofficial GDP in the total GDP. The share of unofficial GDP in Azerbaijan in 1995 constituted 60.6 percent of the total GDP, while in Georgia it was

Table 3.2 Unofficial GDP in the former USSR and the Eastern European countries, 1989–1995

	Share of unofficial GDP in total GDP (%)						
Country	*1989*	*1990*	*1991*	*1992*	*1993*	*1994*	*1995*
USSR							
Armenia	12.0	16.1	20.2	22.0	23.0	27.0	31.6
Azerbaijan	12.0	21.9	22.7	39.2	51.2	58.0	60.6
Belarus	12.0	15.4	16.6	13.2	11.0	18.9	19.3
Estonia	12.0	19.9	26.2	25.4	24.1	25.1	11.8
Georgia	12.0	24.9	36.0	52.3	61.0	63.5	62.6
Kazakhstan	12.0	17.0	19.7	24.9	27.2	34.1	34.3
Latvia	12.0	12.8	19.0	34.3	31.0	34.2	35.3
Lithuania	12.0	11.3	21.8	39.2	31.7	28.7	21.6
Moldova	12.0	18.1	27.1	37.3	34.0	39.7	35.7
Russia	12.0	14.7	23.5	32.8	36.7	40.3	41.6
Ukraine	12.0	16.3	25.6	33.6	38.0	45.7	48.9
Uzbekistan	12.0	11.4	7.8	11.7	10.1	9.5	6.5
CEE							
Bulgaria	22.8	25.1	23.9	25.0	29.9	29.1	36.2
Czech Rep	6.0	6.7	12.9	16.9	16.9	17.6	11.3
Hungary	27.0	28.0	32.9	30.6	28.5	27.7	29.0
Poland	15.7	19.6	23.5	19.7	18.5	15.2	12.6
Romania	22.3	13.7	15.7	18.0	16.4	17.4	19.1
Slovak Rep	6.0	7.7	15.1	17.6	16.2	14.6	5.8

Source: Composed from Gjourgyan and Mirzoyan (2000), Kaufmann and Kaliberda (1996), Lacko (2000), and Shleifer (2005).

equal to 62.6 percent. The share of unofficial GDP in Ukraine in 1995 was reported at 48.9 percent of the total GDP, while in the Russian Federation it was estimated at 41.6 percent.

Data for the former USSR in 1989 are presented as an average for all of the former republics, indicating the same level of unofficial GDP of 12 percent. In the former socialist countries of Central and Eastern Europe, economic transitions have started earlier than in the USSR, and by 1989 the share of unofficial GDP had reached significant value. The share of unofficial GDP in Bulgaria was equal to 22.8 percent, in Romania it was 22.3 percent, and in Hungary 27 percent. By the end of 1995 Bulgaria, Hungary, and Romania remained the leaders in terms of share of unofficial GDP among the countries of Central and Eastern Europe. The share of unofficial GDP in 1995 in Bulgaria was equal to 36.2 percent. Dynamics of the share of unofficial GDP in the Eastern European countries in 1989–1995 are presented in figure 3.4.

Graphs of the share of unofficial GDP in the Eastern European countries in 1989–1995 demonstrate relatively smooth distribution in time almost without sharp increases. The share of unofficial GDP in the countries of the former USSR in 1989–1995 are presented in figure 3.5.

Graphs of the share of unofficial GDP in the countries of the former USSR in 1989–1995 demonstrate very sporadic distribution in time, with a significant increase in some countries. According to the graph, the share of unofficial GDP in Ukraine continuously and steadily increased during the period of 1989–1995, starting from 12 percent in 1989 and reaching

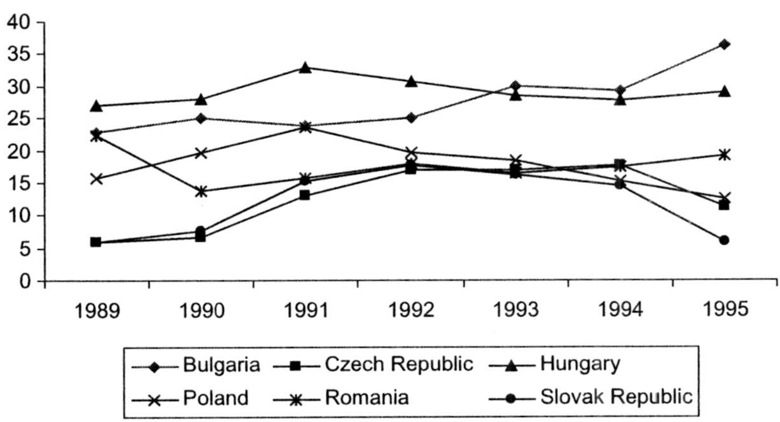

Figure 3.4 Unofficial GDP in the Eastern European countries, 1989–1995.

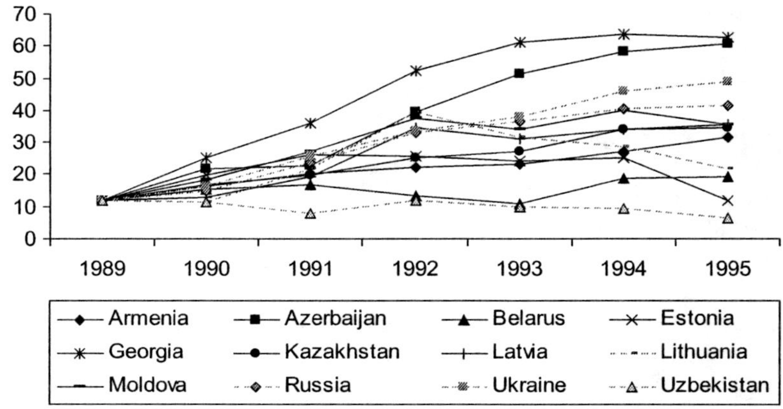

Figure 3.5 Unofficial GDP in the former USSR, 1989–1995.

49 percent in 1995. However, such an increase was not linear, and it accelerated in 1990–1992 and again in 1993–1994. Moreover, an increase in the share of unofficial GDP in Ukraine was taking place when the total GDP was steadily declining. Therefore, an increase in the share of unofficial GDP in Ukraine was not as dramatic as the graphic presentation might make it seem. The share of unofficial GDP in total GDP in the countries of Central and Eastern Europe in the early 2000s is not much higher than the analogous indicator in the countries of Western Europe, United States, Canada, and Australia. Data of the share of the unofficial GDP in the total GDP in the countries of Western Europe, United States, Canada, Japan, and Australia in 1990 are presented in table 3.3.

As is clear from the data, the share of unofficial GDP in Spain and Greece is highest among the developed capitalist countries, comprising 22.9 and 21.8 percent, respectively. The relatively stable economic situation in the countries of Western Europe, United States, Canada, Japan, and Australia points toward an unchanged share of unofficial GDP. Some of the member countries of the European Union Spain and Greece have the lowest levels of per capita income. It is not surprising that rapid economic reforms and relatively low levels of per capita income lead to an increase in the size of the shadow economy in transition societies.

In the USSR in 1989 the share of unofficial GDP in total GDP was more or less the same as it was in the United States, France, and Canada. In 1990 it had achieved the level of Germany and Austria. Within the next few years, the share of unofficial GDP in total GDP in the former Soviet republics went above those of the developed capitalist economies.

Table 3.3 Share of the unofficial DGP in the total GDP (%) in selected countries, 1990

Country	*(%)*	*Country*	*(%)*	*Country*	*(%)*
Spain	22.9	Australia	15.1	France	12.3
Greece	21.8	Germany	14.6	Canada	11.7
Ireland	20.6	Portugal	13.8	Sweden	11.0
Belgium	19.8	Netherlands	13.4	USA	10.5
Italy	19.6	Finland	13.3	Switzerland	10.2
Denmark	16.9	Japan	13.2	Norway	9.3
Austria	15.5	UK	13.1		

Source: Composed from: Lackó (1998).

In considering the share of unofficial GDP in total GDP, we ought to give preference to the weighted average values and focus predominantly on the indicators of the Russian Federation and Ukraine where total GDP was much higher than in the other former Soviet republics. It is possible that the size of the shadow economy in Ukraine and the Russian Federation will be reduced thanks to diligent fiscal policy, with the result that the share of unofficial GDP in total GDP will decrease to the level of the EU countries.

3.1.4 Energy Production and Consumption

One can find quite surprising the fact that the leading international organizations and programs, including the International Monetary Fund (IMF), the World Bank (IBRD), and the United Nations Development Program (UNDP), not only designated Ukraine as a country with a transition economy, but also placed it, all along with the transition economies, on the list of developing countries. This was done with a certain degree of enthusiasm. We ought to consider such categorizations as incorrect. For instance, in his works in 1970s and 1980s, Leontief rightly groups the USSR and socialist countries of Central and Eastern Europe along with capitalist economies of Western Europe and North America, categorizing all of them as developed industrialized nations. In our view, the fact that such a large share of Ukraine's electric energy is produced by nuclear power stations is itself an indication that Ukraine should be listed as an industrialized rather than a developing nation. The country should not be regarded as a developing nation just because of the temporary negative aspects of the transition.

When energy import and decline in energy production are accounted for, the electric energy produced by the nuclear power stations as a share of the total electric energy produced in the country increases as does the weight of nuclear power in general, even if the volume of its production is constant. On the other hand, the presence of a well-developed technologically complex system of energy production by nuclear power plants on an industrial scale indicates that the country cannot be a developing one by definition. Moreover, the electric energy produced by the nuclear power stations as a share of the total electric energy produced in the country has reached 43 percent in 2003 and is at par with the level of developed capitalist countries. In France, the share of electric energy produced by nuclear power stations in the total electric energy produced is approximately 80 percent, but France is something of an exception. The share of electric energy produced by nuclear power stations in the total electric energy produced in Ukraine increased consistently during the entire period of 1992–2003.

The data for energy production and consumption in Ukraine in 1992–2003, including electric energy production and consumption, support our statement that economic decline in Ukraine during the period of 1991–1999 was not as significant as it is presented in numerous sources and should not be considered a deep economic crisis. Electric power consumption declined from 4,308 kWh per capita in 1992 to 2,772.9 kWh per capita in 1998. At the same time registered electric power transmission losses increased from 9 percent in 1992 to 17 in 1998. Electric energy does not dominate the national economy and does not dictate trends in future economic development of the country. In Ukraine in 2002, 5.9 percent of managers surveyed ranked the price of electric energy as a major business constraint. In 2005, this figure declined to 4.9 percent, contrary to expectations.

Energy-efficient technologies in energy-intensive production in metallurgy and machine building are necessary to reduce the national economy's energy dependency. This supports our statement that future development should focus on increasing the effectiveness and efficiency of already existing well-established branches of the national economy. Technological innovations and energy efficiency will protect the national economy from potential shocks caused by energy price fluctuations and energy market volatilities. This, in turn, necessitates a further increase in investment in principal capital, including machines and equipment. Modernization of the nation's basic industries is linked to the creation and development of the stock market, which would facilitate channeling resources into the branches. Human capital accumulation will also be necessary to serve new production technologies.

3.2 Macroeconomic Indicators in Ukraine

Real GDP per capita growth in all of the former Soviet republics was negative during the early and mid-1990s. This situation is generally accepted by the economists and supported by the data. The detailed annual indicators of GDP per capita growth in the CEE and the former USSR for the period of 1991–2004 according to the World Development Indicators database are presented in appendix I. Major macroeconomic indicators in Ukraine for the period of 1989–2010 are presented in appendix II. These data clearly support our suggestion that the output decline have started before the Soviet Union disintegration and indicate stable growth that takes place in the national economies of the former Soviet republics now and in perspective to 2010.

3.2.1 Structure of GDP Growth by Expenditures in Ukraine

One of the ways to consider the structure of GDP growth is by expenditures. Statistical data on the contribution of stock-building, private consumption, government consumption, gross fixed investment, and external balance to real GDP growth in Ukraine for the period of 1991–2010 points to the changing structure of GDP. The data shows that the major emphasis in contribution to real GDP growth in Ukraine is made on private consumption. The literature on growth in Ukraine also points toward increasing private consumption. At the same time role of government consumption declines. External balance has negative effect on growth. This trend will likely continue in the future. Role of investment will continue to grow while investment share will become significantly higher than government consumption. Investment had positive effect on growth starting 1997. It is expected that in the future, the role of the stock-building will be minimal. Statistical data on the structure of contribution of stock-building, private consumption, government consumption, gross fixed investment, and external balance to real GDP in Ukraine for the period of 1993–2010 shows that the share of private consumption in GDP was continuously increasing, beginning in 1993. It increased from 46.667 percent in 1993 to 72.9 in 1998. Such an increase was followed by an insignificant decrease to the level of 64.4 percent in 2004. In 2005 the share of private consumption in GDP was equal to 69.336 percent.

An increase in private consumption is considered a major engine for sustaining present economic growth. It is expected that the share of private consumption in total GDP will fluctuate within a range of 80–88 percent during the period of 2006–2010. This prediction is in line with

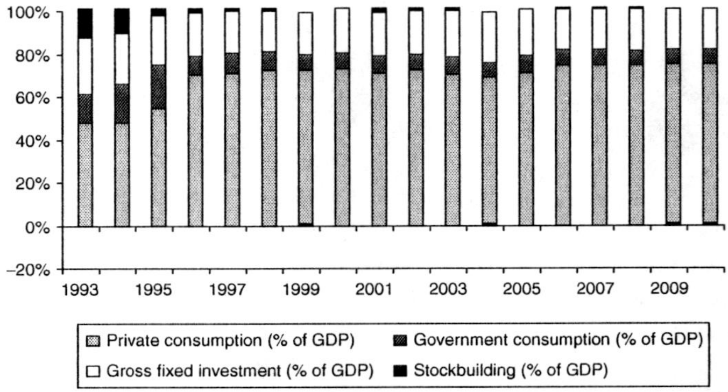

Figure 3.6 Contribution of private consumption, government consumption, gross fixed investment, and stock-building to real GDP in Ukraine (in %), 1993–2010.

the predictions made earlier in the literature on economic growth forecasts in Ukraine. The share of government consumption is expected to remain unchanged during the period of 2005–2010, fluctuating around 8 percent of GDP. The share of government consumption in total GDP increased from 13.3 percent in 1993 to 21.28 in 1995. It has since declined. One factor in such a decline is the shrinking of the public sector due to massive privatization as well as to legalization of a significant part of the shadow economy after 2000. The share of the external trade balance in GDP has declined steadily since 1993. The share of investments is expected to grow further. The contribution of private consumption, government consumption, gross fixed investment, and stock-building to real GDP in Ukraine for the period of 1993–2010 is presented in figure 3.6.

3.2.2 Volume of Direct and Portfolio Investments in Ukraine

Foreign direct investment and portfolio investment flows into a national economy are traditionally considered as one of the major engines of growth. Indeed, such investments may give an impulse to the positive developments in the economy, but only if there is a proper institutional structure in place. Selected indicators for the FDI and portfolio investment flows in Ukraine for the period of 1994–2009 do not point to a significant short-term flow of foreign investments in Ukraine. Statistics show that FDI flow in Ukraine increased from $159 million in 1994 to

$496 million in 1999. The high rate of investment flow in Ukraine continued through 2004. Investment flow increased from $595 million in 2000 to $1,715 million in 2004. The phenomenal growth of FDI flow in Ukraine took place in 2005, when it reached $7,808 million, indicating a four-and-a-half-fold increase in one year. Annual FDI flow in Ukraine during the period of 2006–2009 is expected to be within the limits of $400 million–450 million a year. Portfolio investment flow in Ukraine was positive from 1994 to 1997, reaching $1,605 million. During the period of 1998–2003 it was negative. Portfolio investment outflow was most significant in 2002, reaching $2,177 million. Starting in 2004, Ukraine experienced an inflow of portfolio investment, which is expected to last through 2009. Annual portfolio investment is expected to be within the limits of $500 million–750 million a year.

Foreign direct investment stock in Ukraine increased 10-fold from 1994 to 2001, starting from $483.5 million and reaching $455.3 million. Total volume of FDI in 2006 was equal to $20,775 million. According to the forecasts, FDI stock in Ukraine is to reach $33,275 million by 2009. Despite the increase in FDI, its share in GDP was insignificant over the entire period. The share of FDI in GDP grew from 0.434 percent in 1994 to 1.903 in 2000 and then to 2.084 in 2001 and 2.643 in 2004. Foreign direct investment flow as a share of GDP reached 9.421 percent in 2005 and is expected to fluctuate within the limits of 3.2–4.6 percent per annum. The data indicate that FDI flow as a share of total investment in Ukraine increased from 1.796 percent in 1994 to 9.634 in 2000, that is, more than five times, and reached 42.795 percent in 2005. It is expected that FDI flow as a share of total investment will decline to 13.9 percent in 2009. Foreign direct investment stock as a share of GDP in Ukraine grew continuously from 1.32 percent in 1994 to 12.395 in 2000 and 19.757 in 2005 and is expected to reach 26.3 percent in 2009.

External capital flows in Ukraine were not limited to FDI and portfolio investment inflow. Capital outflow was taking place as well. Foreign direct investment flow as a share of GDP invested abroad increased from 0.055 percent in 1994 to 0.263 in 2005 and could reach 0.7 percent in 2009. Foreign direct investment outflow is insignificant compared to FDI inflow. The proportion was 1 : 7 in 1994, 1 : 3.5 in 2000, and 1 : 36.2 in 2005, and it is expected to be 1 : 4.57 in 2009. The relation of FDI stock in Ukraine to FDI stock abroad as a share of GDP was equal to 37 : 1 in 1994, 23 : 1 in 2000, and 76 : 1 in 2005. According to Economist Intelligence Unit forecasts, the share of FDI stock to GDP in Ukraine will be 38 times higher than FDI stock as a share of GDP outside Ukraine by 2009. Despite the optimistic trends in FDI investment and its balance in Ukraine, one should admit that there is no good reason to accept Leontief's external shock scenario in Ukraine. Theories of exogenous growth based on external shock that comes in the form of massive capital influx in a short period of time are not valid. Total FDI stock and portfolio investment placed in the country constituted only 10 percent of GDP in 1999. Such volume of external investment was unlikely to initiate sustainable and significant economic growth in Ukraine.

We will present some statistics on per capita investment in order to demonstrate insignificant volume of the total external investment inflow and stock. Foreign direct investment per capita in Ukraine was equal to $1.32 in 1994. This indicator grew to $66.36 by 1999. Despite the rapid increase in FDI, the total volume of it remained absolutely insignificant. In 2005 FDI per capita in Ukraine reached $350.27 and is expected to grow to $726.4 in 2009. Total FDI stock of over $700 would possibly be considered significant in early 1990s, but certainly not in 2009. We will continue considering the issue of possible external shock as an initiator of substantial economic growth in Ukraine by addressing trends in statistical data on capital flight and external debt.

3.2.3 Capital Flight, Foreign Debt, and Debt Service in Ukraine

Capital flight from Ukraine during the 1990s is traditionally regarded as significant. The process of capital outflow is assumed to be negative for any national economy and even more so for a transition economy. Economists believe that capital outflow has a negative impact on the speed and success of economic transition in Ukraine and other former socialist countries. Capital outflow from Ukraine was equal to $2,592.5 million in 1998 and then declined to $2,625.1 million in 2002. Capital flight from Ukraine increased to a new high of $11,378.8 million in 2004. This indicator is expected to decline in the future. Similar to Ukraine, in the Russian Federation capital flight in 1998 peaked at $35,205.1 million. The peak it reached in 2005 was $44,816 million. Continuing capital flight from the Russian Federation is expected to reach $64,619.74 million in 2009. It is also expected that starting in 2009 volumes of capital outflow will decline. In Poland, capital outflow started only in 1997, while before 1997 there was capital inflow. Capital outflow also took place from 1999 to 2001. There was a frequent interchange between net capital inflow and net capital outflow in Poland, which were changing each other quite frequently. Hence, it is difficult to identify any sustainable trends in the capital flight. Insignificant net capital outflow is expected starting in 2005. In Hungary, net capital outflow took place from 1995 to 1998, in 2001, and from 2004 to 2006. The most significant capital flight of $8,575 million was observed in 2005.

At the moment of its independence, Ukraine had excellent opportunities for receiving international loans, since all the foreign obligations of the just disintegrated USSR were accepted by the Russian Federation. Foreign debt in Ukraine grew steadily from $550.8 million in 1992 to $13,950.6 million in 1999 and to $26,143.07 million in 2006. It is expected that foreign debt in Ukraine will move beyond $30 billion by the end of 2007, comprising around $30,019.44 million. Data indicate that foreign debt in Ukraine declined slightly only in 2000 and otherwise grew continuously. Foreign debt in Ukraine increases consistently, but its total volume is still insignificant. Indicator of per capita foreign debt grew from $10.6 in 1992 to $282.1 in 1999 and reached $498 only by the end of 2005. According to the Economist Intelligence Unit forecasts, foreign debt per capita in Ukraine will reach $827 in 2010 and will not rise above even the relatively low threshold of $1,000 per capita. It seems obvious that such insignificant amounts of foreign capital inflows in the form of international loans indicated as foreign debt were unlikely to move the industrialized nation of 50 million people toward substantial economic growth. Moreover, the effectiveness of utilizing of international loans is always of great concern. One should admit that international loans in Ukraine and in the Russian Federation were rarely utilized with maximum effectiveness and efficiency.

Size of the foreign debt in Ukraine is significant in respect to total export. Foreign debt was equal to 33.755 percent of export in 1994 and reached its peak of 81.3 percent in 1999. After 1999 the size of foreign debt with respect to total export declined and comprised 49.6 percent in 2006. It is expected that value of this indicator will stay within the limits of 46 to 53 percent till 2010. The indicator of foreign debt to GDP grew continuously starting in 1993 and reached 44.2 percent in 1999. After 1999 one could observe a decline in this indicator to 28.1 percent in 2005. It is expected that the value of this indicator will be around 30 percent till 2010. Debt service was a growing burden for the country and increased from 0.6 percent of GDP in 1993 to 11.7 in 2000. This indicator later declined to 6.3 percent in 2006 and is expected to stay within the limits of 6 percent till 2010.

Foreign debt in the Russian Federation experienced a consistent increase from $78,210.7 million in 1992 to $177,798.3 million in 1998. This increase was followed by a decline to $147,426.9 million in 2002 and then by an increase to $257,497.9 million in 2005. The Russian Federation adopted a course of early repayment of its foreign debt, which was made possible by the rapid increase in the oil and gas prices on the world market. Otherwise the debt could potentially have grown to $307,281.95 million by the end of 2010. The Russian Federation is quite distinct from Ukraine in terms of total debt per head. While in Ukraine total debt per head is insignificant, in the Russian Federation this indicator grew from $526.5 in 1992 to $1,202.7 in 1998 and reached $1,490 by the end of 2005. Earlier it was expected that total debt per head would continue to grow and reach $2,180 by the end of 2010. However, taking into consideration Russia's commitment to repay its debt and the government's strategy to utilize high world prices on oil and gas to repay the debt, one could expect that this indicator would go down much more than has been predicted. During this substantial period of time, the indicator of foreign debt as a percentage of export in the Russian Federation was much higher than in Ukraine. This indicator was equal to 157.185 percent in 1992 and reached its peak of 194.625 in 1999. The value of the indicator has since declined. It declined to 74.3 percent in 2005 and is expected to decline further.

The proportion of total debt to exports of goods and services in the Russian Federation was more significant than in Ukraine and increased from 157.185 percent in 1992 to 194.625 in 1999. After 1999 the value of this indicator declined to 74.3 percent in 2005 and will likely continue to decline. The proportion of total debt to GDP in the Russian Federation grew continuously since 1993 and reached 89.2 percent in 1999. This indicator in the Russian Federation was two times higher than in Ukraine. After 1999, there was a decline in the value of the indicator to 28.1 percent in 2005. The size of the foreign debt in any given year was higher than the FDI inflow in the country. Accordingly, per capita foreign debt was always higher than per capita FDI during the entire period. This means that if foreign debt is to be repaid at any given time during the period of transition, the positive effects of FDI would be nullified. Capital flight from the country was insignificant during the entire period of 1994–2007. It was insignificant compared to foreign debt and FDI. Even in 2005, capital flight did not rise above FDI. Nevertheless, the values of FDI and international credit are not high enough to initiate significant and sustainable growth. The major role of internal resources is obvious.

3.2.4 Unemployment and the Labor Market in Ukraine and other NIS

Indicators of employment, unemployment, the labor market, and workforce dynamics may serve as a link between analyses of the external sources and dynamics of GDP, on the one hand, and data on personal income and income structure of GDP, on the other. In accordance with the logic of this chapter, we present the dynamics of external sources that could potentially be a basis and a moving force for growth and analyze whether they were sufficient for such a task and whether they had a decisive impact on initiation of positive and sustainable economic growth. Indicators of per capita income, personal consumption, and so on are presented to prove that an increase in the population's well-being was the result of economic growth. Indicators of employment and the labor market then serve two purposes. First, they are intended as a link between the two parts listed earlier. Second, dynamics in workforce development and the labor market may reveal not only the potential for growth in the national economies but also the potential sources of that growth.

Data presented by the CIS Official Statistics demonstrate dramatic growth in the number of registered unemployed individuals in Ukraine during the period of 1990–1999. The explanation for such a dramatic increase in registered unemployment is obvious. First of all, there was no registered or officially recognized unemployment in the USSR. At the same time there was hidden unemployment that became obvious once market reforms advanced and enterprises strived for higher efficiency in operation. More importantly, region-wide restructuring on both macro- and micro-level and breaks in the well-established economic ties between the enterprises have led to reduction in production or even closures and lockouts in virtually every enterprise. This process in turn led to rapid growth of unemployment in the former Soviet Bloc. Dynamics of economically active population in the CIS for the period of 1990–1999 are presented in table 3.4.

Indicators of changes in the size of the economically active population in the Russian Federation and Ukraine for the period of 1990–1999 point to the fact that during the second part of the period the number of those who were economically active in both countries had stabilized. Nevertheless, in the Russian Federation it had stabilized at a significantly lower level than it was at the beginning of the reform in 1990 while in Ukraine the economically active population almost reached its initial size. Based on the Economist Intelligence Unit forecast, it is expected that the level of recorded official unemployment in 2010 in Hungary will be equal to 6.4 percent; in Poland, 13.7 percent; in the Russian Federation, 6.1 percent; and in Ukraine, 4.8 percent. This shows that the official level of unemployment in Ukraine in the future will be equal to the level of unemployment in the United States, which has always been traditionally

Table 3.4 Economically active population in the Commonwealth of Independent States (CIS; in thousands), 1990–1999

Country	*1990*	*1991*	*1992*	*1993*	*1994*	*1995*	*1996*	*1997*	*1998*	*1999*
Azerbaijan	3,703	3,736	3,728	3,734	3,655	3,641	3,719	3,732	3,744	3,748
Armenia	1,630	1,671	1,634	1,628	1,593	1,582	1,584	1,538	1,476	1,484
Belarus	5,151	5,025	4,901	4,882	4,790	4,524	4,537	4,528	4,528	4,542
Georgia	2,763	2,524	2,032	1,920	1,814	1,794	2,085	2,351	2,373	—
Kazakhstan	7,806	7,720	7,606	7,004	7,118	7,360	7,490	7,440	7,053	7,055
Kyrgyzstan	1,748	1,731	1,838	1,710	1,716	1,742	1,792	1,792	1,811	1,901
Moldova	2,071	2,070	2,058	1,700	1,699	1,696	1,686	1,671	1,809	1,682
Russia	75,325	73,910	76,008	75,170	73,952	72,639	72,962	72,482	72,229	73,227
Tajikistan	1,938	1,970	1,915	1,876	1,887	1,890	1,777	1,842	1,850	1,780
Uzbekistan	7,941	8,255	8,291	8,288	8,408	8,480	8,595	8,715	8,840	8,930
Ukraine	25,419	25,002	24,576	24,029	23,107	25,162	25,229	24,928	25,286	24,523

Source: CIS Official Statistics. Retrieved from the database on August 8, 2006.

low, and will be significantly lower than the analogous indicator in the Western European countries.

An increase in unemployment negatively impacts the population's personal income and accelerates socioeconomic stratification. Along with redistribution of wealth during the quite contradictory process of privatization, an increase in unemployment led to an increase in socioeconomic inequalities, including inequalities in income distribution, as reflected in the values of the Gini coefficient. According to the data for 2003, presented by the World Development Indicators, the Gini coefficient for the CIS and Baltic states varied within the limits of 0.27–0.4; for the countries of Central and Eastern Europe, from 0.26 to 0.39; and for the countries of Western Europe, from 0.25 to 0.36. Values of the Gini coefficient indicate that inequality in income distribution among different socioeconomic strata of population in the CIS and Baltic states was analogous to income inequalities in the countries of Central and Eastern Europe and was slightly higher than in the countries of Western Europe. The Gini coefficient in Ukraine was equal to the Gini coefficient in Germany and was lower than the average for the CIS countries as well as EU member countries. Hence, by the time Ukraine had successfully formed a predominantly market economy, inequality in income distribution was at a socially acceptable level and at par with the leading world economies.

3.3 Macroeconomic and Social Indicators of the Former Soviet Bloc

An analysis of the Gini coefficient is useful in making a transition to an analysis of statistical data on population's income and well-being in Ukraine, the Russian Federation, Poland, and Hungary. The Gini coefficient reflects the level of income inequality in the society. With the development of economic reforms in the former Soviet Bloc the Gini coefficient was expected to grow in value. The rise in inequality does not mean, however, that the average income per capita has to rise as well, or decline. In fact, average incomes of different socioeconomic strata of population can change along the opposite vectors of development, that is, some strata may experience the rise in per capita income, while others may experience decline.

3.3.1 Population Income in Ukraine

Personal disposable income in Ukraine has increased steadily since 2000 and in the Russian Federation since 1999. Personal disposable income in

Ukraine experienced a decline in 1998–1999 and bottomed out at $15.127 billion in 2000. However, even this minimum was higher than the level of 1993, which was equivalent to $15.127 billion. Personal disposable income in the Russian Federation experienced a decline in 1998–1999, reaching a low of $114.180 billion in 1999. As was the case with Ukraine, the minimum of 1999 in the Russian Federation was higher than the level of 1993, which was equivalent to $88.190 billion. Statistics on personal disposable income in Ukraine for the period of 1993–2010 are presented in table 3.5.

Contrary to common belief, personal disposable income in Ukraine during the period of 1993–1996 was increasing, not decreasing. It more than doubled, growing from $15.127 billion to $34.235 billion. The same can be said about the Russian Federation, where personal disposable income has tripled, increasing from $88.190 billion in 1993 to $273.666 billion in 1996. Real personal disposable income in Ukraine can double during the period of 2004–2010 and reach $83.5 billion. Real personal disposable income in the Russian Federation can double as well, perhaps reaching as much as $625.769 billion in 2010. Data indicate significant and sustainable growth in real personal disposable income in Ukraine

Table 3.5 Personal disposable income in Ukraine (in billion $), 1993–2010

Year	*Personal disposable income*	*Real personal disposable income (1996 prices)*	*Real personal disposable income (% change)*
1993	15.127	38.382	—
1994	17.916	36.130	–5.866
1995	19.864	34.057	–5.740
1996	30.812	30.812	–9.526
1997	34.235	29.620	–3.868
1998	27.460	28.417	–4.062
1999	18.062	25.320	–10.901
2000	17.216	26.275	3.771
2001	22.160	29.166	11.004
2002	26.539	34.566	18.514
2003	30.487	37.981	9.880
2004	38.839	44.528	17.239
2005	54.322	52.810	18.599
2006	69.600	58.000	9.900
2007	80.600	63.100	8.700
2008	93.600	68.900	9.200
2009	106.300	76.200	10.600
2010	119.700	83.500	9.600

Source: Economist Intelligence Unit. Retrieved from the database on August 12, 2006.

since 2000. Real personal disposable income in the Russian Federation has also increased steadily since 2000. An increase in real personal disposable income in Poland and Hungary has occurred since 1996, but the rate of increase in these countries is significantly lower than in Ukraine and the Russian Federation.

The high rate of increase in real personal disposable income in Ukraine that started in 2000 reached a phenomenal 18.5 percent in 2002. This indicator is expected to stay at the average of 10 percent till 2010. The high rate of increase in real personal disposable income in the Russian Federation that started in 2000 reached 13.5 percent in 2003. This indicator is expected to stay at an average of 10 percent till 2010. The financial and currency crisis of 1998 in the Russian Federation is well-reflected as a percentage change in the dynamics of the real personal disposable income. The dramatic decline in real personal disposable income in the country was followed by a no less dramatic increase than 11.3 percent in 2000.

The rate of increase in real personal disposable income in the Russian Federation was negative during the periods of 1993–1995 and from 1998 to 1999. The latter period of decline is explained by the currency crisis, when the Russian economy experienced a more significant negative impact than did the Ukrainian economy. Real personal disposable income in Poland experienced a stable increase since 1991, with only two short-term periods of decline, specifically a decline of 3 percent in 1995 and another decline of 2 percent in 2002.

The rate of increase in real personal disposable income in Poland did not fluctuate as much as it did in Ukraine. The peak here was in 1997 and constituted an increase of 8 percent. Forecasts for the real personal disposable income in Poland are also much more modest than in Ukraine and the Russian Federation, with the annual rate of increase predicted to be around 4.5 percent. Real personal disposable income in Hungary has experienced a stable increase since 1991, with only two short-term periods of negative growth, specifically a decline of 6 percent in 1992 and later a decline of less than 1 percent in 1995. The rate of increase in real personal disposable income in Hungary was at its highest in 1997 when it reached 10 percent. Forecasts for the real personal disposable income in Hungary show an annual rate of increase of 2–4 percent.

3.3.2 Dynamics of Personal Income and Consumer Price Index in Ukraine

Private consumption is traditionally considered a major component of the nation's GDP, especially in the developed countries. In Ukraine and other NIS private consumption is considered a major engine of the demand-driven growth. A steady increase in the share of private consumption is considered a positive trend. The decline in personal consumption during the 1990s is now being compensated by its rapid growth. This growth is especially notable in Ukraine and the Russian Federation. Private consumption in Ukraine experienced an increase during the entire period of 1993–2006, except for 1998 and 1999, when it declined to $30.536 billion and $22.056 billion, respectively. Starting from $21.304 billion in 2000, private consumption grew to $57.47 billion in 2005. Increase in private consumption in the country is expected to reach $124.87 billion by 2010. Real private consumption in constant prices of 1996 in Ukraine was equal to $58.326 billion in 1991. The recovery was achieved only in 2005 with $55.867 billion. This trend is expected to continue with real private consumption reaching $87.159 billion in 2010, that is, 1.5 times higher than in 1991. The rate of growth of private consumption in Ukraine experienced a dramatic decline of 25.9 percent in 1993 but then continued increasing starting in 2000 with highs of 12.4, 13.5, and 16.6 percent in 2004, 2005, and 2006, respectively. It is expected to be positive and vary within the limits of 9–10 percent per annum till 2010.

Private consumption always played a significant role in the structure of GDP growth. Negative trends in private consumption in 1991–999 should be correlated with the negative GDP growth. The impact of private consumption on GDP growth was less significant during its decline and more significant during its increase. It is expected that future GDP growth will rely heavily on an increase in private consumption. Private consumption per capita in Ukraine increased from $297.8 in 1993 to $717.3 in 1997 and then declined to $434.5 in 2000. This decline was followed by an increase to $1,229.3 in 2005. Private consumption per capita is expected to reach $2,740 by 2010.

Nominal private consumption in the Russian Federation has increased continuously since 1993, except for the crisis years of 1998 and 1999. It is expected that nominal private consumption in 2010 will be equal to $752.03 billion, that is, ten times higher than it was in 1993. Real private consumption in 1996 prices in the Russian Federation was declining from $294.536 billion in 1991 to $200.878 billion in 1999. After 1999 there was a steady increase in real private consumption. The level of private consumption in 1991 was achieved in 2003. It is expected that real private consumption in 2010 will be equal to $550.407 billion, that is, two times higher than it was in 1991. Private consumption in the Russian Federation declined starting in 1991, with its most significant decline of 11.766 percent in 1995 and declines of 3.29 percent in 1998 and 2.856 percent in 1999. Starting in 2000, however, there was an increase in private consumption, which reached an annual level of 11–12 percent in 2004–2007.

As is the case with Ukraine, in the Russian Federation private consumption has always played a significant role in the structure of GDP growth. Negative trends in private consumption in 1991–1999 should be correlated with the negative GDP growth. The impact of private consumption on GDP growth was less significant during its decline and more significant during its increase. It is expected that future GDP growth will rely heavily on an increase in private consumption. An increase of 6.4 percent in private consumption in 2006 coincides with the highest level of GDP growth. Personal consumption per capita in the Russian Federation has reached $2,559.5 in 2005 and is expected to grow to $5,340 in 2010.

Except for the crisis year of 1998, when there was a slight decline from $105.8 billion to $104.5 billion, nominal personal consumption in Poland has increased continuously since 1991, and reached $187.6 billion in 2005. It is expected that nominal private consumption in 2010 will be equal to $267.3 billion, that is, six times higher than it was in 1991. Real private consumption in 1996 prices in Poland was equal to $75.738 billion in 1991. A relatively slow but steady increase in real private consumption resulted in a total of $146.467 billion in 2007. It is expected that real private consumption in 2010 will be equal to $165.522 billion, that is, two times higher than it was in 1991.

The most significant percentage increase of 8.729 percent in real private consumption in Poland took place in 1996. The increase in personal consumption in Poland is uniform and not as rapid as in Ukraine and the Russian Federation. Personal consumption in Poland is expected to grow at a rate of 4–4.5 percent per annum starting in 2006. Personal consumption per capita in Poland has doubled during the period of 1991–1996, increasing from $1,185.7 to $2,501.2, and has continued to grow, reaching $5,390 in 2006. Growth in per capita personal consumption is expected to continue till 2010 when it will reach $7,040. The contribution of private consumption was significant during the entire period of transition.

Nominal personal consumption in Hungary has increased continuously since 1991, except for the crisis years of 1995, 1996, and 1997, when there was a slight decline from $29.981 billion in 1994 to $28.283 billion in 1997. Starting from $29.371 billion in 1998, nominal personal consumption reached $74.47 billion in 2005, that is, it almost tripled. It is expected that nominal private consumption in 2010 will be equal to $106.92 billion, that is, four times higher than it was in 1991. Real private consumption in 1996 prices in Hungary was equal to $29.082 billion in 1991. Growth in real private consumption was interrupted slightly in 1992, 1995, and 1996. A relatively slow but steady increase in real private consumption resulted in a total of $46.865 billion in 2007. It is expected that real private consumption in 2010 will be equal to $50.166 billion, that is, 1.7 times higher than it was in 1991.

The most significant percentage decrease of 10.06 percent in real private consumption in Hungary took place in 1991. A significant percentage increase in personal consumption in Hungary started in 1993 with 9.8 percent. Declines in 1995 and 1996 were followed by an especially high annual increase of 6–9.7 percent during 2000–2003. Starting in 2006 the percentage increase in personal consumption is expected to vary within the limits of 1.5–3 percent per annum. Personal consumption per capita in Hungary increased from $2,255.20 in 1991 to $7,520 in 2006. Growth in per capita personal consumption is expected to continue till 2010 when it will reach $10,820. The contribution of private consumption to GDP growth was significant during the entire period of transition.

The rate of increase in nominal private consumption in Ukraine and the Russian Federation is expected to be significantly higher than in Poland and Hungary. There is a certain degree of bias in intercountry statistics on private consumption as well as in other indicators. The bias in statistical data in intercountry analysis is commonplace and is normally checked based on purchasing power parity (PPP) indicators as well as other specific comparisons. This makes intercountry comparisons difficult and somewhat biased. Hence, we focus on intracountry dynamics of countries in transition and not on absolute values of certain national macroeconomic indicators. Then we analyze intercountry dynamics of the previously defined macroeconomic indicators.

Simple intercountry comparisons are less accurate and therefore less useful in the case of transition economies than in the case of Western European economies. Personal consumption per capita in Hungary in 1993 was equal to $2,780, that is, nine times higher than in Ukraine. This demonstrates the partiality of simple comparisons. Problems with simple comparisons are not limited to transition economies and are not unique. Such problems exist to a lesser degree in EU countries. For instance according to statistics, per capita GDP in Luxemburg is 1.5 times higher than in Germany. GDP per capita in Japan in nominal USD is equal to $34,000 in 2005 and is 1.5 times higher than in Canada (around $23,000).

At the same time per capita GDP in terms of PPP in Japan and Canada are about the same and constitute around 77 percent of the United States' per capita GDP. Dynamics of the Consumer Price Index in Ukraine and the Russian Federation for the period of 1992–2010 indicate a high increase.

The Consumer Price Index (CPI) in Ukraine has grown during the entire period of 1992–2010. The most significant increase in consumer prices in terms of constant 1996 prices took place in the early 1990s. The Consumer Price Index percentage change was especially significant during the period of high inflation in 1992–1996. It has declined from 10,111 percent in 1993 to 10 percent in 1997. Starting in 2001, when the CPI was equal to 6 percent, it has crossed the 10 percent threshold twice, amounting to 12.3 percent in 2004 and 10.3 percent in 2005. It is expected that the CPI will stay around 6 percent till 2010, which indicates stabilization in consumer prices. The CPI in the Russian Federation appears to have been less affected by inflation during the first half of the 1990s and to have grown more rapidly starting in 1997.

3.3.3 Labor Productivity and Wages in Ukraine

Labor productivity is fundamental for economic well-being and development. An increase in labor productivity is one of the key factors for sustainable economic growth. High wage serves as an incentive for high productivity of labor. Labor productivity and labor costs in Ukraine varied over the period of transition. Selected indicators of productivity in Ukraine, including labor productivity and labor costs for the period of 1992–2010, are presented in table 3.6.

Data indicate that labor productivity in Ukraine was declining over the period of 1991–1998. Starting 1999, there is a steady increase in labor productivity, reaching as high as 14.4 percent in 2000. Growth in labor productivity in Ukraine becomes a steady trend. Labor costs per hour positively correlate with labor productivity. The rate of growth in average real wages varies year by year. Statistics indicate that the average wage index has stabilized in 1996 and increased significantly since 2000. A continuous increase in real wages is expected till 2010. The trend in labor costs shows that labor becomes more expensive for businesses. We tend to consider such a trend as highly positive for the economy. Higher wages serve as an incentive for more productive labor and extend the base for private consumption, increasing the size of domestic market. Higher levels of human capital in individuals are known to be positively correlated with their earnings.

Table 3.6 Productivity in Ukraine, including labor productivity and labor costs, 1992–2010

Year	*Labor productivity growth (%)*	*Labor costs per hour ($)*	*Annual change in average real wage (%)*	*Index of average wage (1996 = 100)*	*Total factor productivity growth (%)*	*Labor force (million)*
1991	–7.2	—	—	—	–15.8	—
1992	–8.4	0.69	—	261.063	–13.9	—
1993	–12.1	0.35	–46.539	139.567	–14.4	—
1994	–19.9	0.40	–16.547	116.473	–20.0	23.193
1995	–14.4	0.46	9.223	127.215	–13.3	23.795
1996	–8.1	0.51	–21.393	100.000	–7.7	23.436
1997	–0.4	0.59	–1.855	98.145	–0.5	23.128
1998	–0.6	0.47	–2.986	95.215	–0.3	23.125
1999	2.1	0.33	–5.762	89.728	2.0	22.907
2000	14.4	0.32	1.107	90.721	11.2	21.353
2001	10.3	0.44	20.751	109.500	10.1	21.029
2002	4.6	0.54	20.098	131.500	4.9	21.120
2003	9.2	0.66	16.739	153.600	9.3	21.186
2004	11.4	0.85	16.980	179.600	10.9	21.271
2005	0.7	1.20	20.413	216.300	0.8	21.568
2006	4.8	1.50	13.900	246.300	4.3	21.689
2007	5.5	1.70	4.600	257.600	4.6	21.827
2008	5.4	1.92	6.500	274.500	4.4	21.979
2009	5.8	2.14	5.200	288.600	4.6	22.132
2010	5.5	2.38	5.700	305.000	4.1	22.286

Source: Economist Intelligence Unit. Retrieved from the database on August 12, 2006. Composed based on EIU calculations, Ministry of Economy and European Integration; National Bank of Ukraine, State Committee of Statistics, and UNDP.

3.4 Human Capital

An analysis of macroeconomic indicators often underestimates qualitative characteristics. Macroeconomic indicators are aggregates that focus on the quantitative characteristics of national production. Arriving at more precise estimates of the economic situation in Ukraine as well as other transition economies, with their vectors and level of development over the last two decades, requires consideration of such fundamental socioeconomic characteristics as education and health care. Access to education and medical services is crucially important in characterizing living standards and the population's level of personal consumption. It is equally important in an analysis of the reproduction of human capital. Higher education and medical services are two technologically complex branches of the economy that characterize developed nations. Their complexity serves as an indicator of the level of economic development as well as the presence of conditions necessary for economic growth.

3.4.1 Access to Education, Health Care, and Housing

The number of students in higher education institutions per 10,000 population is chosen to analyze the population's access to higher education. This indicator reflects the level or stock of human capital in the countries as well as the dynamics of reproduction of human capital during significant periods of time. The numbers of students in higher education institutions per 10,000 population in the NIS during the period of 1980–1999 are presented in table 3.7.

Contrary to beliefs about the crisis situation in Ukraine, statistics point to continuous growth in the number of students in higher education institutions per 10,000 population. While during independence and the beginning of market reforms in 1991 this indicator in Ukraine was equal to 168, by the year 1999 number of students enrolled in higher education institutions per 10,000 population had reached 259. This indicator is slightly lower than in the Russian Federation, where the number of students per 10,000 population grew from 186 in 1991 to 280 in 1999 Dynamics of the number of students in higher education institutions per 10,000 population in the NIS for the period of 1980–1999 are presented in figure 3.7.

Data for Ukraine indicate that during the transition the total number of students in higher education institutions per 10,000 in the population was increasing consistently since 1993 despite the decline in some other economic indicators. This not only proves the continuous presence of positive developments in the national system of higher education based on the market reforms, but also shows continuous growth in accumulation and concentration of human capital in the national economy.

Positive trends in the development of higher education industry and increasing access of population to higher education characterize such countries as Ukraine, the Russian Federation, and Belarus, but are not necessarily characteristics of all the former Soviet republics. For instance, in Azerbaijan the number of students in higher education institutions per 10,000 in the population as an indicator of access to higher education declined till 1995 and returned to its 1991 level of 147 students only in 1999. This indicator is almost twice lower than in the Russian Federation

Table 3.7 Number of students in higher education institutions per 10,000 population in NIS, 1980–1999

Country	*1980*	*1981*	*1982*	*1983*	*1984*	*1985*	*1986*	*1987*	*1988*	*1989*	*1990*	*1991*	*1992*	*1993*	*1994*	*1995*	*1996*	*1997*	*1998*	*1999*
Azerbaijan	172	172	172	169	163	158	155	149	140	140	146	147	134	125	117	128	132	127	134	147
Armenia	189	188	189	183	173	163	160	161	168	186	191	181	156	124	97	97	142	149	157	160
Belarus	183	183	185	185	186	181	179	177	175	185	184	180	179	169	181	191	203	219	239	258
Georgia	168	170	172	172	169	167	160	160	157	171	190	188	167	168	521	531	239	234	236	248
Kazakhstan	173	176	179	181	180	172	170	168	167	171	171	170	165	163	165	165	176	188	206	245
Kyrgyzstan	151	154	154	151	148	144	142	136	133	136	133	129	119	117	129	142	169	210	274	325
Moldova	127	129	130	128	128	126	123	121	122	127	125	120	109	108	114	149	159	180	199	212
Russia	219	219	218	216	213	206	200	194	190	193	190	186	177	171	171	188	201	221	245	280
Tajikistan	142	138	137	133	131	119	115	114	115	125	128	124	127	121	127	126	127	126	123	130
Turkmenistan	124	125	127	126	122	119	117	117	112	116	113	104	96	90	86	70	62	—	—	—
Uzbekistan	172	172	170	165	162	155	154	155	155	163	165	159	146	123	102	84	71	66	65	68
Ukraine	176	175	175	174	173	167	166	166	165	171	170	168	164	159	172	180	192	220	242	259

Source: Commonwealth of Independent States Official Statistics, retrieved from the database on August 8, 2006.

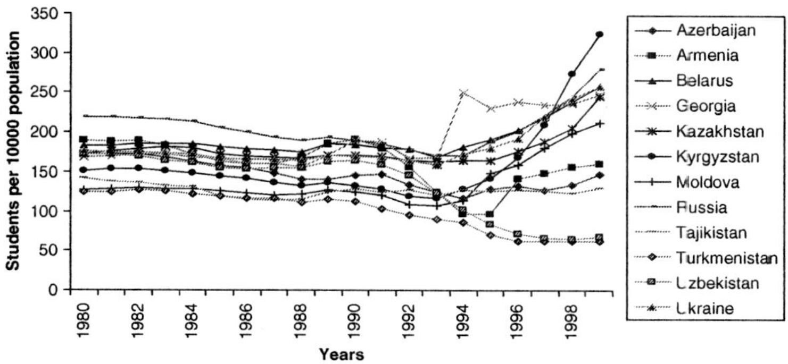

Figure 3.7 Number of students in higher education institutions per 10,000 population in NIS, 1980–1999.

and Ukraine. In Armenia the value of this indicator declined from 191 in 1990 to 97 in 1995 and then increased to 160 in 1999. The differential in access to higher education between Ukraine and the Russian Federation on one hand and Uzbekistan and Turkmenistan becomes even more dramatic when one is to take into account the demographics. In Uzbekistan, over 60 percent of the population is younger than 24 years. This means that the share of population of college age is much higher than in Ukraine. Logically, the number of students attending higher education institutions per 10,000 population should be higher in Uzbekistan, but the data point to the opposite. The advantageous position of Ukraine and the Russian Federation in terms of offering access to higher education to its population is obvious.

In terms of access to higher education some other former republics were not able to attain their 1991 levels. The indicator of the number of students in higher education institutions per 10,000 in the population declined in Uzbekistan from 170 in 1990 to 68 in 1999, and in Turkmenistan from 113 in 1990 to 62 in 1996. These statistics should always be correlated with demographic and migratory processes in the NIS. One should also account for students who receive their education in other countries, predominantly in other member countries of the NIS. The data indicate that despite economic difficulties during the transition period, the number of students in higher education institutions per 10,000 of the population in Ukraine has increased consistently since 1993. This confirms not only continuous and consistent development of the education industry, but also a stable increase in the total volume and concentration of human capital in the country.

The health care industry or the provision of medical services is, along with the education industry, considered one of the fundamental branches of the social sphere. The health care industry is one of the key industries that help accumulate and preserve human capital. One of the major international indicators of a country's socioeconomic development in general and people's access to medical services is the number of physicians per 10,000 population. We offer this indicator as one of the major descriptive sources for the estimation of human capital stock and dynamics of its accumulation. Dynamics of the number of physicians per 10,000 population in the CIS for the selected years during the period of 1980–1999 are presented in table 3.8.

Contrary to beliefs about the critical economic situation in Ukraine, statistics point to the continuous growth in the number of physicians per 10,000 population. While on the eve of independence and the beginning of market reforms in 1990 this indicator in Ukraine was equal to 44, by the year 1999 it had increased 5 percentage points, thus reaching 46. This indicator in Ukraine is slightly lower than in the Russian Federation and Belarus, where the number of physicians per 10,000 thousand population in 1999 was equal to 46.9 and 47.8, respectively. In contrast to Ukraine, in the Russian Federation this indicator did not increase since 1990, when it was equal to 46.9. Moreover, there was a slight decline in the value of this indicator during the period of 1991–1998. Data for Ukraine indicate that during the transition the total number of physicians per 10,000 population increased consistently since 1994 despite the decline in some other economic indicators. Table 3.8 points to an insignificant decline in the indicator in 1992 and 1994. This insignificant decline could potentially be interpreted as a decrease in the capacities of the nation's medical schools. However, that is not so. First, this decline may well be within the limits of statistical error. More importantly, the educational training of a physician takes at least six years. Accounting for the time lag suggests that the significant increase in the number of doctors per 10,000 population since 1997 was a result of an educational process that took place in the early 1990s.

We should also doubt the claim that the decrease in total population was the major cause of the indicator's growth. Indeed, the number of physicians per 10,000 population is a relative value that relates the number of physicians to the total population. However, one would reasonably expect the total number of physicians to decline proportionately to the decline in total population. The consistent increase in the number of physicians per 10,000 population as a measure of access of the public to the medical services in Ukraine is evident. Continuous and persistent growth of the

Table 3.8 Number of physicians per 10,000 population in the CIS, 1980–1999

Country	*1980*	*1981*	*1982*	*1983*	*1984*	*1985*	*1986*	*1987*	*1988*	*1989*	*1990*	*1991*	*1992*	*1993*	*1994*	*1995*	*1996*	*1997*	*1998*	*1999*
Azerbaijan	33.4	33.9	35.9	36.1	36.9	37.8	38.4	38.8	39.4	39.0	38.7	38.4	39.2	38.2	37.7	37.8	37.4	36.7	35.8	35.5
Armenia	35.3	35.5	36.8	37.8	38.3	37.9	38.6	39.2	39.9	40.3	40.5	40.5	39.3	36.9	34.5	33.6	34.0	34.4	34.3	33.2
Belarus	33.8	34.4	35.3	36.0	36.6	37.8	38.4	39.2	39.9	40.6	40.5	40.7	41.4	42.5	43.3	43.6	44.8	45.6	46.3	47.8
Georgia	47.9	49.3	50.5	50.9	52.0	53.5	54.6	55.8	56.9	58.5	57.9	39.4	46.2	42.4	38.2	42.0	41.0	40.5	38.5	—
Kazakhstan	31.9	32.9	33.9	35.4	36.6	37.6	38.5	39.2	40.0	40.9	42.1	41.1	41.8	41.0	39.1	39.7	38.5	36.7	36.3	34.6
Kyrgyzstan	29.1	30.0	30.9	31.7	32.5	33.5	34.5	35.5	36.2	36.6	36.7	36.8	34.9	33.4	33.0	33.2	34.3	32.7	32.1	30.3
Moldova	31.1	32.2	33.4	34.6	35.6	36.8	37.6	38.6	39.4	40.1	40.0	39.2	39.6	39.9	40.1	39.6	39.9	40.2	40.6	36.7
Russia	40.4	41.5	42.6	43.4	44.3	45.1	45.8	46.4	46.8	47.3	46.9	44.3	44.7	45.2	45.1	46.0	47.4	47.6	46.7	46.9
Tajikistan	23.6	24.3	25.2	25.6	26.1	26.7	27.1	27.4	28.6	28.5	27.1	25.5	24.3	23.3	22.7	21.4	20.9	20.1	20.6	21.2
Turkmenistan	28.4	28.7	29.2	30.4	31.2	32.6	33.9	34.9	35.1	35.5	34.6	34.7	33.5	32.9	32.2	31.4	30.2	29.8	—	—
Uzbekistan	28.5	29.8	30.8	31.9	32.9	33.7	34.4	35.1	35.5	35.8	35.8	35.5	35.5	35.2	33.8	33.2	33.4	34.3	—	—
Ukraine	36.5	37.7	38.8	39.6	40.4	41.3	41.8	42.6	43.1	43.9	44.0	44.4	43.8	44.4	44.1	45.1	45.2	45.1	45.5	46.0

Source: Commonwealth of Independent States Official Statistics. Retrieved from the database on August 8, 2006.

number of physicians per 10,000 population in Ukraine during the periods of 1980–1989 and 1990–1999 clearly indicates not only the presence of consistent and sufficient supply of medical services to the population and development of the national system of health care, but also stability in the functioning of medical higher education institutions, including first of all traditionally strong medical schools, as a part of the system of higher education. This demonstrates the presence of continuous positive developments in the national health care during the period of the market reforms, and it also shows continuous growth in accumulation and concentration of human capital in the national economy.

Positive trends in the development of the health care industry and increasing the population's access to medical services characterize such countries as Ukraine, the Russian Federation, and Belarus, but are not necessarily characteristics of all the former Soviet republics. In some other former republics situation with access to medical services did not regain its positions of 1991. For instance, in Azerbaijan the number of physicians per 10,000 of the population as an indicator of access to health care has declined from 38.7 in 1991 to 35.5 in 1999. In Uzbekistan the decline was from 35.8 in 1990 to 34.3 in 1997, in Turkmenistan, from 34.6 in 1990 to 29.8 in 1996, and in Tajikistan, from 27.1 in 1990 to 21.2 in 1999. Similar negative trends characterize many other former republics, including Georgia, Kazakhstan, Kyrgyzstan, and Moldova. These statistics should always be correlated with demographic and migratory processes in the NIS. There is a trend toward the increasing migration of medical professionals from Central Asian states to certain regions in the Russian Federation. While such a trend may be of benefit to the underpopulated regions and rural areas in the Russian Federation, where medical personnel are lacking, it is detrimental to the Asian republics and negatively affects the prospects of their future development.

Some changes in the health care sector may be needed in order to adjust for market changes in the national economy (Osipian, 1997b). The introduction of obligatory health insurance with universal coverage may still be on the agenda since 1990s (Osipian, 1997d). The reform in the provision of health services may be focused on channeling the tax money directly to hospitals and medical centers. For this to happen, a special health care tax may be introduced (Osipian, 2001). The data for Ukraine indicate that despite economic difficulties during the transition period, the number of physicians per 10,000 population increased consistently since 1994. This confirms the presence of continuous and consistent development of the health care industry, increasing access to the medical services, development of medical education, and a stable increase in the total volume and concentration of human capital in the country. Along with access to such necessities as clean water, sufficient nutrition, and such, access to housing is one of the fundamental indicators of the nation's well-being. Development of the housing market in Ukraine as a process of emergence of the real estate market indicates positive trend over the entire period of economic transition. Statistics on the housing space in the CIS for the selected years during the period of 1990–1999 are presented in table 3.9.

Access to housing in Ukraine expressed in terms of square meters per capita was probably the highest among all the CIS countries in 1999. In Ukraine this indicator was equal to 20.4 square meters per capita, and in the Russian Federation it was equal to 19.1 square meters per capita. Dynamics of the average total housing space per inhabitant in Ukraine were positive during the entire period of 1990–1999, with an increase from 17.8 to 20.4 square meters per capita. Growth of this indicator in Ukraine continues thanks to an increase in construction capacities, growing demand for real estate, and an expanding real estate market. Access to education, health care, and housing facilitate accumulation and preservation of human capital. The quality of these services and the level of access to them are the key factors for the population's life expectancy and quality of life. The dynamics of these indicators points to the stable and continuous improvement of the quality of live in Ukraine.

Table 3.9 Average total housing space per inhabitant in the CIS (in square meters), 1990–1999

Country	*1990*	*1991*	*1992*	*1993*	*1994*	*1995*	*1996*	*1997*	*1998*	*1999*
Azerbaijan	12.5	12.2	12.5	12.0	12.3	12.1	12.2	12.2	11.9	12.0
Armenia	15.0	15.8	14.9	15.2	15.3	15.3	15.5	15.7	16.1	—
Belarus	17.9	18.3	18.9	19.3	19.5	19.5	19.7	20.0	20.3	20.8
Georgia	18.8	18.4	19.2	19.1	19.4	19.7	20.0	20.2	20.2	—
Kazakhstan	14.2	14.4	14.5	14.6	15.1	15.4	15.6	16.2	16.3	16.4
Kyrgyzstan	12.1	12.3	12.6	12.8	12.9	12.7	12.6	12.8	12.7	12.5
Moldova	17.9	18.2	18.4	18.4	19.5	19.9	20.1	20.0	20.4	20.7
Russia	16.4	16.5	16.8	17.2	17.7	18.1	18.3	18.6	18.9	19.1
Tajikistan	9.3	9.5	9.0	9.2	8.9	9.1	9.1	9.0	9.0	9.0
Turkmenistan	11.1	11.2	11.4	11.5	11.7	10.8	11.1	11.4	12.3	—
Uzbekistan	12.1	12.2	12.4	12.4	12.7	12.8	13.0	13.0	13.1	13.6
Ukraine	17.8	18.0	18.2	18.5	18.7	19.2	19.2	20.0	20.2	20.4

Source: Commonwealth of Independent States Official Statistics. Retrieved from the database on August 8, 2006.

3.4.2 Life Expectancy

One of the key socioeconomic indicators is average life expectancy at birth. This indicator is to a large extent a function of the population's well-being, including access to education, health care, housing, and personal consumption. At the same time, average life expectancy defines such economic determinants as economically active age, retirement age, and total labor force, as well as the country's overall demographic situation. Statistics on life expectancy at birth for the female populations in the NIS and selected CEE countries for the period of 1990–2004 indicate mixed trends. Life expectancy at birth for the female population in Ukraine stabilized by 1996 and has grown in a stable manner since 1997. Nevertheless, by the year 2007 Ukraine has not reached the level of 1989, when life expectancy at birth for the female population was equal to 75.2 years. Dynamics of life expectancy at birth for the female populations in Ukraine, the Russian Federation, Hungary, and Poland are rather complex. In Poland and Hungary this indicator shows a slow but continuing increase. At the same time this indicator for Poland was always higher than in Hungary. In Ukraine and the Russian Federation the situation was more difficult. Contrary to some perceptions about a rapid decrease in life expectancy at birth for the female population in Ukraine, this indicator had its slight declines and slight increases during the whole period of transition and had stabilized by the end of 2000.

Life expectancy at birth for the male populations in the NIS and CEE countries is not as high as for the female populations. This is common for all the developed countries. Statistics on life expectancy at birth for the male populations in the NIS and selected CEE countries for the period of 1990–2004 indicate negative trends. Dynamics of life expectancy at birth for the male population in Ukraine, the Russian Federation, Hungary, and Poland are rather complex. In Poland and Hungary this indicator shows a slow but continuing increase during the entire period of transition. Specifically, in Hungary the value of this indicator grew from 65.3 years in 1989 to 68.6 years in 2004, and in Poland it went from 66.8 years in 1989 to 70 years in 2004. In Ukraine and the Russian Federation the situation was more complex as was the case with the female population. Despite some people's beliefs about a rapid decrease in life expectancy at birth for the male population in Ukraine and Russia, this indicator declined and increased only slightly during the whole period of transition and had stabilized by the end of 2000. However, in distinction from the analogous indicator for the female population, stabilization of life expectancy at birth for the male population occurred on a lower level than the one achieved before the transition. In the Russian Federation, life expectancy at birth for the male population declined from 64.2 years in 1989 to its lowest level of 57.6 years in 1994 and then stabilized at a level of around 59 years, settling at 58.8 years in 2004. In Ukraine life expectancy at birth for the male population declined from 66.1 years in 1989 to its lowest of 61.8 in 1995 and then stabilized at a level of around 63 years, settling at 62.6 in 2004. Life expectancy at birth for Ukraine's male population was higher than that for the Russian Federation's male population during the entire period of transition.

Despite continuing growth in access to education, health care, and housing, as well as phenomenal growth in the service industries, Ukraine and the Russian Federation experienced negative trends in demographics, including birth rate and life expectancy for the female and male populations. Such negative trends may be explained to a large extent by social problems, including alcohol drinking, increased use of drugs, an unhealthy lifestyle, psychological stress, economic instability during the transition period, increased work loads, an increase in traffic accidences (including fatal ones), and so on. Life expectancy at birth appears to be at an unsatisfactory level for both Ukraine and the Russian Federation. A life expectancy at birth of 59 years for the male population in the Russian Federation is alarming and certainly below the value of the same indicators for other developed nations. It is socially and economically unacceptable. While positive trends are present, the pace of positive changes is slow.

3.4.3 Socioeconomic Progress: Openness and Well-Being

Dynamics of an increase in openness of Ukrainian society and the population's well-being will help us better understand progress in the social and economic life of the country during transition and post-transition development. Primary attention is paid to an increase in consumption of technologically sophisticated or hi-tech products and services. Indicators of the openness of Ukrainian society include access to newspapers, the Internet, and phone communications. The number of Internet users increased from 400 in 1993 to 3,750,000 in 2004, reaching a level of 79 users per 1,000 population. International Internet bandwidth has increased from 15.3 Mbps to 814 Mbps. International tourism and international voice traffic have also increased dramatically. The number of newspapers per 1,000 population increased from 68.66 in 1997 to 174.75 in 2000. The number of mobile phone subscribers reached 13,700,000 in 2004, comprising 289.5 mobile phone subscribers per 1,000 population. The mobile communication market has experienced a real boom since 2000.

The number of phone lines increased from 6,684,200 in 1989 to 12,100,000 in 2004. The indicator for the number of phone lines per 1,000 population grew from 129 in 1989 to 256 in 2004.

The number of personal computers in the country increased from 100,000 in 1990 to 1,327,000 in 2004. The indicator for the number of personal computers per 1,000 population grew from 1.9 in 1989 to 28 in 2004. The number of personal computers used by businesses and individuals increased consistently at a constant rate during the entire period of transition. This indicates that the economic transformation in Ukraine was a productive one. The number of passenger cars increased from 63 per 1,000 population in 1990 to 114 in 2003 and practically doubled during the period of 1990–2004. These data point to revolutionary changes in the sphere of telecommunications, the society's openness, and consumption of hi-tech goods and services. Traffic congestion, information security, and other such problems, previously unknown to the country, are insignificant as compared to the level of openness the society achieved during the period of transition. The idea of following the dynamics of consumption of certain goods and services in order to demonstrate that positive changes have occurred in the society is not new. It has been widely used before. Shleifer says of the 1990s in Russia:

> Average living standards fell little during the decade, and, in some important respects, improved. Retail trade (in constant prices) rose 16 percent between 1990 and 2002... Goskomstat's figures for final consumption of households (in constant prices) rose by about 3 percent during 1990–2002. Average living space increased from 16 square meters per person in 1990 to 19 in 2000, and the share of this living space owned by citizens doubled during the decade, from 26 to 58 percent (Goskomstat Rossii, 2001, p. 200). The number of Russians traveling abroad as tourists rose from 1.6 million in 1993 to 4.3 million in 2000. The shares of households with radios, televisions, tape recorders, refrigerators, washing machines, and electric vacuum cleaners all increased between 1991 and 2000. Private ownership of cars doubled, rising from 14 cars per 100 households in 1991 to 27 in 2000, with large increases occurring in almost all regions (Goskomstat Rossii, 2001, pp. 193–194). (Shleifer, 2005, p. 159)

Shleifer also comments on the population's health, life expectancy, and other social indicators:

> In 1992–93, as the death rate jumped sharply, the Russian Longitudinal Monitoring Survey found no evidence of serious malnutrition in Russia. In fact, the proportion of people whose body weight increased during these

> years exceeded the share that lost weight (Shkolnikov et al., 1998)...The number of doctors per capita, already one of the highest in the world, rose still higher in the 1990s (Goskomstat Rossii, 2001, p. 242). Infant mortality—one indicator of the effectiveness of basic health care—although rising a little initially, fell during the decade, from 17.4 per 1,000 live births in 1990 to 15.3 in 2000 (Goskomstat Rossii, 2001, p. 127). (Shleifer, 2005, p. 161)

Shleifer concludes that "considering the distorted demand, inflated accounting, and uselessness of much of the pre-reform output, Russians today are probably on average better off than they were in 1990" (p. 163). One might argue that radios, televisions, and tape recorders are no longer good indicators of a population's well-being and that weight loss is rather healthy while gaining weight may be the result of a poor diet, but the point in general is well taken—the crisis was not as harsh as it might have appeared to some in 1990s.

3.4.4 R&D in Ukraine

The provision of quality higher education services was on the rise during the entire period of transition and continues to grow after 2005, but the situation in the R&D sector in Ukraine was more complex. Heyets (2001) notes: "Science and education are traditionally assigned the role of facilitators for the hi-tech industries; their development moves at a slow pace, one can feel the loss of personnel with high level qualifications" (p. 1). The R&D sector in Ukraine as well as in other former Soviet republics lost some of its high-skilled employees. One should admit that during the transition the industrial model has experienced certain difficulties, even exhibiting trends toward deindustrialization in some regions and branches of the economy, including the reemergence of primitive forms of production in rural areas. Situation in R&D in Ukraine by categories of employees, scientists, and academics, for 1989–1999 as one of the major indicators of utilization of human capital in production is presented in table 3.10.

The data points to a decrease in the total number of R&D employees in Ukraine during the period of transition. The decline was from 348,645 employees in 1989 to 126,045 in 1999. This significant decline was not proportionate for all of the categories of employees. The number of specialists declined from 292,840 to 94,726, and the number of staff declined from 111,165 to 40,552. The number of technical personnel experienced a less significant decline, from 55,805 to 31,273 employees. The total number of R&D employees has decreased, but this decrease was partially compensated for by the new category of employees, namely, higher

Table 3.10 R&D employment structure in Ukraine, 1989–1999

Year	*Total number of specialists in R&D*	*Number of R&D specialists*	*Number of R&D technicians*	*Higher education faculty in R&D*	*R&D specialists, DSc*	*R&D specialists, PhD*	*Supporting staff*
1989	348,645	292,840	55,805	—	3,299	31,819	111,165
1990	313,079	262,134	50,945	35,995	3,192	29,320	111,924
1991	295,010	243,019	51,991	36,098	3,432	27,843	103,068
1992	248,445	208,058	40,397	39,012	3,843	27,410	89,563
1993	222,127	189,445	32,682	39,201	4,023	25,960	76,876
1994	207,436	171,926	35,510	40,034	3,995	24,277	76,325
1995	179,799	154,253	25,546	41,677	4,099	22,860	62,765
1996	160,103	137,497	22,606	45,395	4,151	21,357	55,681
1997	142,532	124,340	17,841	46,801	4,309	20,637	51,345
1998	134,413	100,912	33,501	48,760	4,510	19,824	45,422
1999	126,045	94,726	31,273	48,414	4,610	19,720	40,552

Source: Commonwealth of Independent States Official Statistics. Retrieved from the database on August 8, 2006.

education faculty working part-time in R&D. The number of employees in this category grew from 35,995 in 1990 to 48,414 in 1999. The explanation for this growth is that with the demand for R&D declining sharply during the 1990s, many R&D specialists with doctoral degrees moved into the rapidly growing industry of higher education services. Moreover, they have retained their work places in the research institutes. The decline in the number of PhD holders working in R&D, from 31,819 in 1989 to 19,720 in 1999, is explained by their employment in educational institutions and private businesses. At the same time the number of R&D employees with a DSc degree (which is a second doctorate, the highest doctoral degree in the country) has increased from 3,299 in 1989 to 4,610 in 1999. Contrary to commonly held opinions, changes in the number of R&D employees in different categories were smooth rather than sharp and unexpected. Dynamics within each category of R&D employees points toward a general decline in the total number of employees with a simultaneous increase in the quality of the total body in proportion to the different categories. This process is still incomplete. Further development of the market economy and market-based relations will lead to an increase in the effectiveness and efficiency of the national research institutes. Positive trends that take place in science and education in Ukraine may be sufficient to maintain the pace of reforms and facilitate industrial development.

3.5 Concluding Remarks

In this chapter, we have proven statistically that the output decline in Ukraine was not as dramatic as it often appears on the official reports, including those presented by the IMF, the World Bank, and such, and lasted for a lesser period than is normally perceived. Official data about cumulative output decline and its continuity should be approached critically. In our view, consecutive output decline in Ukraine continued for no more than six years and the decline itself was significantly smaller than 59 percent of GDP. This statement is proven statistically, when the output decline of 59 percent during the period of 1990–1999 is combined with the reported share of the unofficial or shadow economy, which constituted 48.9 percent in 1995.

Based on the extended analysis of statistical data for Ukraine and other NIS, it is possible to conclude that the so-called economic crisis in Ukraine was to a large extent a myth rather than an adequate description of the economic reality. Indeed, the large scale economic restructuring, privatization, and institutional changes do not offer enough evidence to conclude that the process of transition has resulted in a full-scale continuous economic crisis. Data on electricity consumption and energy consumption confirm our statement that the output decline in Ukraine during the 1990s was not as significant as it is presented in the literature.

The dynamics in the structure of the real GDP during the period of 1991–2007 point to the increasing role of personal consumption and investments in the GDP growth. Growing volumes of personal consumption and investments have positive influence on the GDP per capita growth, while the role of the state spending is less significant and declining. Investments played the positive role starting 1997. The trade balance may have a negative impact on the GDP per capita growth. Further development of the domestic market along with the process of reinvestment will slowly replace government spending as determinants of future economic growth in Ukraine. The data points to the sustainability of economic growth in Ukraine. In the Russian Federation, the rapid GDP per capita growth over the last eight years takes place thanks, in part, to the high prices on carbohydrates. In Ukraine, the rapid economic growth is a result of the endogenous economic change. The national economy is still experiencing a certain dis-balance between the rate of increase in consumer prices and the rate of increase in salaries and wages. Such a dis-balance confirms our thesis about the mismatch in pace of economic reforms and commoditization of labor. Formation of the labor market lags behind the commodity market.

The higher education sector in Ukraine undergoes a rapid development since 1991 and points to the continuous process of accumulation of human capital in the national economy. The reduction in unemployment helps involve the accumulated human capital in the process of production. The hi-tech industries of higher education and health care indicate stable growth in the total social welfare. The increasing openness of the economy and the society, development of the mass media, mobile communications, housing market, and such are all indicators of sustainable economic growth. Among the remaining problems, we would like to underline the decline in population that Ukraine has experienced since independence. While the life expectancy at birth for female and male population has stabilized and continues to increase, the birthrate remains one of the lowest in the world. Unless this trend is reversed, there will be an inevitable demographic problem in the foreseen future. The proportion of people who reached the retirement age increases. The demographic problem will eventually impact the growth rate.

PART IV

EMPIRICAL STUDY

This study analyses the role and impact of human capital on per capita economic growth in Ukraine and uses similar indicators of other post-transition economies, including Hungary, Poland, and the Russian Federation for this analysis. The factors that are associated with the human capital in terms of education levels are analyzed in order to measure this impact. Our approach is to estimate the significance of educational levels for initiating substantial economic growth. The model tests empirically the hypothesis that human capital has a positive impact on per capita economic growth in transition economies. We also estimate a system of linear and log-linear equations accounting for different time lags in the possible impact of human capital on economic growth.

4.1 The Endogenous Model of Economic Growth

For deeper investigation of the potential sources of economic growth in Ukraine and other post-transition economies, we choose an endogenous model of economic growth because the exogenous models of Solow-Swan and Leontief do not adequately describe the transition experience. The debate on whether the accumulation of human capital contributes positively toward raising per capita income growth has reemerged along with the renewed emphasis on the determinants of long-term economic growth. An endogenous model of economic growth appears to be the most appropriate for our evaluation. First, such a model may be applied for cross-sectional analysis, which is probably the best way to analyze economic growth in the countries in transition. Second, the model shows the influence and importance of human capital relative to other key inputs on economic growth and to differences across countries.

Kalaitzidakis et al. (2001) note that while both intuition and several theories of endogenous growth point toward a positive effect of human capital on economic growth, empirical evidence on this issue has been mixed. The purpose of the study is to provide a systematic investigation of the human capital-economic growth nexus. The impact of human capital on economic growth is incorporated according to the Mankiw et al. (1992) framework. Mankiw et al. assume a production function of the form given in equation 1:

$$Y = K_t^{\alpha} - H_t^{\beta}(A_t L_t)^{1-\alpha-\beta}, \tag{1}$$

where Y, K, H, and L represent total output, physical capital stock, human capital stock, and labor, respectively. A is a technological parameter. Technology is assumed to grow exponentially at the rate ϕ.

The Kalaitzidakis et al. model is in some sense a continuation of the Durlauf and Johnson (1995) work but extends their work in one significant direction. Durlauf and Johnson focus on identifying homogenous subgroups of countries, and they assume that the contribution of human capital to economic growth is the same for all countries within each subgroup. Kalaitzidakis et al. (2001) allow the effect of human capital to differ both across countries and also across time. A variety of measures of human capital frequently used in applied growth studies is employed. Kalaitzidakis et al. estimate the unrestricted growth model as follows:

$$\begin{aligned} y_{it} = a_0 + a_1 D_t + a_2 D_j + a_3 \ln S_{it}^k + a_4 \ln(n_{it} + \alpha + \delta + \gamma) \\ + a_5 \ln X_{it} + a_6 \ln h_{it} + \epsilon_{it}, \end{aligned} \tag{2}$$

where Y_{it} refers to the growth rate of income per capita during each period, S^k is the share of output devoted to physical capital accumulation, n_{it} is the rate of growth of the labor force, α is the rate of technical exogenous progress that is constant for all countries in all periods, δ is the depreciation rate of human capital, γ is the depreciation rate of physical capital, X_{it} is per capita income at the beginning of each period, h_{it} is human capital measured either as a stock or as a flow. D_t and D_j are dummy variables for each period and country, that is, Hungary, Poland, the Russian Federation, and Ukraine, respectively.

The model considers a wide variety of measures of education capital, health, and other forms of human capital are not measured. The first measure of education human capital presented by the authors is mean years of schooling for the whole population. This measure is used most frequently in the modern literature on growth. They also examine educational attainment of males and females at the primary, secondary, and postsecondary or tertiary levels. They include educational achievement at the secondary and tertiary level for a number of reasons: "(i) a number of countries have very low or zero values for educational achievement at the tertiary level; (ii) to limit the number of measures of human capital; and (iii) the theoretical mechanisms that link human capital of different educational levels to economic growth draw a distinction between basic education (primary) and education that enables the diffusion of ideas (post primary). Finally, for the purposes of comparison with the early literature on human capital, we consider enrollment rates both at the primary and secondary level and by gender" (p. 234). Human capital in the model is expressed in terms of education only. The rate of depreciation of human capital can be interpreted as a function of health care expenditures. It is not an objective of the model to suggest whether the rate of human capital depreciation is linearly related to health care expenditures, but the model assumes that higher per capita health care expenditures lead to lower rates of human capital depreciation.

4.2 Calculations without the Time Lag

4.2.1 The Data

The data used in the empirical study are for Ukraine, Hungary, Poland, and the Russian Federation, and cover the period of 1990–1999. Selected macroeconomic indicators include GDP per capita growth as percentage, GNI per capita in USD, savings as a percentage of GDP, labor force, number of people employed, and rate of growth of labor force. The data sources include Economist Intelligence Unit and World Development Database. The data demonstrate negative GDP per capita growth in Hungary for the period of 1990–1993 and then substantial per capita economic growth up to 5.635 percent in 1999. Data demonstrate definite fluctuations in GDP per capita growth in Poland. Within the observation period, GDP per capita growth is negative in 1991 and 1994. It is positive for the periods of 1992–1993 and 1995–1999. However, in contrast to Hungary, GDP per capita growth in Poland is not very substantial since it increases from 10.1956 percent in 1995 to 11.575 in 1996 and then decreases to 3.4324 in 1999. Projected GDP growth in Poland for 2001 is 4.0 percent. The trend in GDP per capita growth for the Russian Federation is almost always below the zero line that indicates negative per capita economic growth for the period of 1990–1999. The only two exceptions are 1997 and 1999 with positive GDP per capita growth of 0.717 and 0.633, respectively. The negative trend until 1996 may be explained by the transition crisis and negative GDP per capita growth in 1998 is a consequence of the world currency crisis of 1997–1998. Since 1999 the Russian Federation indicates substantial economic growth of up to 6.4 percent in 2001.

GDP per capita growth in Ukraine remained negative for the period of 1990–1999. It starts from -4.463 percent in 1990 to -0.612 percent in 1999 with the lowest of -21.28 in 1994. Starting in 2000 the economy of Ukraine demonstrates positive real GDP growth of 4.2 percent in 2000, with projected 6.2 percent in 2001, and projected 4.0–6.2 percent for 2002 (IMF, 2001). Assuming constant population decrease, it demonstrates substantial GDP per capita growth. All the data for human capital are from Barro (2000), Barro and Lee (1996) databases, UNESCO, and countries' Ministries of Education databases. Indicators for human capital are measured as the average number of schooling years per person 25 years old and above, and the average number of schooling years per person 15 years old and above. Human capital is also measured as the share of workers with completed secondary education in the labor force.

4.2.2 Empirical Results

This section details the findings from the estimation of the model. The empirical results are summarized in table 4.1. Unlike Kalaitzidakis et al. (2001), we include savings as a percentage of GDP instead of the share of output devoted to physical capital accumulation (the ratio of investment to GDP). The model is estimated using Pooled Least Squares for the growth equation. First, we present results for the model including the share of workers with completed secondary education in the total labor force as our measure of human capital. The regression results for Hungary, Poland, and the Russian Federation are presented in table 4.1.

The coefficient of the human capital variable is negative but statistically insignificant. Savings as a share of GDP has a negative correlation with GDP per capita growth. Increase in savings by 1 percent leads to a decrease in GDP per capita of 2.282 percent. However, the coefficient is statistically insignificant. A 1 percent increase in the gross national income per capita increases GDP per capita growth by 3.372 percent. The coefficient for gross national income per capita is positive but statistically insignificant.

The coefficient for the logarithm of the sum of the rate of growth of the labor force, the rate of technical exogenous progress, and the depreciation

Table 4.1 Regression results for Hungary, Poland, and the Russian Federation

Dependent variable: GNP per capita growth
Method: Pooled Least Squares

Variable	*(1)*	*(2)*	*(3)*	*(4)*
log(GDP)	−2.281950	−4.130292	−3.049124	−1.898404
log(n+a+delta)	211.7075	284.1125	324.8825	468.8184
log(GNIPC)	3.372103	10.60201	8.409283	21.52700
log(SecEd)	−2.432554	—	—	—
log(Ed15)	—	−92.03441	−87.10878	—
log(Ed25)	—	—	—	0.586599
Y1993	—	—	1.150828	—
Y1997	—	—	1.323753	—
HungaryY1993	—	—	—	5.921217
PolandY1993	—	—	—	7.003009
RussiaY1993	—	—	—	−6.587396
HungaryY1997	—	—	—	0.435318
PolandY1997	—	—	—	−6.885087
RussiaY1997	—	—	—	1.095112
Fixed effects				
Hungary	−30.12454	−90.42709	−118.2021	−534.4805
Poland	−25.88381	−76.90207	−105.8910	−522.5860
Russia	−33.83000	−78.51058	−107.8946	−525.3103
Ukraine	—	−69.59642	−100.5148	—
R-squared	0.883036	0.868996	0.874926	0.933623
Adjusted R-squared	0.824554	0.815053	0.799882	0.800869
S.E. of regression	3.040127	3.001439	3.122116	3.238834
Log likelihood	−43.72036	−58.12998	−44.66185	−23.35189
Durbin-Watson stat	2.735736	2.437320	2.459151	3.042483
Mean dependent var	−0.062002	−0.827354	−0.827354	−0.062002
S.D. dependent var	7.258046	6.979211	6.979211	7.258046
Sum squared resid	110.9085	153.1468	146.2141	62.94029
F-statistic	30.19851	37.58905	20.98589	9.376994
Prob(F-statistic)	0.000007	0.000000	0.000003	0.005563

rate for human and physical capital is positive and statistically significant at the 5-percent level of significance. The rate of growth of the labor force is presented as growth of employment only. The rate of technical exogenous progress that is constant for all countries is taken as $\alpha = 1$. The depreciation rate for human and physical capital is taken as $\delta = 0.1$. The coefficient size of 211.7 shows a large effect of growth through employment growths, technical progress, and depreciation on GDP per capita growth. Fixed country effects are negative.

Average years of schooling per person 15 years old and above is the measure of human capital in the GDP per capita growth model for Hungary, Poland, Russia, and Ukraine presented in column 2 of table 4.1. The coefficient on average years of schooling per person 15 years old and above is negative and insignificant at the 5-percent level of significance. Savings as a share of GDP demonstrates a negative correlation with GDP per capita growth. Increasing savings by 1 percent leads to a decrease in GDP per capita of 4.13 percent. However, the coefficient is statistically insignificant. A 1 percent increase in the gross national income per capita increases GDP per capita growth by 10.6 percent. The coefficient of gross national income per capita is positive and statistically significant at the 6-percent level. The coefficient for the logarithm of the sum of the rate of growth of the labor force, rate of technical exogenous progress, and the depreciation rate for human and physical capital is positive and statistically significant at the 5-percent level of significance. The coefficient size of 211.7 shows a large effect of labor growth on GDP per capita growth. Fixed country effects are negative.

The regression with the average years of schooling per person 25 years old and above as the measure of human capital gives similar results. We include two dummy variables in the model to test for shifts in growth over time. Year 1993 is equal to years one for 1993 and earlier and zero for other years. Year 1997 is equal to one for the years 1997 and later and is equal to zero for other years. We estimate the impact of average years of schooling per person 15 years old and above as the measure of human capital on the GDP per capita growth in the regression model for Hungary, Poland, Russia, and Ukraine. The results are presented in column 3 of table 4.1. The coefficient of average years of schooling per person 15 years old and above measure of human capital is negative and insignificant at the 5-percent level of significance. Coefficients for both dummy variables are insignificant at the 5-percent level of significance. This indicates that there is no significant difference for these countries between the periods of time before 1993, from 1993 till 1997, and after 1997 in the GDP per capita growth model.

Regression results for Hungary, Poland, Russia, and Ukraine using the share of workers with completed secondary education in the total labor force as our measure of human capital are presented in column 4. In addition, we test interaction of the countries' fixed effects with the time variables. The coefficient for the share of workers with completed secondary education in the total labor force is negative and insignificant at the 5-percent level of significance. Coefficients for both dummy variables are insignificant at the 5-percent level of significance. This indicates that there is no significant difference for each country between the periods of time before 1993, from 1993 till 1997, and after 1997 in the GDP per capita growth model. Regressions with average years of schooling per person 25 years old and above measure of human capital give similar results.

4.3 Calculations with the Time Lag

4.3.1 The Data

The data used in the empirical study are selected macroeconomic indicators for Ukraine, Hungary, Poland, and the Russian Federation, and cover the period of 1989–2010. These indicators include real GDP growth per head, gross fixed investment, gross national savings rate, and official rate of unemployment. The data sources include Economist Intelligence Unit calculations, U.S. Census Bureau, Ministry of Economy and European Integration, Hungarian Central Statistical Office, State Committee of Statistics, RosStat, Poland Quarterly Statistics, Statistical Yearbook, UN, IMF, and International Financial Statistics. Dynamics of the macroeconomic indicators for Hungary, Poland, the Russian Federation, and Ukraine for the period of 1989–2010 that accounts for the log trajectories are presented in figures 4.1–4.4.

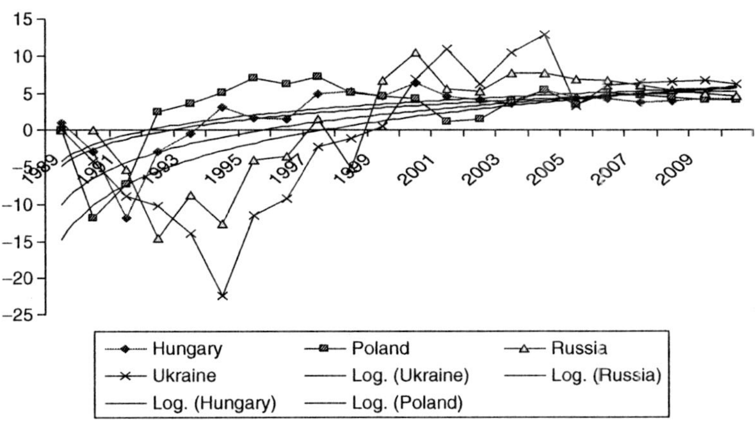

Figure 4.1 Real GDP per capita growth in Hungary, Poland, the Russian Federation, and Ukraine (with the log trajectories), 1989–2010.

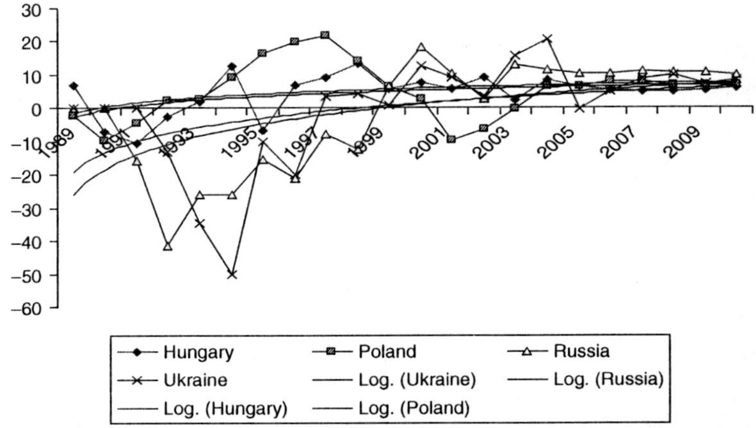

Figure 4.2 Investment in constant capital in Hungary, Poland, the Russian Federation, and Ukraine (with the log trajectories), 1989–2010.

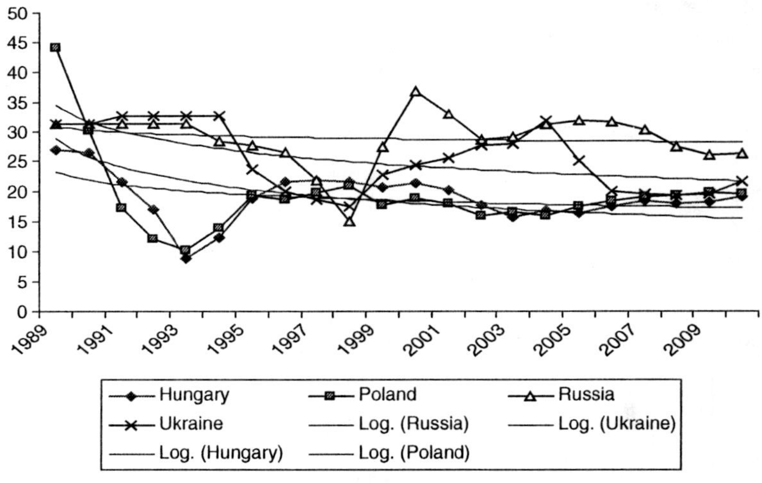

Figure 4.3 Savings rate in Hungary, Poland, the Russian Federation, and Ukraine (with the log trajectories), 1989–2010.

GDP per capita growth in Hungary, Poland, the Russian Federation, and Ukraine was in the different initial position in each country, The convergence of the GDP per capita growth rate in these countries occurs during the period of 1989–2010. Levels of the gross fixed investment in Hungary, Poland, the Russian Federation, and Ukraine were in different

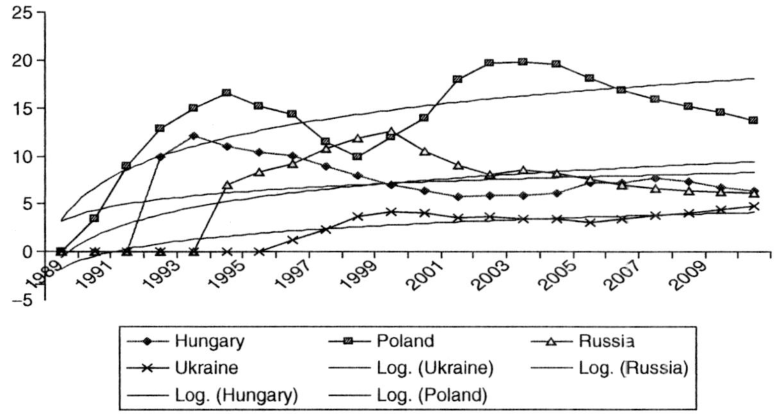

Figure 4.4 Registered level of unemployment in Hungary, Poland, the Russian Federation, and Ukraine (with the log trajectories), 1989–2010.

initial positions in each country. However, gross fixed investment rates converge. The convergence of the gross fixed investment rates in these countries occurs during the period of 1989–2010. Gross fixed investment rates in Poland and Hungary were higher than in the Russian Federation and Ukraine. The process of convergence of the growth gross fixed investment rate coincides with the convergence of the GDP per capita growth in these countries that occurs during the period of 1989–2010. This confirms significant and positive effect of the investment on growth. Levels of the savings rate in Hungary, Poland, the Russian Federation, and Ukraine have not changed significantly during the period of 1989–2010. Sharp decline of the savings rate in the Russian Federation and Ukraine in 1999 can possibly be explained by the world financial crisis of 1997–1998. The official unemployment rate in Hungary, Poland, the Russian Federation, and Ukraine has risen dramatically in early 1990s and has stabilized later. Such a sharp increase in unemployment may be explained in part by the absence of the official unemployment in the USSR and Eastern Europe. Relatively low level of the registered unemployment in the Russian Federation and Ukraine in 1990s should be considered critically as it appears to be much lower than the real unemployment rate.

4.3.2 Empirical Results

The presented calculations are based on the estimation of the system of linear and log-linear equations that account for changes in investment, savings, unemployment, education, and medical services. The independent variables were dropped consequently and the time lags were taken as five-, six, seven, and ten-year time lags. We comment only on the coefficients with 5-percent level of significance. Regression results of GDP per capita growth to investment, savings, and unemployment for Hungary, Poland, the Russian Federation and Ukraine, for the period of 1990–2010, are presented in table 4.2. Regression results indicate positive effects of investments on the GDP per capita growth rate. Contribution of investments to the GDP per capita growth in the Russian Federation is more significant than in Hungary and Poland. Positive effect of investment on per capita GDP growth in Ukraine is

Table 4.2 Regression results of GDP growth to investment, savings, and unemployment for Hungary, Poland, the Russian Federation, and Ukraine, 1990–2010

Country	*Coefficient*	*Std. Error*	*t-Statistic*	*Prob.*
Hungary				
Investment	0.244502	0.068874	3.549997	0.0027
Savings	0.256641	0.055916	4.589727	0.0003
Unemployment	−0.324814	0.111661	−2.908932	0.0102
R-squared	0.669189	Mean dependent var		3.506316
Adjusted R-sq	0.627837	S.D. dependent var		2.184843
Poland				
Investment	0.370721	0.045376	8.169967	0.0000
Savings	−0.290290	0.051233	−5.666129	0.0000
Unemployment	0.435232	0.063468	6.857488	0.0000
R-squared	0.866775	Mean dependent var		3.054571
Adjusted R-sq	0.851973	S.D. dependent var		4.511474
Russia				
Investment	0.435921	0.036696	11.87911	0.0000
Savings	−0.014688	0.055328	−0.265479	0.7945
Unemployment	0.303229	0.176305	1.719908	0.1075
R-squared	0.923170	Mean dependent var		3.181647
Adjusted R-sq	0.912194	S.D. dependent var		6.022545
Ukraine				
Investment	0.537728	0.089562	6.003988	0.0001
Savings	0.112958	0.113220	0.997691	0.3381
Unemployment	−0.265566	0.755503	−0.351509	0.7313
R-squared	0.805419	Mean dependent var		4.713533
Adjusted R-sq	0.772989	S.D. dependent var		5.702856

more significant than that in the Russian Federation, Poland, and Hungary.

The results support theoretical statement made earlier that in transition and post-transition economies savings are not analogous to investments. This means that savings are not necessarily invested in the national economy at full scale. Process of reinvestment is weak. This finding makes obvious underdevelopment of the national stock markets and proves necessary for further development of the capital market, including institutional reform, and strengthening of the national banking sector. Regression results of GDP per capita growth to investment, savings, and unemployment for Hungary, Poland, the Russian Federation, and Ukraine, for the period of 1990–2010 with the constant coefficient are presented in table 4.3.

Regression results presented in table 4.3 indicate positive effects of investments on the GDP per capita growth rate. Contribution of investments to the GDP per capita growth in Ukraine is somewhat lower than in the Russian Federation and is on the same level as in Poland. Increases in savings and investment have positive effect on per capita GDP growth in Ukraine. A 1 percent increase in investment leads to GDP per capita growth of 0.38 percent. A 1 percent increase in savings rate leads to GDP per capita growth of 0.45 percent. The results present empirical evidence in support of the theoretical findings about the necessity of continuing increase of investment in production. This will lead to sustainable economic growth.

Regression results of GDP per capita growth to investment, savings, unemployment, education, and health care for the Russian Federation and Ukraine for the period of 1990–2010 with the constant coefficient (1) and without the constant coefficient (2) are presented in table 4.4. Indicators of the level of access to higher education and medical services are taken with the five-year time lag. Regression results of GDP per capita growth to investment, savings, education, and health care for the Russian Federation and Ukraine for the period of 1990–2010 with the constant coefficient (1) and without the constant coefficient (2) are presented in table 4.5. Indicators of the level of access to higher education and medical services are taken with the six-year time lag. Regression results of GDP per capita growth to investment, savings, health-care, and education for the Russian Federation and Ukraine for the period of 1990–2010 with the constant coefficient (1) and without the constant coefficient (2) are presented in table 4.6. Indicators of the level of access to higher education and health-care are taken with the five-year time lag. Regression results of GDP growth to investment, savings, and education

Table 4.3 Regression results of GDP growth to investment, savings, and unemployment for Hungary, Poland, the Russian Federation and Ukraine, 1990–2010 with the constant coefficient

Country	*Coefficient*	*Std. Error*	*t-Statistic*	*Prob.*
Hungary				
Investment	0.218044	0.065923	3.307547	0.0048
Savings	0.102020	0.099344	1.026938	0.3207
Unemployment	−0.579068	0.173741	−3.332936	0.0045
C	5.009459	2.738086	1.829548	0.0873
R–squared	0.729541	Mean dependent var		3.506316
Adjusted R–sq	0.675450	S.D. dependent var		2.184843
Poland				
Investment	0.377018	0.044253	8.519573	0.0000
Savings	−0.130255	0.120908	−1.077306	0.2964
Unemployment	0.580495	0.117482	4.941147	0.0001
C	−5.103586	3.514660	−1.452085	0.1647
R–squared	0.881476	Mean dependent var		3.054571
Adjusted R–sq	0.860560	S.D. dependent var		4.511474
Russia				
Investment	0.418878	0.038128	10.98601	0.0000
Savings	0.113487	0.112216	1.011325	0.3303
Unemployment	0.504945	0.231460	2.181564	0.0481
C	−5.333275	4.093082	−1.302997	0.2152
R–squared	0.932045	Mean dependent var		3.181647
Adjusted R–sq	0.916363	S.D. dependent var		6.022545
Ukraine				
Investment	0.375891	0.106429	3.531853	0.0047
Savings	0.449317	0.180289	2.492201	0.0299
Unemployment	1.454577	1.013559	1.435119	0.1791
C	−12.98688	5.837625	−2.224685	0.0480
R–squared	0.865800	Mean dependent var		4.713533
Adjusted R–sq	0.829200	S.D. dependent var		5.702856

C: Constant coefficient.

for the Russian Federation and Ukraine for the period of 1990–2010 are presented in table 4.7. Indicators of the level of access to higher education are taken with the five-year time lag.

Regression results of GDP per capita growth to investment, savings, and education for the Russian Federation and Ukraine for the period of

Table 4.4 Regression results of GDP growth to investment, savings, unemployment, education, and health care for the Russian Federation and Ukraine, 1990–2010

Country	*Russian Federation*		*Ukraine*	
Estimation method	*(1)*	*(2)*	*(1)*	*(2)*
Independent variable	*OLS*	*OLS*	*OLS*	*OLS*
Investment	0.544219**	0.349321*	0.341820**	0.384583**
	(0.151921)	(0.088695)	(0.153252)	(0.142531)
	[3.582251]	[3.938462]	[2.230438]	[2.698245]
Savings	−0.038764	0.226039	0.901649	1.196193
	(0.260842)	(0.213105)	(0.728499)	(0.637364)
	[−0.148611]	[1.060695]	[1.237682]	[1.876784]
Unemployment	−1.156294	1.021889	0.410878	0.130104
	(1.554713)	(0.645762)	(1.675531)	(1.609592)
	[−0.743735]	[1.582455]	[0.245223]	[0.080831]
Education	−0.014755	0.041590	−0.066783	−0.060944
	(0.050371)	(0.037368)	(0.089199)	(0.086963)
	[−0.292917]	[1.112996]	[−0.748699]	[−0.700799]
Health care	−2.180633	−0.474601	2.500816	−0.346361
	(1.176011)	(0.366858)	(3.148024)	(0.212904)
	[−1.854263]	[−1.29369]	[0.794408]	[−1.626842]
R–squared	0.959353	0.941654	0.954202	0.941654
Adjusted R–squared	0.918707	0.883307	0.877871	0.883307
Mean dependent var	1.778636	1.778636	3.925778	3.925778
S.D. dependent var	7.173865	7.173865	7.361281	7.361281

Notes: Each column is a separate regression of the growth rate on investment, savings, unemployment, education, and health care.

Standard errors are reported in parentheses. t-statistics are reported in square brackets.

* Indicates statistical significance at the 1-percent level; and ** at the 5-percent level.

1990–2010 with the constant coefficient are presented in table 4.8. Indicators of the level of access to higher education are taken with the six-year time lag (1) and with the seven-year time lag (2).

Regression results indicate positive effects of investments on the GDP per capita growth rate. An increase in investment leads to an increase in per capita GDP growth in all the countries. Other variables are not statistically significant. Effects of the variables that represent access of population to higher education and medical services are within the limits of statistical error. This statement holds when indicators of the level of access to higher education and medical services are

Table 4.5 Regression results of GDP growth to investment, savings, education, and health care for the Russian Federation and Ukraine, 1990–2010

Country	*Russian Federation*		*Ukraine*	
Estimation method	*(1)*	*(2)*	*(1)*	*(2)*
Independent variable	*OLS*	*OLS*	*OLS*	*OLS*
Investment	0.430864*	0.448183*	0.416201*	0.516480*
	(0.042274)	(0.052814)	(0.042274)	(0.105189)
	[10.19206]	[8.486119]	[3.862983]	[4.910021]
Savings	0.133635	0.015774	0.200090	0.394320
	(0.128833)	(0.151186)	(0.128833)	(0.488916)
	[1.037277]	[0.104332]	[0.453996]	[0.806520]
Education	0.017864	−0.001487	−0.040690	0.021822
	(0.022262)	(0.026335)	(0.022262)	(0.083934)
	[0.802457]	[−0.056456]	[−0.500659]	[0.259988]
Health care	−1.484476**	0.053926	5.761747	−0.298297
	(0.645769)	(0.143247)	(0.645769)	(0.186454)
	[0.05510]	[0.376454]	[1.692321]	[−1.599844]
R–squared	0.961679	0.929628	0.950381	0.924120
Adjusted R–squared	0.939781	0.903239	0.917301	0.891600
Mean dependent var	0.908000	0.908000	0.135273	0.135273
S.D. dependent var	7.475416	7.475416	10.96832	10.96832

Notes: Each column is a separate regression of the growth rate on investment, savings, education, and health care.

Standard errors are reported in parentheses. t-statistics are reported in square brackets.

* Indicates statistical significance at the 1-percent level; and ** at the 10-percent level.

taken with the five-, six-, and seven-year time lags. Positive effects of investment in fixed capital in the Russian Federation and Ukraine are higher than in Poland and Hungary. A 1 percent increase in investments in the Russian Federation and Ukraine leads to an increase of the per capita GDP within the limits of 0.37–0.55 percent. While in Poland and Hungary this indicator stays within the limits of 0.22–0.37 percent.

The dependency between the per capita GDP growth and the independent variables we use in the regressions may be nonlinear. We test system of log-linear equations, where all independent variables are taken as logarithms. Initially, we estimate an equation that includes logarithms of all independent variables, including investment, savings, unemployment, education, and health. Then variables of unemployment

Table 4.6 Regression results of GDP growth to investment, savings, education, and health care for the Russian Federation and Ukraine, 1990–2010

Country	*Russian Federation*		*Ukraine*	
Estimation method	*(1)*	*(2)*	*(1)*	*(2)*
Independent variable	*OLS*	*OLS*	*OLS*	*OLS*
Investment	0.452827*	0.454333*	0.430281*	0.523992*
	(0.053285)	(0.046954)	(0.066924)	(0.065638)
	[8.498240]	[9.676147]	[6.429377]	[7.983083]
Savings	-0.014128	-0.018440	0.472994*	0.420083
	(0.155924)	(0.137815)	(0.222495)	(0.273993)
	[-0.090609]	[-0.133805]	[2.125865]	[1.533188]
Education	-0.004705	-0.005694	-0.076373	0.021073
	(0.027358)	(0.022957)	(0.055225)	(0.043700)
	[-0.171966]	[-0.248051]	[-1.382946]	[-0.248051]
Health care	0.029059	0.092991	5.349698**	-0.303923**
	(0.818807)	(0.131469)	(2.468013)	(0.168933)
	[0.035490]	[0.707324]	[2.167614]	[0.109700]
R-squared	0.935410	0.935359	0.953802	0.919064
Adjusted R-squared	0.903115	0.913812	0.927403	0.888713
Mean dependent var	1.363000	1.363000	0.404917	0.404917
S.D. dependent var	7.342776	7.342776	10.49951	10.49951

Notes: Each column is a separate regression of the growth rate on investment, savings, education, and health care.

Standard errors are reported in parentheses. t-statistics are reported in square brackets.
* Indicates statistical significance at the 1-percent level; and ** at the 10-percent level.

and health are consequently taken out from the equations. Indicators of the level of access of population to higher education and medical services are taken consequently with the five-, six-, seven-, and ten-year time lags for all the equations. All combinations of log-linear equations are estimated with and without the constant coefficient. Regression results indicate positive effects of an increase in investment on the per capita GDP growth in the Russian Federation and Ukraine. Investment coefficients are positive and statistically significant in all of the equations with the goodness of fit within the limits of 0.8–0.95. The complete records of the regression results can be obtained from the author. We will consider the most interesting results. Regression results of per capita GDP growth to logarithms of investment, savings, and education with the constant coefficient in

Table 4.7 Regression results of GDP growth to investment, savings, and education for the Russian Federation and Ukraine, 1990–2010

Country	*Russian Federation*		*Ukraine*	
Estimation method	*(1)*	*(2)*	*(1)*	*(2)*
Independent variable	*OLS*	*OLS*	*OLS*	*OLS*
Investment	0.456769*	0.436670*	0.507771*	0.596913*
	(0.050490)	(0.040954)	(0.104841)	(0.101002)
	[9.046741]	[10.66238]	[4.843235]	[5.909940]
Savings	-0.004268	0.048580	0.376908	0.562421
	(0.141282)	(0.117505)	(0.481814)	(0.521962)
	[-0.030207]	[0.413427]	[0.782269]	[1.077514]
Education	-0.006527	0.005975	0.022592	-0.068311
	(0.024251)	(0.016493)	(0.081200)	(0.068011)
	[-0.269131]	[0.362271]	[0.278230]	[-1.004410]
R-squared	0.932750	0.928382	0.926696	0.896375
Adjusted R-squared	0.907531	0.912466	0.895280	0.870469
Mean dependent var	0.908000	0.908000	0.135273	0.135273
S.D. dependent var	7.475416	7.475416	10.968320	10.96832

Notes: Each column is a separate regression of the growth rate on investment, savings, and education.

Standard errors are reported in parentheses. t-statistics are reported in square brackets.

* Indicates statistical significance at the 1-percent level.

the Russian Federation and Ukraine, for the period of 1990–2010, indicate positive effect of an increase in investment in fixed capital, savings, and access to education on the per capita GDP growth. All coefficients of the independent variables are statistically significant. Indicators of the level of access of population to higher education are taken with the ten-year time lag. Regression results of GDP per capita growth to investment, savings, and education for the Russian Federation and Ukraine for the period of 1990–2010 with the constant coefficient (1) and without the constant coefficient (2) are presented in table 4.9. Indicators of the level of access to higher education are taken with the ten-year time lag.

Estimation of the equations that consider indicators of access to higher education and medical services with the seven-year time lag does not bring statistically significant results. This supports our suggestion that an increase in access of population to higher education does not bring positive results for the per capita GDP growth in the short term. Moreover,

Table 4.8 Regression results of GDP growth to investment, savings, and education for the Russian Federation and Ukraine, 1990–2010

Country	*Russian Federation*		*Ukraine*	
Estimation method	*(1)*	*(2)*	*(1)*	*(2)*
Independent variable	*OLS*	*OLS*	*OLS*	*OLS*
Investment	0.451999*	0.449635*	0.517551*	0.513473*
	(0.045165)	(0.041511)	(0.064646)	(0.054756)
	[10.00766]	[10.83167]	[8.005908]	[9.377552]
Savings	-0.011663	-0.014491	0.431738	0.384124**
	(0.131625)	(0.124123)	(0.268069)	(0.204437)
	[-0.088608]	[-0.116749]	[1.610548]	[1.878933]
Education	-0.004157	-0.004167	0.018197	0.042449
	(0.021306)	(0.019454)	(0.040943)	(0.030395)
	[-0.195124]	[-0.214207]	[0.444446]	[1.396600]
R-squared	0.935400	0.935400	0.922793	0.922793
Adjusted R-squared	0.913866	0.913866	0.893841	0.893841
Mean dependent var	1.363000	1.363000	0.404917	0.404917
S.D. dependent var	7.342776	7.342776	10.499510	10.499510

Notes: Each column is a separate regression of the growth rate on investment, savings, and education.

Standard errors are reported in parentheses. t-statistics are reported in square brackets.

* Indicates statistical significance at the 1-percent level; and ** at the 10-percent level.

enrollment in a higher education institution equates to temporary withdrawal from the workforce. Both the level of unemployment and the opportunity costs of obtaining education are of certain concern here. However, an increase in access of population to higher education brings positive results for the per capita GDP growth in the long term. Increasing number of college-educated specialists leads to sustainable economic growth. Apparently, the background for the 2000–2005 rapid economic growth in Ukraine and in the Russian Federation was laid down in early 1990s. This contradicts commonly accepted perception about the crisis decade of 1990s.

Estimation of the system of equations, where all the variables—dependent and independent—were presented in the form of logarithms, confirms positive effect of an increase in investment and per capita GDP growth. For instance, 1 percent increase in investment in fixed capital in Ukraine leads to 0.639 percent increase in per capita GDP growth. Results of the Vector Autoregression Estimates (VAR) and

Table 4.9 Regression results of GDP growth to investment, savings, and education for the Russian Federation and Ukraine, 1990–2010

Country	*Russian Federation*	*Ukraine*	
Estimation method *Independent variable*	*(2)* *OLS*	*(1)* *OLS*	*(2)* *OLS*
Investment	1.461792***	2.141293**	3.389514*
	(0.708749)	(0.698971)	(1.035916)
	[2.062496]	[3.063492]	[3.271996]
Savings	6.209534**	19.06934*	6.853271***
	(1.937277)	(3.728733)	(3.637917)
	[3.205291]	[5.114161]	[1.883845]
Education	-3.356831**	11.31633**	-4.170212***
	(1.194651)	(4.021590)	(2.113641)
	[-2.809885]	[2.813894]	[-1.972999]
R-squared	0.674533	0.893438	0.673608
Adjusted R-squared	0.593166	0.853477	0.601077
Mean dependent var	6.668545	5.854083	5.854083
S.D. dependent var	1.575530	4.683886	4.683886

Notes: Each column is a separate regression of the growth rate on investment, savings, and education.

Standard errors are reported in parentheses. t-statistics are reported in square brackets.

* Indicates statistical significance at the 1-percent level; ** at the 5-percent level; and *** at the 10-percent level.

Impulse Response Function indicate generally positive effects of investment on per capita GDP growth in the short run. In the long run a most significant positive influence of investment in fixed capital on per capita GDP growth occurs during the first two years and then diminishes.

4.4 Concluding Remarks

As follows from the regression results presented in this chapter, investments in fixed capital have positive effect on the GDP per capita growth rate. Contribution of investments to the GDP per capita growth in the Russian Federation is more significant than in Hungary and Poland. Positive effect of investment on per capita GDP growth in Ukraine is more significant than that in the Russian Federation, Poland, and Hungary. Regressions that use average number of schooling years per person 25 years old and above or the average number of schooling years per person 15 years old and above as the human capital measure demonstrate a positive correlation in Poland but a negative correlation in Hungary, even though Hungary has the most sustainable GNP per capita growth. We also show that there is no significant difference in the basic growth model over time. These trend effects did not differ across countries.

Coefficients for total savings as a share of GDP in the regressions indicate a negative but insignificant effect on GNP per capita growth. It confirms our prediction that savings of the population are not invested in production and cannot be considered as a share of output devoted to physical capital accumulation. This reflects the problem of underinvestment in production in Ukraine and the Russian Federation. Gross national income per capita has a positive and significant effect on per capita GNP growth. An increase in income per capita leads to a higher level of growth. This contrasts with the convergence hypothesis presented in the reviewed literature. The empirical model did not examine threshold levels of human capital, but the growth experience of a country may well differ according to which side of the threshold of human capital it is on. This should be examined in the future. The results support theoretical statement made earlier that in transition and post-transition economies savings are not analogous to investments. This means that savings are not necessarily invested in the national economy at full scale. The process of reinvestment is weak. This finding makes obvious underdevelopment of the national stock markets and proves necessary for further development of the capital market, including institutional reform and strengthening of the national banking sector.

Regression results of per capita GDP growth to logarithms of investment, savings, and education with the constant coefficient in the Russian Federation and Ukraine for the period of 1990–2010 indicate positive effect of an increase in investment in fixed capital, savings, and access to education on the per capita GDP growth when indicators of the level of access of population to higher education are taken with the ten-year time lag. An increase in access of population to higher education brings positive results for the per capita GDP growth in the long term. Increasing number of college-educated specialists leads to sustainable economic growth. Apparently, background for the 2000–2005 rapid economic growth in Ukraine and in the Russian Federation was laid down in early 1990s. This contradicts commonly accepted perception about the crisis decade of 1990s. Results of the VAR and Impulse Response Function indicate generally positive effects of investment on per capita GDP growth in the short run. In the long run a most significant positive influence of investment in fixed capital on per capita GDP growth occurs during the first two years and then diminishes. The regression results present strong empirical evidence in support of continuing investment in fixed capital in order to sustain economic growth. Investments in fixed capital are backed by the growing education quality of the workforce.

* * *

4.5 Conclusions and Policy Recommendations

Theories of transition are loosely tied to the theories of growth. While the Western theorists of economic transition focus on such neoliberal concepts and aspects of transition as privatization, inflation, free pricing, supply and demand, economists in Ukraine continue using Marxist and post-Marxist conceptual frameworks for analysis of transition. In their view these frames seem to be more appropriate for understanding the current events and phenomena that take place in the former Soviet Bloc. Relatively successful in explaining the realities of economic downturn, economists were unable to explain rapid economic growth in Ukraine. Transition turned to be more about the redistribution of property and creation of an institutional structure that would preserve the new balance of property rights. As a result, at best the transition can be characterized as a process of creation of new grounds, including institutional grounds, on which the new trajectory of developments is to be based. The emerging new system of coordinates for old and new types of economic agents may have numerous imperfections. At the same time, path-dependent development of Ukraine did not prevent it from accumulating the strength and internal resources to turn the continuing economic decline into rapid economic growth.

The impact of human capital accumulation on economic growth remains controversial. In different research, conclusions reached depend on the definition of human capital, the methodology used, and the time period and set of countries over which the model is estimated. Our objective in this research is to present a study of the possible link between human capital accumulation and GDP per capita growth in Ukraine by using an extended set of macroeconomic indicators and alternative definitions of human capital. As anticipated, parametric estimates reveal no link between the two variables: for different measures of human capital, there is no significant growth effect. The empirical results are supportive of the predictions from the original growth models: an increase in human capital does not correlate with per capita economic growth in countries with a high level of human capital.

The slow initial process of restructuring and institutional changes in Ukraine led to a low level of GDP per capita growth. Nevertheless, positive changes in the economy and the society overall are the result of the structural changes in the economy, institutional reforms, development of the market type of behavior among population, development of market infrastructure, improved management, regional diversification, stabilization of the national currency, slowdown in both "brain drain" and capital outflow, and high level of human capital that served as a ground for economic growth. The consecutive output decline in Ukraine continued for no more than six years and the decline itself was significantly smaller than often stated. The so-called economic crisis in Ukraine was to a large extent a myth.

The state did not hold the initiative in the process of transition, including the social sphere. Poor people, many of whom were poor in the Soviet times, were left aside and failed to integrate in the newly emerging market economy. Hidden poverty came to the surface. As a result, there was an impression about the deep socioeconomic crisis in the nation. Income differentiation and growing corruption in public sector led to an increase in the number of poor families. This process was unavoidable due to the transition to the market. However, the social consequences of the reform could have been mitigated if the government would have a well-developed economic program.

The state has concentrated on such aspects of the reform as privatization and investments, as well as a fundamental political reform. Such a prioritization led to the high social price of the reform. In part, the exogenous type of transformation, that is, an attempt to rebuild the system from the outside by using external forces, was responsible for economic difficulties that were experienced by the large part of the population. Continuing political instability in Ukraine is a natural part of the process of democratization. Corruption, however, may be a challenge. The shift from exogenous to endogenous forms of transformation will lead to the weakening role of the state in the economy. As a result, political instability will have a lesser impact on the development of the national economy.

Overall, results of the study offer policy directions for Ukraine and other transition economies. A high level of human capital needs to be reproduced on an increasing scale. The process of accumulation of human capital will have a positive impact on GDP per capita growth in the long run. An increase in access of population to higher education brings positive results for the per capita GDP growth in the long term. An increasing number of college-educated specialists employed in the industry leads to sustainable economic growth. Apparently, the background for the 2000–2005 rapid economic growth in Ukraine was laid down in early 1990s. This contradicts commonly accepted perception about the crisis decade of 1990s.

While the exogenous resource of economic transition is depleted and the exogenous-type forms of transition are no longer effective, the exogenous growth still has a certain potential in Ukraine. This is explained by the fact that there are still unused labor resources as well as labor migration abroad and capital flight. Repatriation and legalization of capital, return of the labor migrants, and full employment will support economic growth in the short run. However, the sustainable growth will only be possible thanks to technological advancements and innovations. This anticipates endogenous growth. Among the major tasks of post-transition development in Ukraine are strengthening of the labor market and creation of the stock market. Such developments will facilitate better distribution of property and lead to an increase in labor productivity. This will eventually bring higher rate of GDP per capita growth and higher living standards of the population.

The slowdown in the accumulation of amortization funds during 1990s along with the growing depreciation of principal capital was considered as a time bomb for the industry. A significant renovation of principal capital is necessary. During the next decade, that is, from 2008 to 2018, Ukraine will have to renovate at least a third of its principal capital. If a massive technical renovation and incremental growth in production capacities will take place right after the period of significant growth of 2004–2006, then the national economy will enter the stage of cyclical development earlier. If, however, the massive renovation of principal capital will be preceded by the period of economic growth slowdown, predicted for 2007–2010, then the nation's economy will enter the cycle later.

We tend to consider the second scenario as more viable and likely to take place in Ukraine. The slowdown in economic growth will indicate stabilization of the system. Later, based on this already achieved stabilization, renovation of principal capital will began. This renovation will start from the most viable, economically effective, and profitable industries, which are, nevertheless, utilizing old and morally outdated machinery and equipment. Technological changes will be accompanied with the incremental increase in principal capital based on reinvestment of profits, earned in these industries over the last decade.

We believe that the next advancement will become possible based on the process of renovation and investment into principal capital. The process of renovation itself will result in the continuation of strong economic growth. After the renovation, the economy will continue to grow on the basis of new production capacities, technological advancements, and further accumulation of human capital to serve new equipment and technologies. From this perspective, we suggest further institutional and structural changes in Ukraine's economy. It will increase domestic and foreign investment, further develop domestic market, and sustain already achieved substantial GDP per capita growth. Future economic growth in Ukraine will be path-dependent, based on innovations in already existing fundamental branches of the national economy rather than development of new ones.

APPENDICES

Appendix I

GDP per capita growth in the Central and Eastern European countries and the former USSR for 1989–2004 according to World Development Indicators methodology

Table A.1 GDP per capita growth in the NIS and CEE countries, 1989–2004 (annual % change)

Country	*1989*	*1990*	*1991*	*1992*	*1993*	*1994*
Armenia	—	—	−10.88910	−40.75950	−6.66407	7.92383
Azerbaijan	—	—	−2.22959	−23.76380	−24.25940	−20.77810
Belarus	—	—	−1.24847	−9.79468	−7.80756	−11.59640
Georgia	−7.60712	−14.64490	−20.40770	−44.06640	−27.92940	−8.57907
Hungary	1.17239	−3.18942	−11.73020	−2.85762	−0.28636	3.27824
Kazakhstan	—	—	−11.55450	−5.23430	−8.59574	−11.32270
Kyrgyz Rep.	0.84764	3.71923	−9.32709	−14.85480	−15.40350	−20.03240
Latvia	5.05549	−7.48512	−12.30960	−31.34490	−3.29281	3.71394
Lithuania	—	—	−5.82846	−21.17390	−15.84020	−9.14936
Moldova	4.42051	−2.77460	−16.13940	−29.07700	−1.02120	−30.72280
Poland	—	—	−7.30543	2.27828	3.54549	4.96910
Russia	—	−3.37349	−5.25906	−14.56840	−8.56461	−12.46130
Tajikistan	−9.16156	−3.08362	−9.07438	−30.28300	−17.71330	−22.43990
Turkmenistan	−6.71076	−1.94781	−7.36389	−8.01543	−12.51560	−19.40630
Ukraine	3.36751	−6.56001	−8.60169	−9.95838	−14.27370	−22.55080
Uzbekistan	0.65818	−0.78637	−2.82857	−13.26720	−4.50021	−7.19708

Continued

Table A.1 Continued

Country	*1995*	*1996*	*1997*	*1998*	*1999*
Armenia	9.08475	7.49574	4.47080	8.16901	3.93089
Azerbaijan	–12.81000	0.28217	4.78763	8.95741	6.45825
Belarus	–10.11000	3.14401	11.87348	8.91675	3.75033
Georgia	4.51016	12.97227	12.03807	4.34428	4.04866
Hungary	1.80702	1.67659	4.95918	5.28451	4.62847
Kazakhstan	–6.57726	2.03372	3.31959	–0.19201	3.68290
Kyrgyz Rep.	–6.45203	5.54159	8.33332	0.58905	2.21536
Latvia	0.35498	4.79089	10.09487	6.46092	4.15124
Lithuania	4.02949	5.46120	7.75511	8.03369	–1.02755
Moldova	–1.12771	–4.93707	1.89016	–6.22572	–3.10236
Poland	6.87799	5.91654	6.71159	4.75625	4.12193
Russia	–4.01735	–3.33770	1.69944	–5.03891	6.82906
Tajikistan	–13.63280	–17.85890	0.31857	3.91586	2.40589
Turkmenistan	–9.23495	–8.38468	–12.61530	5.63697	15.07709
Ukraine	–11.50330	–9.19777	–2.11217	–1.01931	0.74547
Uzbekistan	–2.80287	–5.09000	3.56561	2.79826	2.84094

Country	*2000*	*2001*	*2002*	*2003*	*2004*
Armenia	6.62080	10.17418	13.40822	14.37812	7.39263
Azerbaijan	10.19537	9.05170	9.77781	10.36072	9.22415
Belarus	6.11723	5.09021	5.52430	7.59642	11.59918
Georgia	2.99955	6.00316	6.68616	12.30461	7.29727
Hungary	6.46820	2.66074	4.10215	3.69470	4.88081
Kazakhstan	10.13077	13.69281	9.79520	8.93349	8.78317
Kyrgyz Rep.	4.35562	4.48742	–0.78627	6.06591	5.93741
Latvia	7.70275	8.60470	7.40345	7.79689	8.90686
Lithuania	4.85244	6.93392	7.13757	10.16636	7.24767
Moldova	2.43334	6.46148	8.17064	6.95878	7.64027
Poland	3.97790	2.06496	1.42045	3.93548	5.48004
Russia	10.00451	5.34647	5.21216	7.86771	7.70229
Tajikistan	7.03137	8.99007	7.95287	9.04633	9.38949
Turkmenistan	17.08336	18.75855	—	—	—
Ukraine	6.97137	10.30354	6.20298	10.34161	12.95349
Uzbekistan	2.33658	2.70548	2.49454	2.68234	6.13382

Source: World Development Indicators. Retrieved from the database on August 10, 2006.

Appendix II

Major GDP indicators in Ukraine for 1989–2006 and in the forecasts till 2010.

Table A.2 Selected indicators of GDP in Ukraine, 1989–2010

Year	*Nominal GDP (US$ at PPP; bln USD)*	*Real GDP (bln UAH)*	*Real GDP (PPP US$ at 1996 prices; bln USD)*	*Real GDP (US$ at 1996 prices; bln USD)*	*Nominal GDP (bln UAH)*	*Nominal GDP (US$; bln USD)*	*Real GDP at factor cost (bln UAH)*
1989	373.629	118.856	448.236	107.942	—	—	—
1990	374.084	114.102	430.307	103.624	—	—	—
1991	353.486	104.175	392.870	94.609	—	—	2.001
1992	325.816	93.861	353.976	85.242	—	—	1.729
1993	286.006	80.533	303.711	73.138	1.500	33.094	1.482
1994	225.197	62.091	234.161	56.389	12.000	36.639	1.142
1995	201.768	54.516	205.594	49.510	54.500	36.997	1.002
1996	185.034	49.064	185.034	44.559	81.519	44.559	0.903
1997	182.470	47.592	179.483	43.222	93.365	50.151	0.875
1998	180.988	46.688	176.073	42.401	102.593	41.883	0.859
1999	183.240	46.594	175.721	42.316	130.442	31.581	0.856
2000	198.279	49.344	186.088	44.813	170.070	31.261	0.797
2001	221.716	53.884	203.209	48.936	204.190	38.009	0.867
2002	237.098	56.686	213.775	51.480	225.810	42.393	0.937
2003	264.061	62.127	234.298	56.422	267.344	50.133	1.020
2004	300.825	69.645	262.648	63.249	345.113	64.881	1.146
2005	317.266	71.455	269.477	64.894	424.741	82.881	1.187
2006	343.948	75.386	284.298	68.463	464.876	92.055	1.265
2007	375.248	79.758	300.787	72.434	492.751	96.998	1.351
2008	410.882	84.543	318.834	76.780	571.732	111.666	1.445
2009	449.150	89.785	338.601	81.540	653.722	126.690	1.549
2010	488.671	94.992	358.239	86.269	754.717	145.418	1.655

PPP: Purchasing power parity.

Source: Economist Intelligence Unit. Retrieved from the database on August 12, 2006. Composed based on EIU calculations.

REFERENCES

Ukrainian and Russian Sources

Abalkin, L.I. (Ed.). (1997). Kurs perehodnoj ekonomiki. Uchebnik dlja vuzov [Transition economics: textbook]. M.: Finstatinform.

Aleksandrova, V.P. (2003a). Perspektivi finansuvannja NTR. [Perspectives of R&D funding]. In V.M. Heyets (Ed.). *Ekonomika Ukrainy: strategija i politika dovgostrokovogo rozvitku* (pp. 417–423). Kyiv: IEP, Feniks.

———. (2003b). Strategija finansuvannja innovacijnoï dijal'nosti jak zasib upravlinnja ïï naprjamkami. [The strategy of funding innovations as a tool of managing directions for development]. In Heyets (Ed.). *Ekonomika Ukrainy* (pp. 391–416).

Arhangel'skij, U., Radzievskij, A., and Alekseev, A. (2006). Bednost', nalogi i ekonomicheskij rost [Poverty, taxes, and economic growth]. *Ekonomika Ukrainy*, 5, pp. 63–71.

Arkhiyereyev, S. (1998). Institucional'nye preobrazovanija i transakcionnye izderzhki [Institutional reforms and transaction costs]. *Biznes Inform*, 11, pp. 20–22.

Balabanova, A.V. (2004). Upravlenie ekonomicheskim rostom: modeli i strategii [Managing economic growth: models and strategies]. M.: Ros. akad. Predprinimatel'stva.

Baranovs'kij, O.I. (2003). Reformuvannja bankivs'koï sistemi Ukrainy [Banking system reform in Ukraine]. In Heyets (Ed.). *Ekonomika Ukrainy* (pp. 629–640).

Bazhal, U.M. (Ed.). (2002). Ekonomichna ocinka derzhavnih prioritetiv tehnologichnogo rozvitku [Economic estimates of the state priorities in technological development]. Kyiv: IEP.

Bazhal, U.M., and Odotjuk, I.V. (2003). Investicijni resursi ta prioritetni naprjami innovacijnogo rozvitku [Investment resources and the primary directions of innovative development]. In Heyets (Ed.). *Ekonomika Ukrainy* (pp. 684–694).

Bessonov, V.A. (2005). Problemy analiza rossijskoj makroekonomicheskoj dinamiki perehodnogo perioda [The problems of analysis of macroeconomic dynamics during the transition in Russia]. M.: MAKS Press.

Bliznjuk, V.V. (2003). Trudovi vidnosini ta rinok praci [Labor relations and the labor market]. In Heyets (Ed.). *Ekonomika Ukrainy* (pp. 298–313).

Bolhovitinova, O.U. (2003). Investicijnij potencial amortizacijnoï politiki [Investment potential of the reinvestment policy]. In Heyets (Ed.). *Ekonomika Ukrainy* (pp. 668–683).

Bolhovitinova, O.U., and Mar'enko, A.V. (2003). Renovacijni prioriteti investicijnoï politiki Ukrainy [Renovation priorities of the investment policy in Ukraine]. In Heyets (Ed.). *Ekonomika Ukrainy* (pp. 659–667).

Bondarenko, M.I., and Hrytsenko, A.A. (1993). Ekonomicheskaja teorija: V 5 [Economic theory, Vol. 5. Introduction]. Kharkov: HGU.

Borejko, V. (2005). Ob obespechenii uskorennogo razvitija ekonomiki Ukrainy [Facilitating rapid economic development in Ukraine]. *Ekonomika Ukrainy*, 8, pp. 20–24.

Bridun, E.V. (2003). Innovacijnij rozvitok ta perspektivi vnutrishn'ogo rinku mashinobudivnoï produkciï [Innovative development and perspectives of the domestic market for machine building]. In Heyets (Ed.). *Ekonomika Ukrainy* (pp. 809–826).

Buzgalin, A. (1995). Zakonomernosti perehodnoj ekonomiki: teorija i metodologija [Laws of the transition economy: theory and methodology]. *Voprosy ekonomiki*, 2, pp. 32–44.

Chechelev, T.V., et al. (2001). Effektivnyj ekonomicheskij rost: teorija i praktika: Investicii. Rost. Effektivnost'. Social'noe razvitie. Intellektual'nyj kapital. Rossija v mirovom hozjajstve [Effective economic growth: theory and practice. Investment. Growth. Effectiveness. Russia in the global economy]. M.: Finansovaja akad. pri Pravitel'stve RF.

Cherednichenko, L.G. (2004). Konceptual'nye osnovanija ekonomicheskogo rosta v transformiruemoj hozjajstvennoj sisteme [Conceptual grounds of economic growth in the changing economy] Dis....d-ra ekon. nauk: 08.00.01 Rossijskaja ekonomicheskaja akademija im. G.V. Plehanova. M.

Cherevko, G., and Lukash, V. (1998). Chelovecheskij aspekt social'no-ekonomicheskoj effektivnosti [Human aspect of socio-economic effectiveness]. *Ekonomika Ukrainy*, 3, pp. 47–51.

Chukhno, A. (1996). Problemy teorii perehodnogo perioda: ot komandnoj k rynochnoj ekonomike [Theory of transition: from the command economy to the market economy]. *Ekonomika Ukrainy*, 4, pp. 4–21.

Dan'ko, M.S. (2003). Perspektivi institucijnogo zabezpechennja innovacijnogo rozvitku [Istitutional grounds for the innovative development]. In Heyets (Ed.). *Ekonomika Ukrainy* (pp. 448–462).

Danilishin, B., and Kucenko, V. (2006). Intellektual'nye resursy v ekonomicheskom roste: puti uluchshenija ih ispol'zovanija [Intellectual resources in economic growth: ways of increasing effectiveness of their utilization]. *Ekonomika Ukrainy*, 1, pp. 71–79.

Dem'janenko V.V. (2003a). Ljuds'kij kapital v Ukraïni v konteksti postindustrial'nogo rozvitku [Human capital in Ukraine in the context of postindustrial development]. In Heyets (Ed.). *Ekonomika Ukrainy* (pp. 250–263).

———. (2003b). Strategichni cili rozvitku ljuds'kogo potencialu ta zasobi ïh dosjagnennja v Ukraïni [Strategic goals for the human capital development and the means for their realization in Ukraine]. In Heyets (Ed.). *Ekonomika Ukrainy* (pp. 233–249).

Dem'janenko V.V., and Timenko N.M. (2003). Strategichni naprjamki rozvitku osviti [Strategic directions for educational development]. In Heyets (Ed.). *Ekonomika Ukrainy* (pp. 276–297).

Dubjanskaja, G.U. (2005). Ekonomika razvitija, osnovannaja na znanijah: idejno-konceptual'nye osnovy [Economics of development for a knowledge-based economy; conceptual grounds]. M.: MAKS Press.

Evstigneeva, R.P., and Evstigneev, L.N. (2005). Ekonomicheskij rost = Economic growth: liberal'naja al'ternativa [Economic growth = Economic growth: the liberal alternative]. M.: Nauka.

Fedorenko, A.V. (2003). Fondovij rinok [Stock market]. In Heyets (Ed.). *Ekonomika Ukrainy* (pp. 566–576).

Fridman, L.A., Vidjasov, M.V., and Mel'jancev, V.A. (1998). Gosudarstvennye rashody (potreblenie) i ekonomicheskij rost [Public expenditures (consumption) and economic growth]. M.: Ros. ekon. shk.

Gal'chins'kij, A.S., et al. (2004). Strategija ekonomichnogo i social'nogo rozvitku Ukraïni (2004–2015) "Shljahom evropejs'koï integracïi" [The strategy of economic and social development in Ukraine (2004–2015) "On the road to European integration"]. Kyiv: IVC Derzhkomstatu Ukraïni.

Gal'chinskij, A., and Levochkin, S. (2004). Stanovlenie investicionnoj modeli ekonomicheskogo rosta Ukrainy [Making the investment model of economic growth in Ukraine]. *Ekonomika Ukrainy*, 6, pp. 4–11.

Garipova, Z.F., Gizatulin H.N., and Garipov, F.N. (2005). Trudovoj potencial i ekonomicheskij rost [Labor force and economic growth]. Ekaterinburg: In-t ekonomiki UrO RAN.

Golikov, V.I., and Fedorenko, A.V. (2003). Zahist prav vlasnosti jak skladova institucijnoï arhitektoniki [Protection of property rights as a basis for institutional development]. In Heyets (Ed.). *Ekonomika Ukrainy* (pp. 190–203).

Golikova, N.V. (2003). Rozvitok osviti - shljah do ekonomiki znan' [Development of education as a way to the knowledge-based economy]. In Heyets (Ed.). *Ekonomika Ukrainy* (pp. 264–275).

Golub, K.U. (2006). Stabilizacija finansovogo sektora kak sredstvo obespechenija ustojchivogo ekonomicheskogo rosta [Financial sector stabilization as a tool for sustainable economic growth]. Saratov: Sarat. gos. soc.-ekon. un-t.

Gosh, A. (1997). Uchebnaja koncepcija "obshecivilizacionnogo processa" [The concept of "global process"]. *Ekonomika Ukrainy*, 10, pp. 91–93.

———. (1998). Ob ob'ektivnom ekonomicheskom stroe postsocialisticheskoj Ukrainy [Economic formation in the post-socialist Ukraine]. *Ekonomika Ukrainy*, 6, pp. 57–64.

Grushevskaja, L.S. (2004). Problemy formirovanija institucional'noj sredy kak faktora ekonomicheskogo rosta v sovremennoj Rossii [The problems of creation of the institutional environment for economic growth in the modern Russia]. Dis.... kand. ekon. nauk : 08.00.01 Novosibirsk.

Heyets, V.M. (2000). Nestabil'nist' ta ekonomichne zrostannja [Instability and economic growth]. Kyiv: IEP, Feniks.

———. (2001). Rinkova transformacija v 1991–2000 rokah: zdobutki, trudnoshi, uroki [The market transformation of 1991–2000: the results, the difficulties, and the lessons]. *Visnik NAN Ukrainy*, 2, pp. 1–17.

———. (2003a). Nacional'na innovacijna sistema ta innovacijno-investicijna dijal'nist' [The national innovative system and innovations and investments activities]. In Heyets (Ed.). *Ekonomika Ukrainy* (pp. 351–372).

———. (2003b). Paradigma strategiï dovgostrokovogo rozvitku [The paradigm of long run development strategy]. In Heyets (Ed.). *Ekonomika Ukrainy* (pp. 71–86).

———. (2003c). Scenarii ta prognozi dovgostrokovogo rozvitku ekonomiki Ukraïni [Scenarios and forecasts of the long run economic development in Ukraine]. In Heyets (Ed.). *Ekonomika Ukrainy* (pp. 120–135).

———. (2003d). Strategichni skladovi ekonomichnogo rozvitku [Strategic components of economic development]. In Heyets (Ed.). *Ekonomika Ukrainy* (pp. 87–94).

———. (2003e). Innovativno-innovacijnij shljah rozvitku—modernizacijnij proekt strategiï rozvitku ekonomiki i suspil'stva. [Innovation-innovative way of development: project of modernization for the economic and social development strategy]. In Heyets (Ed.). *Ekonomika Ukrainy* (pp. 337–350).

Heyets, V.M. (Ed.). (1999). Sektoral'ni modeli prognozuvannja ekonomiki Ukraïni [The sector models of economic forecasting in Ukraine]. Kyiv: Feniks.

———. (2000). Ekonomika Ukraïny: pidsumki peretvoren' ta perspektivi zrostannja [Economy of Ukraine: summary of changes and perspectives for growth]. H.: Fort.

———. (2003a). Ekonomika Ukraïny: strategija i politika dovgostrokovogo rozvitku [Economy of Ukraine: strategy and policy for the long run development]. Kyiv: IEP, Feniks.

———. (2003b). Transformacijni procesi ta ekonomichne zrostannja v Ukraïni [Transformation and economic growth in Ukraine]. Kharkiv: Fort.

Heyets, V.M., and Kireev S.I. (2003). Zagrozi rozvitku nacional'noï ekonomiki ta ïh vidvernennja [Threats to the national economy and their prevention]. In Heyets (Ed.). *Ekonomika Ukrainy* (pp. 135–154).

Heyets, V.M, and Kvasnjuk, B. (2003). Transformacijni peretvorennja (pereosmisljujuchi projdene) [Transformational changes (rethinking the past)]. In Heyets (Ed.). *Ekonomika Ukrainy* (pp. 39–70).

Heyets, V.M., and Shums'ka S.S. (2003). Valjutno-kursova politika Ukraïni v seredn'ostrokovij perspektivi [Currency exchange rate policy in Ukraine in the long run]. In Heyets (Ed.). *Ekonomika Ukrainy* (pp. 615–628).

Heyets, V.M., and Skripnichenko M.I. (2003). Vid ekzogenno zalezhnoï do endogenno orientovanoï strategiï rozvitku ekonomiki [From exogenously dependent to endogenous strategy of economic development]. *Ekonomika i prognozuvannja*, 1, pp. 34–46.

Hristenko, V., et al. (2002). Innovacii i ekonomicheskij rost [Innovations and economic growth]. M.: Nauka, 2002.

Hrytsenko, A.A. (1997). Struktura rynochnoj transformacii inversionnogo tipa [The structure of the inversion-type market transformation]. *Ekonomika Ukrainy*, 1, pp. 4–10.

———. (2003). Osoblivosti institucijnoï arhitektoniki ukrains'kogo suspil'stva XXI stolittja [Essential features of the institutional development in Ukrainian society in the 21st century]. In Heyets (Ed.). *Ekonomika Ukrainy* (pp. 155–171).

Ivanter, V.V. (2004). Prognozy ekonomicheskogo rosta v Rossii [Economic growth forecasts in Russia]. Tsikl publichnyh lekcij "Akademiki RAN-studentam GUU" M.: GUU, 2004.

———. (2006). Problemy ekonomicheskogo rosta Rossii [Problems of economic growth in Russia]. M.: GOUVPO "GUU."

Ivlev, A.F. (2004). Teorija oplaty naemnogo truda kak ekonomicheskoj kategorii, otvetstvennoj za ekonomicheskij rost [The theory of wage as an economic category that contributes to economic growth]. SPb.: Info-da.

Kalinina, I.L. (2005). Formirovanie i realizacija effektivnoj fiskal'noj politiki, stimulirujuwej ekonomicheskij rost [Development of the fiscal policy that stimulates economic growth]. Dis.... kand. ekon. nauk : 08.00.05 M.

Kendjuhov, A. (2005). Motivacija tvorcheskogo intellektual'nogo truda: issledovanie osnovnyh podhodov [Motivation for the creative intellectual work: study of the major approaches]. *Ekonomika Ukrainy*, 3, pp. 49–55.

Kireev, S.I. (2003). Ukraïna v sistemi єvropejs'kih ta єvroaziats'kih procesiv integracii: problema viboru optimal'nogo vektora [Ukraine in the system of European and Euro-Asian processes of integration: the problem of choosing the optimal vector]. In Heyets (Ed.). *Ekonomika Ukrainy* (pp. 835–843).

Kireev, S.I., and Shnipko, O.S. (2003a). Mizhnarodna konkurentospromozhnist' Ukraïni u XXI stolitti: peredumovi, chinniki ta skladovi formuvannja [International competitiveness of Ukraine in the 21st century: preconditions, factors, and components]. In Heyets (Ed.). *Ekonomika Ukrainy* (pp. 867–883). Kyiv: IEP, Feniks.

———. (2003b). Innovacijna komponenta zabezpechennja konkurentospromozhnosti kraïni [Innovations in the competitiveness of the national economy]. In Heyets (Ed.). *Ekonomika Ukrainy* (pp. 921–941).

Kolganov, A. (1995). Zakonomernosti perehodnoj ekonomiki: ekonomicheskie tendencii i modeli [Laws of the transition economy: economic tendencies and models]. *Voprosy ekonomiki*, 2, pp. 50–60.

Koropec'kij, I.S. (1995). Deshcho pro minule, nedavne minule ta suchasne ukraïns'koï ekonomiki [Something about the past, resent past, and the present of the Ukrainian economy]. Kyiv: Libid'.

Kosenkov, R.A. (2005). Sistemnyj analiz i prognozirovanie faz innovacionnogo rosta ekonomiki: informacionnaja tehnologija SAPFIR [Systemic analysis and forecasting of the stages of economic growth: information technology package SAPFIR]. M.: Finansy i statistika.

Koshkin, A.V., and Shabaev, V.A. (2004). Institucional'nye faktory ekonomicheskogo rosta [Institutional determinants of economic growth]. Kemerovo: Kuzbassvuzizdat.

Krichevs'ka, T.O. (2003). Groshovi instituti v arhitektonici ukraïns'kogo suspil'stva [Monetary institutions in the structure of the Ukrainian society]. In Heyets (Ed.). *Ekonomika Ukrainy* (pp. 204–220).

Krjuchkova, I.V. (2000). Makroekonomichne modeljuvannja ta korotkostrokove prognozuvannja [Macroeconomic modeling and the short run forecasting]. Harkiv: Fort.

———. (2003). Tsinova konkurentospromozhnist' ekonomiki Ukrainy [Price competitiveness of the Ukrainian economy]. In Heyets (Ed.). *Ekonomika Ukrainy* (pp. 914–921).

Kushlin, V.I. (2005). Kachestvo ekonomicheskogo rosta: nauchnye razrabotki i rossijskaja praktika: materialy nauch.-prakt. konf., 21 sent. 2004 g [Quality of economic growth: research and practice in Russia. Collection of works]. M.: Izd-vo RAGS.

Kuznetsova, N.P. (2000). Ekonomicheskij rost: istorija i sovremennost' [Economic growth: past and present]. SPb.: Sentjabr'.

Kvashnina, N.A. (2004). Ekonomicheskij rost i investicionnyj process: voprosy metodologii, teorii i praktiki: Regional'nyj aspekt [Economic growth and investment process: issues of methodology, theory, and practice. Regional aspect]. Dis.... d-ra ekon. nauk: 08.00.01, 08.00.05. Ivanovo.

Kvasnjuk, B.E. (2000). Nacional'ni zaoshchadzhennja ta ekonomichne zrostannja [National savings and economic growth]. Kyiv: MP Lesja.

———. (2003a). Derzhava i strategija ekonomichnogo ta social'nogo progresu [The state and the strategy of economic and social progress]. In Heyets (Ed.). *Ekonomika Ukrainy* (pp. 107–119).

———. (2003b). Rol' derzhavi u dovgostrokovomu ekonomichnomu zrostanni [Role of the state in the long run growth]. Kyiv: IEP; Kharkiv: Fort.

L'vov, D.S. (2004). Ekonomicheskij rost i kachestvo ekonomiki [Economic growth and quality of the economy]. M.: Russkaja kniga.

Lapko, O.O., and Aleksandrova, V.P. (2003). Naukovo-tehnichnij potencial ta jogo rozvitok [Scientific and technical potential and its development]. In Heyets (Ed.). *Ekonomika Ukrainy* (pp. 373–390).

Lashov, B.V., and Spizharskaja, L.S. (2004). Sovokupnyj spros i ekonomicheskij rost v Rossii [Aggregate demand and economic growth in Russia]. SPb.: Leningrad. gos. un-t im. A.S. Pushkina.

Lavrov, E.I., and Kapoguzov, E.A. (2006). Ekonomicheskij rost. Teorii i problemy: ucheb. posobie [Economic growth: theories and problems. Textbook]. Feder. agentstvo po obrazovaniju, Om. gos. un-t im. F.M. Dostoevskogo.

Lir, V.E., and Podolets, R.Z. (2003). Strukturni zmini na rinkah energoresursiv ta perspektivnij energetichnij balans Ukraïny [Structural changes in the energy market and the future energy balance in Ukraine]. In Heyets (Ed.). *Ekonomika Ukrainy* (pp. 771–793).

Lisovitsky, V.N. (1992). Osnovy teorii rynochnoj ekonomiki [Principles of market economy]. Kharkov: HGU.

Ljuds'kij rozvitok regioniv Ukraïny: metodika ocinki ta suchasnij stan [Human development in the regions of Ukraine: present situation and methodology of evaluation]. (2002). Kyiv: RVPS NANU.

Lunina, I.O. (2000). Derzhavni finansi Ukraïni v perehidnij period [Public finance in Ukraine during the transition]. Harkiv: Fort.

———. (2003). Reformuvannja mizhbjudzhetnih vidnosin ta rozvitok regioniv [The reform of the budgetary relations and regional development]. In Heyets (Ed.). *Ekonomika Ukrainy* (pp. 510–525).

Makarkin, N.P. (2005). Aktual'nye problemy kachestvennogo ekonomicheskogo rosta: materialy Vseros. nauch.-prakt. konf. (Saransk, 20–21 okt. 2005) [Modern problems of economic growth quality. Collection of works]. Saransk: Krasnyj Oktjabr.

Mar'enko, A.V. (2003). Konceptual'ni osoblivosti investicijnoï politiki [Conceptual specifics of the investment policy]. In Heyets (Ed.). *Ekonomika Ukrainy* (pp. 641–658).

Mocherny, S.V. (1993). Osnovy ekonomichnoï teoriï [Economics]. Ternopil': AT Tarneks, 1993.

Mudrak, R. (2005). Prodovol'stvennye rashody v kontekste ekonomicheskogo rosta Ukrainy [Food expenditures in the context of economic growth]. *Ekonomika Ukrainy*, 6, pp. 73–78.

———. (2006). Derzhavna reguljatorna politika jak skladova ekonomichnogo rozvitku [The state regulatory policy as a component of economic development]. *Ekonomika Ukrainy*, 7, pp. 34–40.

Novitskij, V. (2005). Institucionalizm v dialektike sovremennogo ekonomicheskogo razvitija [Institutionalism in the dialectics of the modern economic development]. *Ekonomika Ukrainy*, 7, pp. 49–57.

Olijnik, O.S. (2003). Rozvitok rinku intelektual'noï vlasnosti [Intelelctual property market development]. In Heyets (Ed.). *Ekonomika Ukrainy* (pp. 482–493).

Onishko, S.V. (2003). Ekonomichne stimuljuvannja innovacijnogo rozvitku [Economic stimuli of innovation-based development]. In Heyets (Ed.). *Ekonomika Ukrainy* (pp. 463–481).

Osadchaja, I. (2005). Ekonomicheskij rost i raspredelenie dohodov: prjamaja i obratnaja svijaz' [Economic growth and income distribution: direct and reverse links]. *Chelovek i trud*, 6, pp 12–22.

Osipian A.L. (1997a). Uchastie v obshestvenyh rabotah i massovaya bezrabotitsa [Participation in Public Work and Mass Unemployment]. *Business Inform*, 6, pp. 44–45.

———. (1997b). Problemy organizatsii meditsinskogo strahovaniya v Ukraine [Problems of Organization of Health Insurance in Ukraine]. *Business Inform*, 8, pp. 45–46.

Osipian A.L. (1997c). Puti reformirovaniya pensionnoj sistemy [Pension System Reform]. *Business Inform*, 10, pp. 42–43.

———. (1997d). Meditsinskoe strahovanie: problemy i perspektivy [Health Insurance: Problems and Perspectives]. *Business Inform*, 18, pp. 47–50.

———. (1998a). Sotsial'noe strahovanie ot bezrabotitsy [Social Insurance from Unemployment]. *Business Inform*, 4, pp. 71–73.

———. (1998b). Pensionnoe strahovanie [Pension Insurance]. *Business Inform*, 5, pp. 72–74.

———. (1998c). Organizatsionnye formy zanyatosti v usloviyah povysheniya urovnya bezrabotitsy [Organizational Forms of Employment in the Stage of Unemployment Rate Increasing]. *Actual Problems of Economic and Humanitarian Development of Ukraine on the Border of Centuries*. Kramatorsk, vol. 1, pp. 24–30.

———. (1999). Vektor regional'nyh interesov: usloviya I tendentsii zashchity [The Vector of Regional Interests: Conditions and Tendencies of Protection]. *Journalist*, 5–6, pp. 19–21.

———. (2001). Ekonomika gosudarstva blagosostojanija: osnovy i formirovanie v uslovijah rynochnoj transformacii [Economy of the welfare state: foundations and creation under the conditions of market transformation]. Donetsk: Lebed.

———. (2007). Ekonomichesky rost: obrazovanie kak factor proizvodstva [Economic Growth: Education as a Factor of Production]. Kramatorsk: KEHI Press.

Ostashko, T.O., and Mishchenko, N.M. (2003). Strukturni zmini v agrarnomu sektori i rozvitok agrarnogo rinku [Structural changes in the agricultural production and development of the market of agricultural products]. In Heyets (Ed.). *Ekonomika Ukrainy* (pp. 755–771).

Ovchinnikova, N.V. (2004). Ekonomiko-matematicheskoe modelirovanie vlijanija prjamyh inostrannyh investicij na ekonomicheskij rost v razvivajushihsja stranah [Mathematical models to study effects of foreign direct investment on economic growth in developing countries]. Dis.... kand. ekon. nauk: 08.00.13 M.

Panova, E.I. (1998). "Tenevoj" sektor i ekonomicheskij rost [Shadow economy and economic growth]. M.: RESH.

Pavlenko, U.V. (2003). Sociokul'turni zasadi integracijnih procesiv Ukraïni [Socio-cultural grounds of the integrational processes in Ukraine]. In Heyets (Ed.). *Ekonomika Ukrainy* (pp. 829–835).

Pavlov, O. (2006). Paradigma sil's'kogo rozvitku [Paradigm of agricultural development]. *Ekonomika Ukrainy*, 7, pp. 41–48.

Pavlova, N.A. (2001). Modelirovanie vlijanija obrazovanija na ekonomicheskij rost [Modeling effects of education in economic growth]. Dis.... kand. ekon. nauk : 08.00.13 M.

Perepelkin, V.A. (2001). Teorija i politika ekonomicheskogo rosta [Theory and politics of economic growth]. Samara : Samar. un-t.

Perminov, S.B., Egorova, E.N., and Pjatkovski, M. (Eds). (2004). Vlijanie sovremennyh informacionnyh tehnologij na ekonomicheskij rost v Rossii i stranah Vostochnoj Evropy v 1990–2001 godah. [Impact of the modern information technologies on economic growth in Russia and Eastern Europe in 1990–2001]. M.: Centr. ekon.-mat. in-t Ros. akad. nauk.

Petkova, L. (2005). K voprosu o kachestve ekonomicheskogo rosta Ukrainy [Issues of the quality of economic growth in Ukraine]. *Ekonomika Ukrainy*, 6, pp. 45–49.

Pokrytan, A. (1997). Rynochnaja transformacija i problemy prioritetov v ekonomike Ukrainy [Market transformation and problem of priorities in the economy of Ukraine]. *Ekonomika Ukrainy*, 12, pp. 18–27.

Ponomarev, V.M. (2004). Makroekonomicheskie zakonomernosti i tendencii formirovanija struktury ekonomicheskogo rosta [Macroeconomics and tendencies of the structural changes in economic growth]. Dis.... d-ra ekon. nauk: 08.00.01 Saratov.

Popova, V., and Popov, V. (2005). Realii i perspektivy ekonomicheskogo rosta v Ukraine [Realities and perspectives of economic growth in Ukraine]. *Ekonomika Ukrainy*, 6, pp. 23–29.

Prihod'ko, T.I. (2003a). Posilennja dii zovnishnih faktoriv ekonomichnogo rozvitku ta nakopichuvannja deformacij u strukturi zovnishn'otorgovel'nogo oborotu [Increasing influence of the exogenous factors of economic development and accumulation of the structural problems in foreign trade]. In Heyets (Ed.). *Ekonomika Ukrainy* (pp. 726–731).

———. (2003b). Spad virobnictva ta jogo vidnovlennja jak strukturoformujuchij chinnik [Decrease in production and industrial renovations as a factor that shapes structure of the economy]. In Heyets (Ed.). *Ekonomika Ukrainy* (pp. 706–710).

———. (2003c). Strategija i politika racional'nih strukturnih zmin u 2003–2012 rr. [Strategy and policy of the rational structural changes in 2003–2012]. In Heyets (Ed.). *Ekonomika Ukrainy* (pp. 732–754).

———. (2003d). Strukturoutvorjujuchi faktori v ekonomici Ukraïni u 1991–2002 rr. [Factors that determine structure of the national economy in Ukraine in 1991–2002]. In Heyets (Ed.). *Ekonomika Ukrainy* (pp. 706–716).

———. (2003e). Vpliv zmini tsin ta inshih faktoriv na strukturni zrushennja u virobnictvi [Influence of price changes and other changes on the structural changes in the industry]. In Heyets (Ed.). *Ekonomika Ukrainy* (pp. 710–717).

———. (2003f). Inertsijnist' strukturnih peretvoren' za umov pasivnoï roli derzhavi [Inertia of the structural changes and the passive role of the state]. In Heyets (Ed.). *Ekonomika Ukrainy* (pp. 718–725).

Revenko, A.P. (2003). Ljuds'kij rozvitok i cili novogo tisjacholittja [Human development and the goals of the new millenium]. In Heyets (Ed.). *Ekonomika Ukrainy* (pp. 221–232).

Rokochaja, V., and Moroz, D. (1998). K voprosu o vybore optimal'nogo puti rynochnoj transformacii [The issue of choosing the optimal path for the market transformation]. *Ekonomika Ukrainy*, 9, pp. 53–59.

Romanova, T.G. (2002). Institucional'nye preobrazovanija kak faktor ekonomicheskogo rosta [Institutional reforms as factors of economic growth]. SPb.: Izd-vo S.-Peterb. gos. un-ta ekonomiki i finansov.

Sacks, J., and Pivovars'kij, O. (1996). Ekonomika perehidnogo periodu [The transition economy]. Kyiv: Osnova.

Saktoev, V.E. (1999). Transformacii rossijskoj makroekonomicheskoj modeli i ekonomicheskij rost [Economic transition in Russia and economic growth]. Dis.... d-ra ekon. nauk: 08.00.01 SPb.

Salijchuk, V.F. (2004). Ekonomicheskij rost: teoreticheskie aspekty [Economic growth: theoretical issues]. Kurgan: Kurgan. gos. un-t.

Samojlov, A.V. (2005). Metody analiza i ocenki ekonomicheskogo rosta [Methods of analysis and estimation of economic growth]. SPb.: Izd-vo S.-Peterb. gos. un-ta ekonomiki i finansov.

Savchenko, M.I. (2005). Ekzogennye faktory ustojchivogo ekonomicheskogo rosta Rossii [Exogenous determinants for sustainable economic growth in Russia]. Dis.... kand. ekon. nauk: 08.00.14 Krasnodar.

Seleznev, A.Z. (2001). Nematerial'noe proizvodstvo i ekonomicheskij rost [Non-material production and economic growth]. M.: Nauka.

Shchedrina T.I. (2003a). Transfer tehnologij ta jogo rol' u realizacii innovacijnoï modeli rozvitku [Technology transfer and its role in the innovation-based model of development]. In Heyets (Ed.). *Ekonomika Ukrainy* (pp. 424–438).

———. (2003b). Perspektivna politika shchodo transferu tehnologij [Technology transfer: policy for the future]. In Heyets (Ed.). *Ekonomika Ukrainy* (pp. 439–447).

Shnipko, O.S. (2003). Institucijni faktori posilennja konkurentospromozhnosti nacional'noï ekonomiki [Institutional determinants for the increase in competitiveness of the national economy]. In Heyets (Ed.). *Ekonomika Ukrainy* (pp. 941–953).

Shubravskaja, E. (2005). Ustojchivoe ekonomicheskoe razvitie: ponjatie i napravlenie issledovanij [Sustainable economic development: tehc ategory and direction for research]. *Ekonomika Ukrainy*, 1, pp. 36–41.

Shums'ka, S.S. (2003). Monetarna politika ta ekonomichne zrostannja [Monetary policy and economic growth]. In Heyets (Ed.). *Ekonomika Ukrainy* (pp. 594–614).

Sidenko, V.R. (2003a). Prioriteti evrointegracijnoï strategiï Ukraïni u sferi ekonomiki [The strategic economic priorities of Euro-integration in Ukraine]. In Heyets (Ed.). *Ekonomika Ukrainy* (pp. 843–850).

Sidenko, V.R. (2003b). Ukraïna v procesah mizhnarodnoï integraciï [Ukraine in the processes of international integration]. Kharkiv: Fort.

Sidenko, V.R., and Liu Kong Than' (2003). Perspektivi vkljuchennja Ukraïni v global'ni ekonomichni procesi ta rozvitok vidnosin iz SOT [Perspectives of integration in the global economic processes for Ukraine and development of cooperation with the WTO]. In Heyets (Ed.). *Ekonomika Ukrainy* (pp. 859–866).

Sidenko, V.R., and Timchenko, O.G. (2003). Rozvitok vzaєmodiï Ukraïni z institutami ES ta regional'nih ekonomichnih organizacij [Development of the links between Ukraine and the EU institutions and regional economic organizations]. In Heyets (Ed.). *Ekonomika Ukrainy* (pp. 850–859).

Sidorovich, A.V. (Ed.). (1997). Kurs ekonomicheskoj teorii. Obshie osnovy ekonomicheskoj teorii, mikroekonomika, makroekonomika, perehodnaja ekonomika: Uchebnoe posobie [Economic theory: microeconomics, macroeconomics, transition economics]. M.: Dis.

Simkina, L.G., et al. (2002). Innovacionnyj ekonomicheskij rost: rossijskie vozmozhnosti i ih realizacija [Innovations-based economic growth: opportunities in Russia]. Sb. nauch. tr. M-vo obrazovanija Ros. Federacii. S.-Peterb. gos. izhener.-ekon. un-t; SPb.: SPbGIEU.

Snigir, L.Ya., and Shums'ka, S.S. (2003). Finansovi resursi ekonomichnogo rostu [Financial resources of economic growth]. In Heyets (Ed.). *Ekonomika Ukrainy* (pp. 545–565).

Sokolik, M.P. (2003). Formuvannja rivnja zhittja naselennja [Living standards of populaiton]. In Heyets (Ed.). *Ekonomika Ukrainy* (pp. 314–333).

Sokolovskij, O.A. (2001). Ekonomicheskij rost v uslovijah sistemnoj transformacii: Obshie zakonomernosti i osobennosti v perehodnyj period [Economic growth under the conditions of systemic transformation: general laws and specifics of transition]. Dis.... d-ra ekon. nauk: 08.00.01 Saratov.

Solovejkina, M.P. (2002). Ekonomicheskij rost, vozmozhnosti i granicy v transformirujushchejsja ekonomike: Metodologija i teorija analiza [Economic growth: potential and limits in the transition economy. Methodology and theory of analysis]. Dis.... kand. ekon. nauk: 08.00.01 Rostov n/D.

Spirjagin, V.I. (2005). Issledovanie problem ekonomicheskogo rosta [Problems of economic growth]. Syktyvkar izd-vo Komi nauch. centra UrO RAN.

Suhorukov, A. (2006). Innovacijna paradigma ekonomichnogo rozvitku Ukraïni [The innovation-based paradigm of economic development in Ukraine]. *Ekonomika Ukrainy*, 7, pp. 92–95.

Tarasevich, V.M., Yaremenko, O.L., and Art'omova, T.O. (2003). Institucijne reguljuvannja social'no-ekonomichnoï dinamiki [Institutional regulation of the socio-economic dynamics]. In Heyets (Ed.). *Ekonomika Ukrainy* (pp. 181–189).

Temchuk, P.P., and Palamarchuk, V.O. (1994). Narisi z ekonomichnoï teoriï [Issues in economic theory]. Kyiv: ISDO.

Tjurina, V.U. (2005). Rossijskaja ekonomika: problemy i protivorechija ekonomicheskogo rosta [Russian economy: problems and contradictions of economic growth]. Saratov: Nauch. kn.

Tochilin, V.O. (2001). Rozvitok sektoriv i tovarnih rinkiv Ukrainy [Development of the industries and commodity markets in Ukraine]. Uzhgorod: IVA.

———. (2004). Formuvannja galuzevih rinkiv Ukrainy: perehidnij period [Creation of the branch-based markets in Ukraine]. Kyiv: Feniks.

Tolmachev, P.I. (2005). Ekonomicheskij rost kak osnova ustojchivogo razvitija nacional'nyh ekonomik: Vneshneekonomicheskie faktory [Economic growth as a basis for sustainable development of the national economies: external factors]. Dis. . . . d-ra ekon. nauk: 08.00.14, 08.00.01 M.

Tomas, V., et al. (2001). Kachestvo rosta [Quality of growth]. M.: Ves' Mir.

Ungaeva, M.A. (2005). Ekonomicheskij rost: rol' struktury i institutov [Economic growth: the role of the structure and the institutions]. Dis. . . . kand. ekon. nauk: 08.00.01 SPb.

Vahnenko, T.P. (2000). Derzhavnij borg Ukraïni ta jogo ekonomichni naslidki [Domestic debt in Ukraine and its economic consequences]. Kyiv: Al'terpres.

———. (2003). Borgova politika derzhavi [Government borrowing policy]. In Heyets (Ed.). *Ekonomika Ukrainy* (pp. 526–535).

Veretennikova, I.I. (2005). Faktory i uslovija ekonomicheskogo rosta [Factors and conditions of economic growth]. SPb.: Himizdat.

Vilenskij, A.V., et al. (2002). Predprinimatel'stvo, rynok i ekonomicheskij rost [Entrepreneurship, market, and economic growth]. M.: In-t ekonomiki RAN.

Vorobyev, E.M., Hrytsenko, A.A., and Kim, M.N. (Eds). (1997). Ekonomicheskaja teorija [Economic theory]. Har'kov: Fortuna-Press.

Vosproizvodstvo i ekonomicheskij rost: Sbornik [Reproduction and economic growth: Collection of works]. (2001). Mosk. gos. un-t im. M. V. Lomonosova. M.: TEIS.

Vovkanich, S. (2005). Sociogumanisticheskij kontekst naukoemkoj ekonomiki innovacionnogo obshestva [Socio-humanistic context of the knowledge-based economy in an innovative society]. *Ekonomika Ukrainy*, 3, pp. 42–48.

Vozhzhov, A. (2004). Ob ocenke ispol'zovanija kreditnogo mul'tiplikatora dlja obespechenija ekonomicheskogo rosta [Estimating the effectiveness of credit multiplicator for economic growth]. *Ekonomika Ukrainy*, 7, pp. 18–24.

Yaremenko, O.L. (2003). Institucijni riziki social'no-єkonomichnogo rozvitku Ukraïni. In Heyets (Ed.). *Ekonomika Ukrainy* (pp. 172–180).

Yatskevich, V. (2006). Problema "predelov rosta" i sistemnaja optimizacija [The issue of growth limits and systemic optimization]. *Ekonomika Ukrainy*, 3, pp. 4–11.

Zadorozhny, G.V. (1996). Sobstvennost' i ekonomicheskaja vlast' [Property and economic power]. Kharkiv: Osnova.

Zagors'ka, T.P., and Gumenjuk, K.V. (2003). Strukturni zmini v metalurgiï ta rozvitok vnutrishn'ogo rinku metaloprodukciï [Structural changes in the metallurgic industry and development of the domestic market for the products of the industry]. In Heyets (Ed.). *Ekonomika Ukrainy* (pp. 793–809).

Zas'ko, V.N. (2004). Vzaimodejstvie vneshnih i vnutrennih faktorov ekonomicheskogo rosta v uslovijah usilenija integracionnyh processov [Interactions between external and internal factors of economic growth under the conditions of strengthening integration]. Dis. . . . d-ra ekon. nauk: 08.00.05 M.

Zemskova, E.S. (2005). Konechnoe potreblenie kak predposylka ekonomicheskogo rosta v transformacionnoj ekonomike [Final consumption as a precondition for economic growth in a transition economy]. Dis.... kand. ekon. nauk: 08.00.01 M.

Zhabin, A.P., and Hasaev, G.R. (2004). Problemy kachestva ekonomicheskogo rosta: materialy Mezhdunar. nauch. kongr., 17–28 maja 2004 [Quality of economic growth: Collection of works]. Samara: Sam. gos. ekon. akad.

Zhits, G.I. (2000). Innovacionnyj potencial i ekonomicheskij rost [Innovations and economic growth]. Saratov: Sarat. gos. tehn. un.

Zverev, O.A. (2005). Modeli makroekonomicheskogo ravnovesija i rosta [Models of macroeconomic equilibrium and growth]. SPb.: Izd-vo S.-Peterb. un-ta.

Other Sources

Abramovitz, M. (1956). Resource and output trends in the United States since 1870. *American Economic Review*, 46, pp. 5–23.

Acemoglu, D. (1994). Search in the Labor Market, Incomplete Contracts, and Growth. *CEPR Discussion Paper* no. 1026.

———. (1996). A Microfoundation for Social Increasing Returns in Human Capital Accumulation. *Quarterly Journal of Economics*, 3, pp. 779–804.

———. (1997). Training and Innovation in an Imperfect Labor Market. *Review of Economic Studies* 64(3), pp. 445–464.

Aghion, P., and Blanchard, O. (1993). On the Speed of Transition in Central Europe. *NBER Macro Annual*, Cambridge, MA.

Aghion, P., and Howitt, P. (1998a). Capital Accumulation and Innovation as Complimentary Factors in Long-Run Growth. *Journal of Economic Theory*, 2, pp. 34–60.

Aghion, P., and Howitt, P. (1998b). Endogenous Growth Theory. Cambridge: The MIT Press.

Alesina, A., and Rodrik, D. (1994). Distributive Politics and Economic Growth. *Quarterly Journal of Economics*, 109, pp. 465–490.

Alesina, A., Ozler, S., Roubini, N., and Swagel, P. (1996). Political Stability and Economic Growth. *Journal of Economic Growth*, 1, pp. 189–211.

Amendola G., Guerrieri, P., and Padoan, P. (1992). International Patterns of Technological Accumulation and Trade. *Journal of International and Comparative Economics*, 2, pp. 235–252.

Anechiarico, F. and Jacobs, J. (1995). *The Pursuit of Absolute Integrity: How Corruption Control Makes Government Ineffective*. Chicago, IL: University of Chicago Press.

———. (1996). Panopticism and Financial Controls: The Anticorruption Project in Public Administration. *Crime, Law and Social Change*, 22, pp. 361–379.

Arrow, K. (1962). The Economic Implications of Learning by Doing. In Robert Becker and Edwin III Burmeister (Eds). *Growth Theory. Volume I. Descriptive Growth Theories* (pp. 122–145). Vermont: Edward Elgar Publishing, 1991.

Arrow, K., Chenery, H., Minhas, B., and Solow, R. (1961). Capital-Labor Substitution and Economic Efficiency. *Review of Economics and Statistics*, 43, pp. 225–250.

Aslund, A. (2000). Why Has Ukraine Failed to Achieve Growth? In A. Aslund and G. de Menil (Eds). *Economic Reform in Ukraine: The Unfinished Agenda* (pp. 255–277). Armonk, NY: M. E. Sharpe.

———. (2001). Ukraine's Return to Economic Growth. *Post-Soviet Geography and Economics*, 42(5), pp. 313–328.

———. (2002a). *Building Capitalism: The Transformation of the Former Soviet Bloc.* New York: Cambridge University Press.

———. (2002b). Why Has Ukraine Returned to Economic Growth? Retrieved May 2006, from http://pdc.ceu.hu/archive/00001669/.

Banajan, K. (1999). *The Ukrainian Economy since Independence.* London: Edward Elgar Publishing.

Barro, R. (1997). *Determinants of Economic Growth: A Cross-Country Empirical Study.* New York: Cambridge University Press.

———. (2000). Inequality and Growth in a Panel of Countries. *Journal of Economic Growth*, 1, pp. 5–32.

Barro, R., and Lee, J. (1996). International Measures of Schooling Years and Schooling Quality. *American Economic Review*, 86, pp. 218–223.

Barro, R., and Sala-i-Martin, X. (1999). *Economic Growth.* Boston: The MIT Press.

Bazhal, A., Galkovska, T., Skripnik, O., and Surzhik, L. (2006). Znannya optom i vrozdrib, abo Nezruchni zapytannja do ministra osvity i nauky, *Dilovyj Tyzhden'*, June 5, 2006. Retrieved June 12, 2007, from http://www.osvita.org.ua/articles/218.html.

Bellver, A., and Kaufmann, D. (2005). Transparenting Transparency: Initial Empirics and Policy Applications. World Bank Policy Research Working Paper. Washington, DC.

Benhabib, J., and Spiegel, M. (2000). The Role of Financial Development in Growth and Investment. *Journal of Economic Growth*, 4, pp. 341–360.

Berthelemy, J., Pissarides, C., and Varoudakis, A. (2000). Human Capital and Growth: The Cost of Rent Seeking Activities. In M.S. Oosterbaan, Thijs de Ruyter van Steveninck, and N. van der Windt (Eds). *The Determinants of Economic Growth* (pp. 209–229). New York: Kluwer Academic Publisher, 2000.

Besançon, M. (2003). Good Governance Rankings: The Art of Measurement. World Peace Foundation Report 36, Washington, D.C. Retrieved October 1, 2008, from doi: http://siteresources.worldbank.org/EXTWBIGOVANTCOR/Resources/wpf36governance.pdf.

Bhagwati, J. (1982). Directly unproductive, profit-seeking (DUP) activities. *Journal of Political Economy*, 90, pp. 988–1002.

Black, J. (1962). The Technical Progress Function and the Production Function. *Economica*, 5, pp. 35–48.

Blanchard, O. (1997). *The Economics of Transition in Eastern Europe.* Cambridge: Clarendon Press.

Bleaney, M., and Nishiyama, A. (2002). Explaining Growth: A Contest between Models. *Journal of Economic Growth*, 1, pp. 43–56.

Boon, P. (1996). Politics and the Effectiveness of Foreign Aid. *European Economic Review,* 40(2), pp. 289–329.

Burnside, C., & Dollar, D. (2000). Aid, Policies and Growth. *American Economic Review,* 90, pp. 847–867.

Cantwell, A. (1989). *Technological Innovations and Multinational Corporations.* Oxford: Basic Blackwell.

Carlberg, M. (1997). *International Economic Growth.* Berlin: Phisica-Verlag.

Chakraborty, S., and Das, M. (2005). Mortality, Human Capital and Persistent Inequality. *Journal of Economic Growth,* 10(2), pp. 159–192.

Chesnais, F. (1986). Science, Technology and Competitiveness. *OECD STI Review,* 1.

Chmelarova, V., and Papageorgiou, C. (2005). Nonlinearities in Capital-Skill Complementarity. *Journal of Economic Growth,* 10(1), pp. 59–89.

Chowdhury, A., and C. Kirkpatrick. (1994). *Development Policy and Planning: An Introduction to Models and Techniques.* London: Routledge.

CityNews (2006). Byvshy rector luganskogo filiala MAUP prisvoila 831,9 tysyach griven, *CityNews,* December 25, 2006. Retrieved March 24, 2007, from http://www.citynews.net.ua/5/8925_1.html.

Dabrowski, M. (2002). Is the Economic Growth in Ukraine Sustainable? In S. Cramon-Taubaden and I. Akimova (Eds). *Fostering Sustainable Growth in Ukraine* (pp. 69–85). Berlin: Physica-Verlag.

Darden, K. (2008). The Integrity of Corrupt States: Graft as an Informal State Institution, *Politics & Society,* 36(1), pp. 35–59.

De Haan, J., and Siermann, C.L.J. (1996). New evidence on the relationship between democracy and economic growth. *Public Choice,* 86, pp. 175–198.

———. (1998). Further evidence on the relationship between economic freedom and economic growth. *Public Choice,* 95, pp. 363–380.

De Haan, J., and Sturm, J. (2000). On the relationship between economic freedom and economic growth. *European Journal of Political Economy,* 16, pp. 215–241.

———. (2003). Does more democracy lead to greater economic freedom? New evidence for developing countries. *European Journal of Political Economy,* 19, pp. 547–563.

———. (2004). Economic freedom and economic growth: a robust relationship? Mimeo.

De Haan, J., Lundstrom, S., and Sturm, J. (2006). Market-oriented institutions and policies and economic growth: a critical survey. *Journal of Economic Surveys,* 20(2), pp. 157–191.

De Vanssay, X., and Spindler, Z. (1994). Freedom and growth: do constitutions matter? *Public Choice,* 78, pp. 359–372.

Demsetz, H. (1967). Towards a Theory of Property Rights. *American Economic Review,* 57(2), pp. 61–70.

Dinopoulos, E., and Waldo, D. (2005). Gradual product replacement, intangible-asset prices and Schumpeterian growth. *Journal of Economic Growth,* 10(2), pp. 135–158.

Dodonov, B., Hirschhausen, C., Opitz, P., and Sugolov, P. (2002). Efficient infrastructure supply as a condition for economic development—the case of Ukraine. In Cramon-Taubaden and Akimova (Eds). *Fostering Sustainable Growth in Ukraine* (pp. 213–226).

Domar, E. (1946). Capital expansion, rate of growth and employment. *Econometrica*, 14, pp. 137–147.

———. (1970). Capital expansion and growth. In Amartya Sen (Ed.). *Growth Economics* (pp. 232–260). Baltimore: Penguin Books.

Dorfman, R., Samuelson, P., and Solow, R. (1958). *Linear Programming and Economic Analysis*. New York: Penguin.

Dornbush, R. (1996). *Stabilization, Debt, and Reform. Policy Analysis for Developing Countries*. London: Prentice Hall.

Dosi, G., Pavitt, K., and Soete, L. (1990) *The Economics of Technical Change and International Trade*. Brighton: Wheatsheaf.

Durham, B. (1999). Economic growth and political regimes. *Journal of Economic Growth*, 1, pp. 81–111.

Durlauf, S., and Johnson, P. (1995). Multiple regimes and cross-country growth behavior. *Journal of Applied Econometrics*, 10, pp. 365–384.

Dye, T. (1966). *Politics, Economics, and the Public*. Chicago: Rand McNally.

Easterly, W. (1993). How much do distortions affect growth? *Journal of Monetary Economics*, 32, pp. 187–212.

———. (2001). The middle class consensus and economic development. *Journal of Economic Growth*, 4, pp. 317–335.

Ebner, A. (2008). *The Institutions of the Market: Organizations, Social Systems, and Governance*. New York: Oxford University Press.

Economist Intelligence Unit Database. New York: Bureau van Dijk Electronic Publishing.

Eremenko, I. (2002). Reserve requirements and implicit taxation of commercial banks in Ukraine. In Cramon-Taubaden and Akimova (Eds). *Fostering Sustainable Growth in Ukraine* (pp. 201–212).

Ernst, D., and O'Connor, D. (1989). *Technology and Global Competition: The Challenge for Newly Industrializing Economies*. Paris: OECD.

Fischer, S. (1993). The role of macroeconomic factors in growth. *Journal of Monetary Economics*, 32, pp. 485–512.

Fisher, S., Sahay, R., and Vegh, C. (1996). Stabilization and growth in transition economies: the early experience. *Journal of Economic Perspectives*, 2, pp. 45–66.

Foster, J., and Székely, M. (2000). How good is growth? *Asian Development Review*, 18(2), pp. 59–73.

Fosu, A. (1992). Political instability and economic growth: evidence from sub-Saharan Africa. *Economic Development and Cultural Change*, 40(4), pp. 829–841.

Freeman, C., and Foray, D. (1993). *Technology and the Wealth of Nations*. New York: Pinter Publisher and OECD.

Galor, O., and Tsiddon, D. (1997). The distribution of human capital and economic growth. *Journal of Economic Education*, 1, pp. 28–43.

Gavrilenkov, E. (2002). Achievements of missed opportunities: factors of economic growth in Russia. What lessons are relevant to Ukraine? In Cramon-Taubaden and Akimova (Eds). *Fostering Sustainable Growth in Ukraine* (pp. 13–27).

Gavriliuk, V., and Malenkov, V. (2004). Grazhdanstvennost', patriotism i vospitanie molodezhi [Civic-mindedness, patriotism, and upbringing of young people]. *Sotsiologicheskie issledovaniya*, 4, pp. 44–50.

Ghost, A. (1999). *A Macroeconomic Framework for Sustained Economic Growth*. London: Prentice Hall.

Gjourgyan, G., and Mirzoyan, J. (2000). Methodology to Develop More Accurate Measures of Value Added: Experience of Armenia. Report presented at the Joint Workshop on Measurement of the Non-observed Economy, OECD, EuroStat, and Goskomstat of the Russian Federation, Moscow.

Glaeser, E., La Porta, R., Lopez-de-Silanes, F., and Schleifer, A. (2004). Do institutions cause growth? *Journal of Economic Growth*, 9(3), pp. 271–303.

Gong, T. (1997). Forms and characteristics of China's corruption in the 1990s: with continuity. *Communist and Post-Communist Studies*, 30(3), pp. 277–288.

———. (2002). Dangerous collusion: corruption as a collective venture in contemporary China. *Communist and Post-Communist Studies*, 35(1), pp. 85–103.

Gorodnichenko, Y., and Sabirianova, K. (2006). Public Sector Pay and Corruption: Measuring Bribery from Micro Data. Paper submitted to the NEUDC annual conference, Ithaca, NY.

Gould, E., Moav, O., and Weinberg, B. (2001). Precautionary demand for education, inequality, and technological progress. *Journal of Economic Growth*, 4, pp. 285–315.

Grafts, N. (1995). Exogenous or endogenous growth? The industrial revolution reconsidered. *The Journal of Economic History*, 4, pp. 745–773.

Greenwood, J., and Uysal, G. (2005). New goods and the transition to a new economy. *Journal of Economic Growth*, 10(2), pp. 99–134.

Guerrieri, P. (1992). Technological and trade competition: the changing position of US, Japan and Germany. In M.C. Harris and G.E. Moore (Eds). *Linking Trade and Technology Policies* (pp. 29–59). Washington, D.C.: National Academy Press.

———. (1998). Trade Patterns, FDI, and Industrial Restructuring of Central and Eastern Europe. BRIE Working Paper 124. Center for German and European Studies, University of California, Berkeley.

Guerrieri, P., and Tylecote, A. (1994). National competitive advantages and microeconomic behaviour. *Journal of Economic Innovation and New Technology*, 3, pp. 49–76.

Gylfason, T. (2002). Natural resources and economic growth: what is the connection? In Cramon-Taubaden and Akimova (Eds). *Fostering Sustainable Growth in Ukraine*.

Haber, S., Razo, A., and Maurer, N. (2003). *The Politics of Property Rights: Political Instability, Credible Commitments, and Economic Growth in Mexico, 1876–1929*. New York: Cambridge University Press.

Hansen H., and Tarp, F. (2001). Aid and Growth Regression. *Journal of Development Economics,* 64(2), p. 547–570.

Hansen, P., and Nanivska, V. (Eds). *Economic Growth with Equity: Ukrainian Perspectives.* Washington, D.C.: IBRD/World Bank, 1999.

Harrod, R. (1937). Review of Joan Robinson's 'Essays on the Theory of Employment'. *Economic Journal,* 49, p. 326–330.

———. (1939). An Essay in Dynamic Theory. *Economic Journal,* 49, pp. 14–33.

———. (1948). Towards a Dynamic Economics: Some Recent Developments of Economic Theory and Their Applications to Policy. London: Macmillan.

———. (1970). Dynamic theory. In Sen (Ed.). *Growth Economics* (pp. 261–289).

Hausmann, R., Pritchett, L., and Rodrik, D. (2005). Growth accelerations. *Journal of Economic Growth,* 10(4), pp. 303–330.

Havrylyshyn, O. (1999). *Growth Experience in Transition Countries, 1990–98.* Washington, D.C.: International Monetary Fund.

———. (2007). Fifteen Years of Transformation in the Post-Communist World: Rapid Reformers Outperformed Gradualists. CATO Institute report 4.

Havrylyshyn, O., Izvorski, I., and Rooden, R. (1999). Growth in transition economies 1990–1997: an econometric analysis with application to Ukraine. In A. Siedenberg and L. Hoffman (Eds). *Ukraine at the Crossroads: Economic Reforms in International Perspective* (pp. 22–57). Berlin: Physica-Verlag.

Havrylyshyn, O., Lissovolik, B., and Shadman-Valavi, M. (2002). Ecoonmic growth in Ukraine: what if reforms and economic recovery had started earlier? In Cramon-Taubaden and Akimova (Eds). *Fostering Sustainable Growth in Ukraine* (pp. 96–115).

Heyd, J. (2008). Comments from a fly on the wall: an outsider's inside view of Ukrainian education. In R. McGee (Ed.). *Accounting Reform in Transition and Developing Economies* (pp. 343–354). New York: Springer.

Heyets, V. (2002). Is there any economic growth in Ukraine? In Cramon-Taubaden and Akimova (Eds). *Fostering Sustainable Growth in Ukraine* (pp. 86–95).

Heyneman, S. (2004). Education and corruption. *International Journal of Educational Development,* 24, pp. 638–658.

———. (2007). Three universities in Georgia, Kazakhstan and Kyrgyzstan: the struggle against corruption and for social cohesion. *Prospects: Quarterly Review of Comparative Education,* 37(3), pp. 305–318.

Heyneman, S., Anderson, K., and Nuraliyeva, N. (2008). The cost of corruption in higher education. *Comparative Education Review,* 52(1), pp. 1–26.

Hicks, J. (1932). *The Theory of Wages.* London: Macmillan.

Hilgard, E. (1956). *Theories of Learning.* New York: Appleton-Century-Crofts.

Hirschman, A. (1958). *The Strategy of Economic Development.* New Haven, CT: Yale University Press.

Howitt, P., and Aghion, P. (1996). R&D in the growth process. *Journal of Economic Growth,* 1, pp. 49–74.

Huntington, S. (1968). *Political Order in Changing Societies.* New Haven, CT: Yale University Press.

IMF Concludes Article 4 Consultation with Ukraine. Public Information Notice (PIN) 3 01/5, 2001. Retrieved August 12, 2004, from www.imf.org.

IMF, Ukraine: Recent Economic Development, 2001. Retrieved August 12, 2004, from www.imf.org.

Jahnke, J. (2002). Finance and growth in Ukraine. In Cramon-Taubaden and Akimova (Eds). *Fostering Sustainable Growth in Ukraine* (pp. 116–128).

Johansen, L. (1959). Substitution vs. fixed production coefficients in the theory of economic growth: a synthesis. *Econometrica*, 27, pp. 157–176.

Jones, C., and Williams, J. (2000). Too much of a good thing? The economics of investment in R&D. *Journal of Economic Growth*, 1, pp. 65–86.

Justman, M., and Teubal, M. (1991). A structuralist perspective on the role of technology in economic growth and development. *World Development,* 19(9), pp. 43–58.

Kalaitzidakis, P., Mamuneas, T., Savvides, A., and Stengos, T. (2001). Measures of human capital and nonlinearities in economic growth. *Journal of Economic Growth*, 3, pp. 229–254.

Kaldor, N. (1955–1956). Alternative theories of distribution. *Review of Economic Studies*, vol. XXIII, 2.

———. (1961). Capital accumulation and economic growth. In F.A. Lutz and D.C. Hague (Eds). *The Theory of Capital* (pp. 177–222). New York: St. Martin's Press.

Kaldor, N., and Mirrlees, J. (1969). A new model of economic growth. In J.E. Stiglitz and H. Uzawa (Eds). *Readings in the Modern Theory of Economic Growth* (pp. 384–402). Cambridge, MA: MIT Press

Kaufmann, D. (2005). Myths and realities of governance and corruption. Social Science Research Network SSRN, doi: http://ssrn.com/abstract=829244. Accessed October 1, 2008.

Kaufmann, D., and Kaliberda, A. (1996). Integrating the unofficial economy into the dynamics of post-socialist economies. In B. Kaminski (Ed.). *Economic Transition in the Newly Independent States* (pp. 81–120). Armonk, NY: M. E. Sharpe.

Kaufmann, D., and Kraay, A. (2003). Governance Matters III: New Indicators for 1996–2002 and Addressing Methodological Challenges. The World Bank Institute Working Papers, Washington, D.C.: The World Bank.

Kaufmann, D., and Vicente, P. (2005). Legal Corruption. Social Science Research Network SSRN. doi: http://papers.ssrn.com/sol3/papers.cfm?abstract_id=829844&rec=1&srcabs=829244. Accessed October 1, 2008.

Kaufmann, D., Hellman, J., Jones, G., and Schankerman, M. (2000). Measuring Governance, Corruption, and State Capture: How Firms and Bureaucrats Shape the Business Environment in Transition Economies. World Bank Policy Research Working Paper No. 2312. Social Science Research Network SSRN, doi: http://ssrn.com/abstract=236214. Accessed October 1, 2008.

Kelly, M., and Hageman, A. (1999). Marshallian externalities in innovation. *Journal of Economic Growth*, 1, pp. 39–54.

Kendrick, J. (1976). *The Formation and Stock of Total Capital.* New York: Columbia University for NBER.

Keynes, J. (1935). *The General Theory of Employment, Interest and Money.* New York: Harcourt.

Klein, L., and Kushnirsky, F. (2005). Econometric modeling at mixed frequencies. *Journal of Economic and Social Measurement*, 30(4), pp. 251–277.

Klitgaard, R. (1986). *Elitism and Meritocracy in Developing Countries.* Baltimore: John Hopkins University Press.

———. (1988) *Controlling Corruption.* Berkeley and Los Angeles: University of California Press.

———. (1991). Gifts and bribes. In R. Zeckhauser (Ed.). *Strategy and Choice* (pp. 211–240). Cambridge, MA: MIT Press.

Knack, S., and Keefer, P. (2008). Institutions and economic performance: cross-country tests using alternative institutional measures. *Economics & Politics*, 7(3), pp. 207–227.

Kofanova, E., and Petukhov, V. (2006). Public opinion of corruption in Russia. *Russian Social Science Review*, 47(6), pp. 23–45.

Kravchuk, R. (2002). *Ukrainian Political Economy: The First Ten Years.* New York: Palgrave MacMillan.

Kregel, J. (1973). *The Reconstruction of Political Economy: An Introduction to Post-Keynesian Economics.* London: Macmillan.

Krueger, A. (1974). The political economy of the rent-seeking society. *The American Economic Review*, 64, pp. 291–303.

———. (1990). Government failures in development. *Journal of Economic Perspectives,* 4, pp. 9–23.

Krueger A., and Lindahl, M. (2000). Education for Growth: Why and For Whom? NBER Working Paper 7591.

Kuznets, S. (1966). *Modern Economic Growth: Rate, Structure, and Spread.* New Haven: Yale University Press.

Lackó, M. (1998). The hidden economies of visegrád countries in international comparison: a household electricity approach. In L. Halpern and C. Wyplosz (Eds). *Hungary: Towards a Market Economy* (pp. 128–152). Cambridge: Cambridge University Press.

———. (1999). Do Power Consumption Data Tell the Story? Electricity Intensity and Hidden Economy in Post-Socialist Countries. Budapest Working Papers on the Labor Market. Budapest: Institute of Economics, Hungarian Academy of Sciences.

———. (2000). Hidden economy—an unknown quantity? Comparative analysis of hidden economies in transition countries, 1989–95. *Economics of Transition*, 8(1), pp. 117–149.

Lal, D. (2000). Institutional development and economic growth. In M.S. Oosterbaan, Thijs de Ruyter van Steveninck, and N. van der Windt (Eds). *The Determinants of Economic Growth* (pp. 169–197). New York: Kluwer Academic Publisher, 2000.

Lall, S. (1990). *Building Industrial Competitiveness in Developing Countries*. Paris: OECD.

Lancaster, T., and Montinola, G. (1997). Toward a methodology for the comparative study of political corruption. *Crime, Law & Social Change,* 27(3–4), pp. 185–206.

Lensink, R., and Kuper, G. (2000). Recent advances in economic growth: a policy perspective. In Oosterbaan, van Steveninck, and van der Windt (Eds). *The Determinants of Economic Growth* (pp. 235–266).

Lensink, R., and Morrissey, O. (1999). Aid Instability as a Measure of Uncertainty and the Positive Impact of Aid on Growth. *CREDIT Research Paper* 99/6, University of Nottingham.

Leontief, W. (1938). The significance of Marxian economics for present-day economic theory. *American Economic Review,* 28, pp. 1–9.

———. (1958). Theoretical note of time-preference, productivity of capital, stagnation, and economic growth. *American Economic Review,* 1, pp. 105–111.

———. (1966). *Essays in Economics: Theories and Theorizing.* Oxford: Oxford University Press.

———. (1990). *Ekonomicheskie Esse: Teorii, Issledovaniya, Fakty i Politika* [*Essays in Economics: Theories, Research, Facts, and Politics*]. Moskva: Politizdat.

Lewis, A. (1984). *The Rate of Growth of the World Economy.* Nankang: Institute of Economics, Academia Sinca.

Lindeen, J., and Willis, G. (1975). Political, socio-economic, and demographic patterns of support for public higher education. *Western Political Quarterly,* 28, pp. 528–541.

Lipset, S. (1960). *Political Man: The Social Basis of Modern Politics.* New York: Doubleday.

Little, I. (1982). *Economic Development.* New York: Basic Books.

Lucas, R. (1987). On the mechanics of economic development. In Donald P. Jacobs, Ehud Kalai, and Morton I. Kamien (Eds). *Frontiers of Research in Economic Theory.* (pp. 82–102). New York: Cambridge University Press, 1998.

———. (1988). On the mechanics of economic development. *Journal of Monetary Economics,* 22, pp. 33–54.

Mankiw, G., Romer, D., and Weil, D. (1992). A contribution to the empirics of economic growth. *The Quarterly Journal of Economics,* 2, pp. 407–437.

Mankovska, N., and Dean, J. (2002). The relationship between foreign direct investment and trade flows in transition economy: the case of Ukraine. In Cramon-Taubaden and Akimova (Eds). *Fostering Sustainable Growth in Ukraine* (pp. 252–263).

Marshall, R., and Tucker, M. (1992). *Thinking for a Living: Education and the Wealth of Nations.* New York: Basic Books.

McCandless, G., and Wallance, N. (1991). *Introduction to Dynamic Macroeconomic Theory: an Overlapping Generations Approach.* Cambridge: Harvard University Press.

McDermott, J. (1999). Mercantilism and modern growth. *Journal of Economic Growth*, 1, pp. 55–80.

Mincer, J. (1996). Economic development, growth of human capital, and the dynamics of the wage structure. *Journal of Economic Growth*, 1, pp. 29–48.

Mokyr, J. (1990). *The Lever of Riches*. New York: Oxford University Press.

Morris, B. (1961). *Economic Growth and Development*. New York: Pitman Publishing Corporation.

Mulligan, C., and Sala-i-Martin, Xavier. (2000). Measuring aggregate human capital. *Journal of Economic Growth*, 3, pp. 215–252.

Murphy, K., Shleifer, A., and Vishny, R. (1991). The allocation of talent: implications for growth. *Quarterly Journal of Economics*, 106, pp. 503–530.

Nehru, V., and Dhareswar, A. (1994). New Estimates of Total Factor Productivity Growth for Developing and Industrial Countries. Policy Research Working Paper 1313, The World Bank.

Nelson, R. (1956). A theory of the low-level equilibrium trap in undeveloped economies. *American Economic Review*, 46(5), pp. 894–908.

———. (1996). *The Sources of Economic Growth*. Cambridge: Harvard University Press.

Nerlove, M. (1965). *Estimation and Identification of Cobb-Douglas Production Function*. Chicago: Rand McNally&Co.

Nickell, S., and Layard, R. (1999). Labor market institutions and economic performance. In O. Ashenfelter and D. Card (Eds). *Handbook of Labor Economics*, vol. 3 (pp. 3029–3084). London: Elsevier.

Nikandrov, N. (2007). Vospitanie I sotsializatsiya v sovremennoj Rossii: riski I vozmozhnosti [Upbringing and socialization in contemporary Russia: risks and opportunities]. *Pedagogika*, 1, pp. 3–14.

North, D. (1990). *Institutions, Institutional Change, and Economic Performance*. New York: Cambridge University Press.

———. (1992). *Transaction Costs, Institutions, and Economic Performance*. San Francisco, CA: ICS Press.

———. (2006). *Understanding the Process of Economic Change*. Princeton, NJ: Princeton University Press.

———. (2007). Institutions, transaction costs and economic growth. *Economic Inquiry*, 25(3), pp. 419–428.

Nurske, R. (1953). *Problems of Capital Formation in Underdeveloped Countries*. Oxford: Blackwell.

O'Rourke, K., and Williamson, J. (2005). From Malthus to Ohlin: trade, industrialization and distribution since 1500. *Journal of Economic Growth*, 10(1), pp. 5–34.

Olson, M. (1982). *The Rise and Decline of Nations: Economic Growth, Stagflation, and Social Rigidities*. New Haven, CT: Yale University Press.

———. Big bills left on the sidewalk: why some nations are rich, and others poor. *Journal of Economic Perspectives*, 10(2), pp. 3–24.

———. *Power and Prosperity: Outgrowing Communist and Capitalist Dictatorships*. New York: Basic Books.

Olson, M., Sarna, N., and Swamy, A. (2000). Governance and growth: a simple hypothesis explaining cross-country differences in productivity growth. *Public Choice*, 102(3–4), pp. 341–364.

Olsson, O. (2005). Technological opportunity and growth. *Journal of Economic Growth*, 10(1), pp. 35–58.

Oosterbaan, M.S., Thijs de Ruyter van Steveninck, and van der Windt, N. (Eds). *The Determinants of Economic Growth*. New York: Kluwer Academic Publisher, 2000.

Osipian, A. (2007a). Corruption in higher education: conceptual approaches and measurement techniques. *Research in Comparative and International Education*, 2(4), pp. 313–332.

———. (2007b). Corruption hierarchies in education in developing and transition societies. In D. Thompson and F. Crampton (Eds). *UCEA Conference Proceedings for Convention 2007*, doi: http://coe.ksu.edu/ucea/2007/Osipian1_UCEA2007.pdf.

———. (2007c). Replacing university entry examinations with standardized tests in Russia: will it reduce corruption? In D. Thompson and F. Crampton (Eds). *UCEA Conference Proceedings for Convention 2007*, doi: http://coe.ksu.edu/ucea/2007/Osipian2_UCEA2007.pdf.

———. (2007d). "Feed from the Service": Corruption and Coercion in the State—University Relations. Annual Conference of the *Central Eurasian Studies Society* (CESS, Harvard), University of Washington, Seattle, WA, October 17, 2007. The Education Resources Information Center (ERIC), US Department of Education, doi: http://www.eric.ed.gov/ERICDocs/data/ericdocs2sql/content_storage_01/0000019b/80/3f/98/a8.pdf.

———. (2007e). Higher education corruption in Ukraine: opinions and estimates. *International Higher Education*, 49, pp. 21–22.

———. (2008a). Political graft and education corruption in Ukraine: compliance, collusion, and control. *Demokratizatsiya: The Journal of Post-Soviet Democratization*, 16(4), pp. 323–344.

———. (2008b). Corruption hierarchies in higher education in the former Soviet Bloc. *International Journal of Educational Development*, 29(3), pp. 321–330.

———. (2008c). Corruption in higher education: does it differ across the nations and why? *Research in Comparative and International Education*, 3(4), pp. 345–365.

———. (2008d). Book Review of *Corrupt Schools, Corrupt Universities: What Can Be Done?* Paris: Institute for International Educational Planning by Jacques Hallak and Muriel Poisson. *Canadian and International Education Journal*, 37(2), pp. 99–101.

———. (2008e). Corruption and coercion: university autonomy versus state control. *European Education: Issues and Studies*, 40(3), pp. 27–48.

———. (2008f). Misdeeds in the U.S. higher education: illegality versus corruption. The Education Resources Information Center (ERIC), US Department of Education. doi: http://www.eric.ed.gov/ERICDocs/data/ericdocs2sql/content_storage_01/0000019b/80/3c/85/2f.pdf.

Osipian, A. (2008h). Higher education corruption in Ukraine as reflected in the nation's media. The Education Resources Information Center (ERIC), US Department of Education. doi: http://www.eric.ed.gov/ERICDocs/data/ericdocs2sql/content_storage_01/0000019b/80/3b/6f/a4.pdf.

———. (2009a). Corruption and reform in higher education in Ukraine. *Canadian and International Education Journal*, 38(1).

———. (2009b). Vouchers, tests, loans, privatization: will they help tackle corruption in russian higher education? *Prospects: Quarterly Review of Comparative Education*, forthcoming.

———. (2009c). Investigating corruption in American higher education: the methodology. *FedUni Journal of Higher Education*, forthcoming.

Osipian, A., and Osipian, A. (2006). Why Donbass votes for Yanukovych: confronting the Ukrainian Orange Revolution. *Demokratizatsiya: The Journal of Post-Soviet Democratization*, 14(4), pp. 495–519.

Page, J. (2006). Strategies for pro-poor growth: pro-poor, pro-growth or both? *Journal of African Economies*, 15(4), pp. 510–542.

Pavitt, K. (1984). Sectoral patterns of technical change: toward a taxonomy and theory. *Research Policy*, 13, pp. 22–42.

———. (1988). International patterns of technological accumulation. In N. Hood and J. Vahlne (Eds). *Strategies in Global Competition* (pp. 287–314). London: Croom Helm.

Perotti, R. (1996). Growth, income distribution, and democracy: what the data say. *Journal of Economic Growth*, 1, pp. 149–187.

Petrov, G., and Temple, P. (2004). Corruption in higher education: some findings from the states of the former Soviet Union. *Higher Education Management and Policy*, 16(1), pp. 83–99.

Pomfret, R. (2000). *Development Economics*. New York: Prentice Hall.

Posner, R. (1975). The social costs of monopoly and regulation. *Journal of Political Economy*, 83, pp. 807–827.

Pritchett, L. (1996). Where Has All the Education Gone? Washington, D.C.: World Bank, Working Paper 1581.

Ramsey, F. (1928). A mathematical theory of saving. In R. Becker and E. Burmeister (Eds). *Growth Theory. Volume II. Optimal Growth Theories*. Vermont: Edward Elgar Publishing, 1991.

Redding, S. (1996). Low-skill, low-quality trap: strategic complementarities between human capital and R&D. *Economic Journal*, 106, pp. 458–470.

Reid, G. (1989). *Classical Economic Growth: An Analysis in the Tradition of Adam Smith*. New York: Basic Blackwell Ltd.

Robinson, J. (1937). *Essays in the Theory of Employment*. London: Macmillan.

———. (1955–1956). The Classification of Inventions. *Review of Economic Studies*, 5, pp. 139–142.

———. (1956). *The Accumulation of Capital*. Homewood: Richard D. Irwin.

Romer, P. (1986). Increasing returns and long run growth. *Journal of Political Economy*, 5, pp. 1002–1037.

———. (1989a). Capital accumulation in the theory of long run growth. In R. Barro (Ed.). *Modern Business Cycle Theory* (pp. 51–127). Cambridge: Harvard University Press.

———. (1989b). Human Capital and Growth: Theory and Evidence. NBER Working Paper 3173.

———. (1990). Capital, labor and productivity. *Brookings Papers on Economic Activity*, Microeconomics Special Issue, pp. 337–367.

———. (1990). Endogenous technological change. *Journal of Political Economy*, 5, pp. 71–102.

———. (1994). The origins of endogenous growth. *Journal of Economic Perspectives*, 1, pp. 3–22.

Rose-Ackerman, S. (1978). *Corruption: A Study in Political Economy*. New York: Academic Press.

———. (1999). *Corruption and Government: Causes, Consequences and Reform*. Cambridge: Cambridge University Press.

Rosenberg, N. (1976). *Perspective on Technology*. Cambridge: Cambridge University Press.

———. (1982). *Inside the Black Box*. Cambridge: Cambridge University Press.

Rosenberg, N., and Birdzell, L. (1985). *How the West Grew Rich: The Economic Transformation of the Industrial World*. New York: Basic Books.

Rosenstein-Rodan, P. (1957). *Notes on the Theory of the "Big Push."* Cambridge: MIT.

———. (1961). International Aid for Underdeveloped Nations. *Review of Economics and Statistics*, May, pp. 22–38.

Rostow, W. (1990). *Theorists of Economic Growth from David Hume to the Present; with a Perspective on the Next Century Including a Mathematical Appendix by Michael Kennedy and Walt W. Rostow*. New York: Oxford University Press.

Ruth, J. (1998). Economic growth and investment in education; how allocation matters. *Journal of Economic Growth*, 4, pp. 337–360.

Sachs, J., and Warner, A. (1995). Economic reform and the process of global integration. *Brookings Papers on Economic Activity*, 0(1), pp. 1–95.

Samuelson, P. (1991). A theory of induced innovation along Kennedy-Weisacker lines. In Robert Becker and Edwin III Burmeister (Eds). *Growth Theory. Volume I. Descriptive Growth Theories* (pp. 34–63). Vermont: Edward Elgar Publishing.

Satarov, G. (2006). Corruption process in Russia: level, structure, trends. In G. Satarov (Ed.). *Diagnostics of Corruption in Russia: 2001–2005*. Moscow: INDEM Foundation. Retrieved May 12, 2006, from http://www.indem.ru/en/publicat/2005diag_engV.htm.

Sayed, T., and Bruce, D. (1998). Police corruption: towards a working definition. *African Security Review*, 7(1), pp. 1. Retrieved May 20, 2002, from http://www.iss.co.za/ASR/7No1/SayedBruce.html.

Scherbakov, A. (2002). A restructuring trap in transition economies: where does it lead? In Cramon-Taubaden and Akimova (Eds). *Fostering Sustainable Growth in Ukraine* (pp. 276–288).

Schmookler, F. (1966). *Invention and Economic Growth*. Cambridge, MA: Harvard University Press.

Schuler, P. (2004). Implementation of WTO regulatory rules in Ukraine: challenges and opportunities. In I. Burakovsky, L. Handrich, and L. Hoffmann (Eds). *Ukraine's WTO Accession: Challenge for Domestic Economic Reforms* (pp. 85–102). Berlin: Physica-Verlag.

Schultz, T. (1963). *The Economic Value of Education*. New York: Columbia University Press.

———. (1970). *Investment in Human Capital: The Role of Education and of Research*. New York: Free Press.

———. (1981). *Investing in People: The Economics of Population Quality*. Berkeley: University of California Press.

———. (1990). *Restoring Economic Equilibrium: Human Capital in the Modernizing Economy*. Oxford, Cambridge: Blackwell.

———. (1993). *Origins of Increasing Returns*. Oxford, Cambridge: Blackwell.

Schumpeter, J. (1911). *Theory of Economic Development*. New York: Harper & Brothers.

———. (1934). *The Theory of Economic Development: An Inquiry into Profits, Capital, Credit, Interest, and the Business Cycle*. Cambridge: Harvard University Press.

———. (1939). *Business Cycles: A Theoretical, Historical, and Statistical Analysis of the Capitalist Process*. New York: McGraw Hill.

———. (1947). *Capitalism, Socialism, and Democracy*. New York: Harper & Brothers.

Scott, M. (1989). *A New View of Economic Growth*. Oxford: Oxford University Press.

Segerstorm, P. (2000). The long-run growth effects of R&D subsidies. *Journal of Economic Growth*, 3, pp. 277–305.

Semenov, V. (2007). Tsennostnye orientatsii sovremennoj molodezhi [Value orientations of contemporary youth]. *Sotsiologicheskie issledovaniya*, 4, pp. 37–43.

———. (2008). The value orientations of today's young people. *Russian Social Science Review*, 4, pp. 38–52.

Sen, A. (1970). *Growth Economics*. Baltimore: Penguin Books.

Sengupta, J. (1998). *New Growth Theory: An Applied Perspective*. Northampton: Edward Elgar Publishing.

Shadnaya, O. (2006). Vzyatka: mif, o kotorom vse slyshali, no nikto ne videl? *Context*, February 2, 2006. Retrieved June 12, 2007, from http://www.osvita.org.ua/articles/50.html.

Shaw, P. (2005). The Determinants of Educational Corruption in Higher Education: The Case of Ukraine. Paper presented at the 2005 NEUDC Conference, Yale University, New Haven, CT.

Shearer, S. (1961). Concept of economic growth. *Kyklos*, 4, pp. 497–512.

Shen, R. (1996). *Ukraine's Economic Reform: Obstacles, Errors, Lessons*. New York: Praeger Publishers.

Shioji, E. (2001). Public capital and economic growth: a convergence approach. *Journal of Economic Growth*, 3, pp. 205–228.

Shkolnikov, V., Cornia, G., Leon, D., and Mesle, F. (1998). Causes of the Russian mortality crisis: evidence and interpretations. *World Development Report*, 26, pp. 1995–2011.

Shleifer, A. (2005). *A Normal Country: Russia after Communism*. Cambridge, MA: Harvard University Press.

Shleifer, A., and Treisman, D. (2003). A Normal Country. NBER Working Paper 10057. Retrieved January 4, 2004, from www.nber.org/papers/w10057.

Siedenberg, A. and Hoffmann, L. (Eds). *Ukraine at the Crossroads: Economic Reforms in International Perspectives*. Berlin: Phisica-Verlag, 1999.

Snooks, G. (1999). *Global Transition: A General Theory of Economic Development*. London: Macmillan Press.

Sokoloff, K., and Engerman, S. (2000). Institutions, factor endowments, and path of development in the new world. *Journal of Economic Perspectives*, 14, pp. 217–232.

Solomon, P., and Foglesong, T. (2000). The two faces of crime in post-Soviet Ukraine. *East European Constitutional Review*, Summer, pp. 72–76.

Solow, R. (1957). Technical change and the aggregate production function. *Review of Economics and Statistics*, 39, pp. 312–320.

———. (1960). Investment and technical progress. In K.J. Arrow, S. Karlin, and P. Suppes (Eds). *Mathematical Methods in Social Sciences* (pp. 89–104). Stanford: Stanford University Press.

———. (1970). *Growth Theory: An Exposition*. Oxford: Clarendon Press.

———. (1988). *Growth Theory: An Exposition*, revised edn. Oxford: Oxford University Press.

Sorensen, A. (1999). R&D, learning, and phases of economic growth. *Journal of Economic Growth*, 4, pp. 429–445.

Storesletten, K., and Zilibotti, F. (2000). Education, educational policy and growth. *Swedish Economic Policy Review*, 7, pp. 39–70.

Streeten, P. (1995). *Thinking about Development*. New York: Cambridge University Press.

Svensson, J. (2005). Eight questions about corruption. *Journal of Economic Perspectives*, 19(3), pp. 19–42.

Swan, T. (1969). Economic growth and capital accumulation. In J. Stiglitz and H. Uzawa (Eds). *Readings in the Modern Theory of Economic Growth* (pp. 88–116). Cambridge, MA: MIT Press.

Swensson, J. (2005). Eight questions about corruption. *Journal of Economic Perspectives*, 17(3), pp. 19–42.

Thieben, U. (2001). Fiscal federalism in Western European and other countries: centralization or decentralization? What is better for economic growth? Are there implications for Ukraine? In L. Hoffman and F. Mollers (Eds). *Ukraine on the Road to Europe* (pp. 255–277). Berlin: Physica-Verlag.

Thiel, E. (2002). The investment environment in Russia and Ukraine: common weaknesses in the institutional and policy framework. In Cramon-Taubaden and Akimova (Eds). *Fostering Sustainable Growth in Ukraine* (pp. 173–189).

Transparency International. (2008), Corruption Perceptions Index. Retrieved October 1, 2008, from http://www.transparency.org/policy_research/surveys_indices/cpi.

Tridico, P. (2007). Institutions, human development and economic growth in transition economies. *European Journal of Development Research*, 19(4), pp. 569–593.

Tullock, G. (1967). The welfare costs of tariffs, monopolies and theft. *Western Economic Journal*, 5, pp. 224–232.

Ukraine: Recent Economic Developments. IMF Staff Country Report 96/21. Washington, D.C.: IMF, 1996. Retrieved May 1, 2001, from www.imf.org.

Uzawa, H. (1967). Neutral inventions and the stability of growth equilibrium. In J. Stiglitz and H. Uzawa (Eds). *Readings in Modern Theory of Economic Growth*. Cambridge, MA: MIT Press.

Uzawa, H, and Watanabe, T. (1960). A Note on the Classification of Technical Inventions. Technical Report 85. Stanford: Stanford University Press.

Valdes, B. (1999). *Economic Growth: Theory, Empirics, and Policy*. Northampton: Edward Elgar Publishing.

Vanek, J. (1968). *Maximal Economic Growth. A Geometric Approach to Von Neumann's Growth Theory and the Turnpike Theorem*. Ithaca: Cornell University Press.

Verdoorn, P. (1956). Complementary and long-range projections. *Econometrica*, 24, pp. 429–450.

Vitrenko, Y. (1999). Policy in education. In J. Hansen and V. Nanivska (Eds). *Economic Growth with Equity: Ukrainian Perspectives* (pp. 21–36). Washington, D.C.: IBRD.

Volkwein, J., and Malik, S. (1997). State regulation and administrative flexibility at public universities. *Research in Higher Education*, 38(1), pp. 17–43.

Von Neumann, J. (1945–1946). A model of general economic equilibrium. *Review of Economic Studies*, XIII, pp. 1–9.

Waite, D., and Allen, D. (2003). Corruption and abuse of power in educational administration. *The Urban Review*, 35(4), pp. 281–296.

World Development Indicators Database. (2005). Retrieved August 12, 2006, from www.worldbank.org.

Woronowycz, R. (2003). Nationwide Survey Reveals Culture of Corruption in Ukraine, *Ukrainian Weekly*, 4.

Yeager, T. (1999). *Institutions, Transition Economies, and Economic Development*. Oxford: Westview Press.

Zagler, M. (1999). *Endogenous Growth, Market Failures and Economic Policy*. New York: St.Martin's Press.

Zimring, F., and Johnson, D. (2005). On the comparative study of corruption. *British Journal of Criminology*, 45, pp. 793–809.

Zon, H. (2000). *The Political Economy of Independent Ukraine*. New York: St. Martin's Press.

INDEX